KOREAN WOMEN

View from the Inner Room

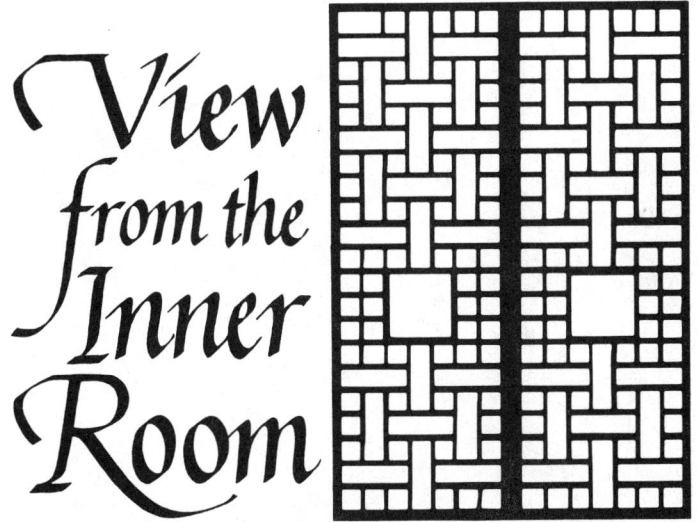

Contributors

MARTINA DEUCHLER
EDWARD W. WAGNER
MARK PETERSON
YOUNGSOOK KIM HARVEY
CLARK SORENSEN
HAEJOANG CHO
LAUREL KENDALL
BRIAN WILSON
DAVID R. McCANN
BARBARA E. YOUNG
HESUNG CHUN KOH

Edited by
LAUREL KENDALL and MARK PETERSON

ISBN 0-910825-02-5

LIBRARY OF CONGRESS CATALOG CARD NUMBER: 82-084450
COPYRIGHT © 1983 BY LAUREL KENDALL AND MARK PETERSON
ALL RIGHTS RESERVED
PRINTED IN THE UNITED STATES OF AMERICA

To Youngsook Kim Harvey (1934-1983),
a remarkable Korean woman

Publisher's Note

The interdisciplinary nature of this volume has resulted in some differences in romanization, as in the accounts of the fieldwork of Cho and Harvey, which reflect the actual sound of the local dialects as heard in the field. The editors have respected their contributors' choices in romanization in this respect and have provided appropriate cross-references in the glossary and index.

Contents

MARTINA DEUCHLER
Preface   1

LAUREL KENDALL and MARK PETERSON
Introduction   5
"Traditional Korean Women" — A Reconsideration

EDWARD W. WAGNER
Two Early Genealogies and Women's Status in Early Yi Dynasty Korea   23

MARK PETERSON
Women without Sons: A Measure of Social Change in Yi Dynasty Korea   33

YOUNGSOOK KIM HARVEY
Minmyŏnuri: The Daughter-in-Law Who Comes of Age
in Her Mother-in-Law's Household   45

CLARK SORENSEN
Women, Men, Inside, Outside:
The Division of Labor in Rural Central Korea   63

HAEJOANG CHO
The Autonomous Women: Divers on Cheju Island   81

LAUREL KENDALL
Korean Ancestors: From the Woman's Side   97

BRIAN WILSON
The Korean Shaman: Image and Reality   113

DAVID R. MCCANN
Formal and Informal Korean Society: A Reading of Kisaeng Songs   129

BARBARA E. YOUNG
City Women and Divination: Signs in Seoul   139

HESUNG CHUN KOH
Korean Women, Conflict, and Change:
An Approach to Development Planning   159

Glossary   175

Index   182

Contributors

MARTINA DEUCHLER teaches Korean language and history at the University of Zurich. She received her Ph.D. in history and Far Eastern languages from Harvard University. Her main interest is the social and intellectual history of late Koryŏ and early Yi. She is currently doing research on Koryŏ society. Her works include *Confucian Gentlemen and Barbarian Envoys* (1977) and "The Tradition: Women during the Yi Dynasty," in *Virtues in Conflict: Tradition and the Korean Woman Today*.

LAUREL KENDALL is Assistant Curator in charge of Asian ethnographic collections at the American Museum of Natural History. She has done fieldwork in Korea and among Korean immigrant women in Honolulu. She holds a Ph.D. in anthropology from Columbia University and has published several articles on her dissertation topic, Korean shamanism. She has taught at the University of Kansas, and she was a postdoctoral trainee in medical anthropology at the University of Hawaii. She was first entranced by Korean shamans as a Peace Corps Volunteer.

CONTRIBUTORS

MARK PETERSON is currently a professor of Korean Studies at Brigham Young University. He studied at Utah State University and then at Brigham Young University, where he received a B.S. in Anthropology and Asian Studies. In 1973, his Master's degree was obtained from Harvard University in Regional Studies—East Asia. He passed the general examination for the Ph.D. degree at Harvard in 1976 and was a Fulbright doctoral dissertation research grantee in 1977. From 1978 to 1983, he served as Executive Director of the Korean-American Educational (Fulbright) Commission and taught Korean history at the Ewha University International School and at the Kansas-at-Ewha Program. His dissertation is entitled "The Confucian Transformation of the Korean Family: An Examination of Inheritance, Marriage and Adoption in the mid Yi Dynasty." He has published several articles on topics relating to social history.

EDWARD W. WAGNER is Professor of Korean Studies at Harvard University. He received an A.B. degree in Government in 1949; an A.M. in Regional Studies—East Asia in 1951; and a Ph.D. in History and Far Eastern Languages in 1959, all at Harvard. His publications include: *The Literati Purges: Political Conflict in Early Yi Korea* (1975); "The Korean *Chokpo* as a Historical Source" (1971); "The Ladder of Success in Yi Dynasty Korea" (1972); "Social Stratification in Seventeenth-Century Korea: Some Observations from a 1663 Seoul Census Register" (1972); "A Computer Approach to Genealogical Research in East Asia" (1971); and "The Civil Examination Process as Social Leaven: The Case of the Northern Provinces in the Yi Dynasty" (1975). As is evident from the titles of the publications listed above, his research has been closely related to the questions of the structure of Yi dynasty society and the composition of the Yi ruling class elite. The use of genealogies as historical source material has been and continues to be a central focus of his research.

YOUNGSOOK KIM HARVEY was born in Hwanghae Province in what is now North Korea. She received her Ph.D. in anthropology from the University of Hawaii in 1976 and served on the faculty of Chaminade University in Honolulu. Her works include *Six Korean Women: The Socialization of Shamans*, as well as several articles on Korean women, mental health, religion, and the immigrant experience. She was also an assistant editor of *Biography: An Interdisciplinary Quarterly*. She died in 1983.

CONTRIBUTORS

CLARK W. SORENSEN is presently Assistant Professor of Anthropology at Vanderbilt University. He received his Ph.D. from the University of Washington in 1981, with a dissertation entitled, "Household, Family, and Economy in a Korean Mountain Village," which was based on sixteen months of fieldwork conducted in 1976 and 1977 in western Kangwŏn Province, Republic of Korea.

HAEJOANG CHO was born in Pusan, Korea. She graduated from Yonsei University in 1971 with a B.A. in history and received her master's degree from the University of Missouri and her Ph.D. in anthropology from the University of California, Los Angeles. In 1979, she returned to Korea to teach anthropology at Yonsei University and at the Seoul National University. Since 1981, she has been Assistant Professor of Sociology at Yonsei University. Her current research interests lie in women's studies and in the organizational principles of Korean society. She has written several articles on women, sex roles, and social change.

BRIAN WILSON is Professor of Anthropology at St. Norbert College and a Ph.D. candidate at the University of Wisconsin-Madison. As a Fulbright grantee, he did fieldwork on Korean shamanism in 1978-79. He is the author of a paper on "Values and Religion," which appeared in *A City in Transition: Urbanization in Taegu, Korea*, edited by Man-gap Lee and Herbert Barringer. His long acquaintance with Korea began in 1960, when he assumed a teaching position at the University of Foreign Studies in Seoul just four days before the advent of the Student Revolution that overthrew Syngman Rhee.

DAVID R. MCCANN holds a Ph.D. in Korean literature from Harvard University. At Cornell University, he has taught Japanese and Korean literature and a course on Folk Literature of East Asia. He is the translator of *The Middle Hour: Selected Poems of Kim Chi Ha*, and *Winter Sky, Poems by So Chongju*; the editor of the literary anthologies, *Black Crane, 1* and *2*; a co-editor of *Studies on Korea in Transition*; and the author of several articles on Korean literature, as well as a collection of his own poems, *Keeping Time*.

CONTRIBUTORS

BARBARA E. YOUNG graduated with honors from Mills College in 1967, receiving a B.A. degree in sociology and anthropology. She did graduate work at Columbia as a student of Margaret Mead and received an M.A. degree in 1970. After working at the Burke Museum in Seattle, she received a Ph.D. in anthropology at the University of Washington in 1980. Her fieldwork in Korea in 1976-77 was supported by a Fulbright Fellowship and a National Service Research Award. Her dissertation is entitled "Spirits and Other Signs: An Ethnography of Divination in Seoul, Republic of Korea." She is presently employed in the field of medical research in Seattle.

HESUNG CHUN KOH is Director of Research and Development at the Human Relations Area Files, and she also teaches seminars on Korean Society and Culture at Yale University. She holds a Ph.D. degree in Sociology from Boston University, and she did postdoctoral work in Chinese Studies as an NDEA Fellow at Harvard and Georgetown Universities. Mrs. Koh served as first chairperson of the Korean Studies Committee for the Association for Asian Studies. She has taught seminars on East Asian Law and Society at the Yale Law School, as well as other courses elsewhere on Korean Culture and Society and on Sex Roles and Women in Cross-Cultural Perspectives. Recently she served as Visiting Professor at the National Museum of Ethnology in Osaka, Japan. Her books include studies on religion and social structure of Yi dynasty Korea, Korean family and kinship, and Korean and Japanese women. She has also written numerous articles on these topics, including "Yi Korean Women in the Public Domain: A New Perspective on Social Stratification" (1975) and "Religion and Socialization of Women in Korea: Biographies of Buddhist Nuns Compared with Shamans" (in press).

Acknowledgments

Many of the papers in this volume were originally presented in a symposium on Korean women at the Association for Asian Studies Annual Meeting in 1979 in Los Angeles. Laurel Kendall, David McCann, Mark Peterson, Ellen Salem, Clark Sorensen, and Barbara Young read papers; Martina Deuchler, Hesung Chun Koh, and Hanna Papanek were discussants. Three extraordinary women facilitated the transformation of this event from symposium to book. Hesung Chun Koh suggested that we publish our papers and brought the manuscript to East Rock Press. Elizabeth P. Swift masterfully edited our prose and was the patient and diplomatic mainstay of this project. Sandra Mattielli helped us choose our title and designed our book jacket, incorporating the pattern of a Korean door lattice.

Eugene H. Chai of the Columbia University Library kindly helped us to make the Glossary conform with the McCune-Reischauer system of romanization and provided the calligraphy for all vernacular characters included in it.

KOREAN WOMEN

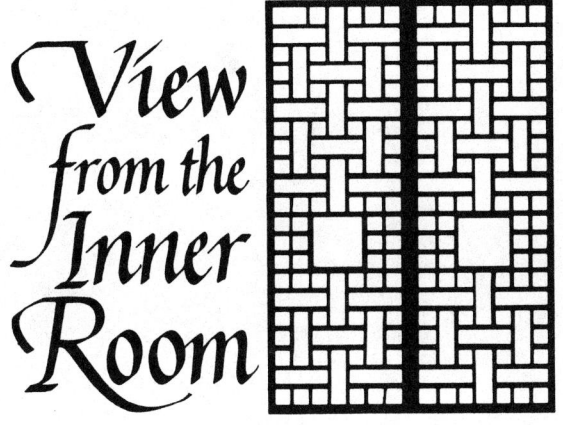

View from the Inner Room

Preface

Martina Deuchler

Westerners traveling through Korea in the late nineteenth century expressed surprise at the apparent absence of women in that country. A land without the opposite sex? Until very recently, readers of historical and ethnographic literature on Korea may have had similar doubts. Both the casual observer and the serious researcher have been under the spell of a century-old social creed — a creed that has given Korean society and Korean studies a distinct male orientation.

Confucianism, adopted by the founders of the Yi dynasty (1392-1910) as the basis of their sociopolitical program, introduced into Korean society the principle of agnation: it made men alone the structurally relevant members of society and relegated women to social dependence. This Confucian view of Korean society has also shaped, to a large degree, the point of view of many modern researchers: preoccupied with analyzing the Confucian patrilineage, they have tended to neglect women's concerns.

Fortunately, recent researchers have begun to correct this distorted perspective by drawing attention to the hitherto dimly-lit inner rooms of the Confucian house. Confucian-inspired stereotypes have come under scrutiny, and the social significance of female roles and activities has come to light. The study of Korean women, moreover, has brought momentum to the deceptively static Confucian social world. The focus on women, variables in the status equation over time and space, has demanded a more differentiated analysis of social change and, as a result, has substantially advanced our understanding of Korean Confucianization.

Women were not always marginal and dependent members of Korean society. During the Koryŏ period (918-1392), women were, to great extent, in command of their own lives. Residence patterns, inheritance rules, and social and ritual recognition provided women with a firm and independent standing in Koryŏ society. In fact, the high status of Koryŏ women indicates that Korean society during that period was structurally quite different from the society that developed later on during the Yi dynasty. The introduction of Confucianism brought about a decisive change. Propagating the duality of female (*yin*) and male (*yang*) — with male ascendant — as the basis of the natural order and as the normative force for the social order, Confucianism subordinated women to men, assigned them to stereotypic social categories — chaste woman, devoted wife, dedicated mother — and confined them spatially in the inner rooms of the house.

Confucianism could not put all women behind walls, however. Although it was pervasive as the model of a perfect social order for all of Yi society, not all status groups adhered to Confucian practice to the same degree. Could it be that Confucianism never managed to put its roots as deeply into Korean soil as scholars have heretofore assumed? Only a comparatively small upper class could afford to approximate ideological purity in daily life: separate living quarters for men and women and sequestered women who went abroad only in sedan chairs or at night. All others, although guided by Confucian principles, were economically unable to confine their women. Even the aristocratic household had female servants who walk unveiled beside the lady's sedan chair. Perhaps even more important, living on the periphery of Confucian consciousness, the lower classes were only mildly indoctrinated, and they preserved older social patterns.

Two categories of women have always lived outside the walls of social tradition and Confucian ideology: the professional shaman (*mudang, mansin*) and the professional entertainer (*kisaeng*). Although treated with contempt, these women rendered indispensable professional services. Early documents hint of their importance in Koryŏ society. The shaman received official recognition, and the state called upon her to pray for rain in time of drought. The shaman's most valued function, however, was healing. This was evident even to a Chinese observer. The Koreans, he writes, never use medicine; instead, they call the shaman to exorcise the bad spirits that are supposed to have caused the sickness.* And shamans were feared for their power to communicate with spirits.

The Confucian founders of the Yi dynasty confronted a strong shaman tradition. Confucian officialdom viewed the shaman as a dangerous manipulator who subjected the rational human world to the irrational, and therefore unpredictable, world of spirits. The scholar-officials tried to neutralize the shamans' influence by relegating them to base status and by banning them from cities. Shamanism, however, survived five hundred years of Confucian suppression—vivid testimony to its inherent strength in Korea's religious tradition. The paucity of references to shamanism in literary sources does not signify a Confucian victory over indigenous "superstition." The shaman's lore was transmitted orally from generation to generation. This body of knowledge and practice, never pressed into the expressive categories of the scholar-official's literary language, undoubtedly retains elements that tie present-day shaman ritual to the pre-Confucian past.

This collection of articles presents an amazing variety of female roles and certainly belies the stereotype of the powerless and dependent Korean woman. Korean women, whether ideologically confined to the inner rooms or cast out to the periphery of society, created for themselves positions of influence radiating across the narrow ideological and social confines of the Confucian family. Insiders or outsiders? As everywhere else, right in the mainstream of life.

---

* Hsu Ching, *Koryŏ togyŏng* (reprinted by Asea Munhwasa, Seoul, 1972), p. 83.

Introduction

"Traditional Korean Women": A Reconsideration

Laurel Kendall
Mark Peterson

We offer a view from the inner room, Korean society from another perspective. We focus on Korean women not merely as a much-neglected topic but as a strategy for re-examining our working assumptions on the form, variation, and historical transformation of Korean society. "View from the inner room" is an apt metaphor of our intentions. In a traditional Korean house, the inner room—the *anbang*—was hidden away behind the great house gate. Invisible to passersby in the fields and lanes outside the house, life within the housewalls radiated from the *anbang*. The inner room was women's domain; some have claimed that the inner room was women's prison.

The higher a woman's status, the more she sequestered herself. In Seoul at the turn of the century, officials' wives and female relatives were carried through the streets in closed sedan chairs from one walled compound to the women's quarters in another walled compound. The respectable woman who walked abroad wore a loose veil that covered her head and shaded her face. Commoner women were distinguished from elite *yangban* women by the legally designated styles of their veils (Hulbert 1906: 352: EWU 1972: 2, 207-09). When a lady could send her slave women to draw water from the well and do the marketing, she herself would travel abroad only after nightfall. The tolling of a bell would clear Seoul's thoroughfares of men, and the "pitch dark streets presented the singular spectacle of being tenanted solely by bodies of women with servants carrying lanterns" (Bishop 1897: 47). Freedom of movement and absence of the veil were the marks of slave women or women in outcaste professions. Slave women, as they appear in antique genre paintings and in old photographs, accompany a lady's sedan chair, pound laundry beside a stream, or gossip together on the way home from the market. Insofar as modesty was a status attribute, the slave's costume—a brief jacket and short skirt over pantaloons—was a mark of degradation. As described in 1906, a decade after the legal abolition of slavery: "She will be seen carrying water home from the well on her head, and not only will her face be uncovered but there will be a startling hiatus between her short jacket and her waist band which leaves the breasts entirely exposed" (Hulbert 1906: 359).

Most students of Korean society have thus far respected the privacy of virtuous women and preserved the inner room's functional invisibility. Men held the public domain, men practiced statecraft and schemed at local politics. Men made and wrote official history. An occasional woman won passing mention in dynastic chronicles as a good man's virtuous wife or as an evil man's devious consort. In the palace, women worked their wiles for good or ill from behind the scenes, where they made admirable targets for historiographic scapegoating. Where Korean social philosophers deemed woman a morally inferior being, necessarily constrained by rule and precept, tales of scheming concubines who plotted sorcery with avaricious female shamans proved the point. The missionaries and travelers who gave the West its first glimpse of Korea stood this image of Confucian womanhood on its head; the Korean woman was now the wretched and depraved product of oppressive patriarchy. Juxtaposed to the ideal Confucian family was the missionary's vision of the enlightened Christian family, wherein ". . . woman's ideal is to love and be loved" (*Korea Review* 1906: 54; see also Moose 1911: 233 ff.; Underwood 1904: 239). The Reverend Gifford lamented the social and moral condition of Korean womanhood: "In what a narrow world do they pass their lives! And then the women are universally spirit worshippers and live in constant dread of evil spirits. In view of these facts; can we wonder that the habitual thinking of Korean women is petty, or superstitious, or vulgar? Poor things!" (Gifford 1898: 61).

Although they were appalled by the Korean woman's low social esteem and jural status, these early observers acknowledged in their writings the force of character by which, according to Jones, ". . . she has risen superior to circumstances and occupies a higher position than men would grant her" (Jones 1896: 223). He comments further that ". . . woman has exercised in Korean national and private life a degree of influence out of all proportion to her theoretical position in society." As a mother-in-law, ". . . her sway is as despotic as any absolute monarchy on earth" (Jones n.d.: 4, 6). As one doughty gentlewoman traveler commented: "There is no doubt that the Korean woman, in addition to being a born intrigante, exercises a certain direct influence, especially as a mother and mother-in-law, and in the arrangement of marriages" (Bishop 1897: 342).

While the exercise of women's power was either covert or contained within the family, women's personalities were far from deferential. Describing the topknot that was a traditional male grooming in Korea, Underwood provides this refreshing image:

> . . . It is a great pity men do not wear their hair in this way in America. We women who favor women's rights would soon find it a mighty handle by which to secure them, for in the hands of a discerning woman it is indeed an instrument of unlimited possibilities. . . . By one of these well-tied arrangements have I beheld a justly irate wife dragging home her drunken husband from the saloon; and firmly grasping this, I have seen more than one indignant female administering that corporal punishment which her lord and master no doubt richly deserved. [Underwood 1904: 50].

Gale recounts how, stopping at a desolate riverside village, he was cross-examined by "a number of clarion-voiced females." He goes on: "One able-bodied Amazon, smoking a long pipe, pushed to the front, saying: 'I'm going to have a look at him—wouldn't they want to see me if I were in his country?' Here I was confronted by one who, like John Knox, feared not the face of man. It was for me to speak in accents humble and low" (Gale 1898: 49).

In missionary accounts, one reads of women who stubbornly clung to their new-found faith despite the opposition of husbands and in-laws and of women who, with equal stubbornness, refused to follow their husbands' new faith until swayed by the force of prayer or the intervention of the holy spirit (Underwood 1904: 165; Scranton 1897: 296-97; Kim 1934: 79). In her biography of "Deaconess Chang," Harvey provides a vivid contemporary example (Harvey 1979: 205-34).

Elsewhere, and with less fascination, Korean women are described as "violent and insubordinate, [they] sow division and ruin in their households, fight with their mothers-in-law, take revenge on their husband by making his life unbearable, and continually provoke scenes of wrath and scandel" (Dallet 1954: 123). We are told that "their subjects of conversation are confined to gossip, scandal, and squabbling. What an unlovely picture!" (Wagner 1908).

Present-day ethnographers, if less inclined to evaluate Korean women's moral fiber, have been equally disinclined to intrude upon the *anbang*. Village mores are changing, but, not so many years ago, Brandt reported that village men discreetly hampered his attempts to converse with village women (Brandt 1971: 134). Osgood cavalierly bows to the village wife," . . standing in the background under the eaves of the house" (Osgood 1951: 34).

Unavailable for comment, women seem all but irrelevant. Osgood (1951), Mills (1960), Knez (1959), and Han (1977) provide general descriptions of rural life. Brandt (1971) analyzes patterns and styles of male association. Lee (1960), Kim (1964), and Pak and Gamble (1975) consider the effect of the presence or absence of strong lineages on social and economic life. Biernatzki (1967) describes lineage organization, the Janellis (1975, 1978) present an ethnography of ancestor worship in a single-lineage village and an analysis of lineage organization, and Dix (1977, 1979) discusses the relationship between Confucian ideology and social life. Han's (1949) study at a distance of a North Korean village includes a rare appreciation of women's social and economic activities, but, with this one exception, we have until recently read almost exclusively of men, ancestor worship, Confucian ideology, and the lineage. Korean men consider these to be the essential underpinnings of social life, and ethnographers have taken them at their word.

Insofar as Korean scribes, foreign missionaries and travelers, and anthropologists have written with accuracy and detail, the researcher studying women finds much of interest and some surprises in their work. Even so, our understanding of traditional Korean society is lopsided, all but womanless. As a consequence, anyone familiar with China reads accounts of Korean life with a smothering sense of déjà vu. Families are patrilineal; marriage is patrilocal. Ancestor worship adds an ethical imperative to the birth of boy children, who will work upon and eventually inherit the family's lands and sustain the family's ancestors with periodic feasts. One point of contrast, the Chinese sons' inheritance is partible. Koreans hark back to an older Chinese pattern, acknowledging the primacy of the first-born son in families and the senior line's primacy in lineage organization. The eldest son takes on the household headship and, with it, the responsibility to worship ascendant generations of family ancestors (*chesa* or *ch'arye*). Secondary sons establish "little houses" (*chagŭnjip*) subordinate to the eldest brother's "big house" (*k'ŭnjip*). Secondary sons, grandsons, and nephews gather in the "big house" for ancestor worship and, through this exclusive male rite, they map the ties that bind them.

Lineage rites project the metaphor of close kin and common ancestors onto a larger collectivity of related households linked through agnatic ties to illustrious distant kin. The senior heir of the senior line leads all of the others, by seniority, at graveside rites (*sije, sihyangje*). Lineage ancestor rites reify genealogical relationships.

One could diagram Korean families and lineages as connected triangles, the anthropologist's shorthand for men in kinship diagrams. Circles signifying women—mothers, wives, aunts, and daughters—provide no significant interface. Sometimes they are omitted. Concerning women, Chinese cliches echo through Korean ethnography. Korean men cite the Confucian homily, "*Namjon, yŏbi*:" "Men are honored, but women are abased." A daughter is a "robber woman" (*todŭngnyŏ*), who carries household wealth away when she marries. Sons are the desired births, the foundation of a woman's security in her affinal household. Both male and female informants cite failure to produce a son as grounds for "sending back" a bride. A bride leaves her own home and village to live with strangers under a mother-in-law's tyrannical sway. Her only consolation: the sorry bride will one day herself become a tyrannical mother-in-law.

These have been our working assumptions, but they are now being challenged from two directions. As a consequence of the development of women's studies in the 1970s and interest in this discipline on at least one Korean campus (Yoon 1979), we are reading more about Korean women. At the time of this writing, five volumes and a number of articles cover such diverse topics as women in Korean history, Korean women and the law, palace women, working women, and women in proverbs.[1] Scholars have gone beyond their initial laments that little enough is known about most women in most societies and have taken "women-issues" to the field, some in Korea. Tantalized by the hypothesis that a woman's participation in public production will have a positive effect on her social standing, Yoon (1977) and Cho (1979a, 1979b) describe male and female work, ritual, and family roles in Cheju villages, where diving women enjoy a unique status and consciousness. Koh (1975) describes Yi dynasty women in the public domain. Harvey (1979, 1980) presents six female shamans' vivid and detailed life histories; she suggests that women seize the shaman's initiation sickness (sinbyŏng) as a way out of the impasse of a housewife's role. Harvey (1976), Kendall (1977a, 1977b, 1977c, 1979), and Yoon (1977) discuss the relationship between shaman ritual and other aspects of women's social experience. Dix (1980) discusses points of occlusion between women-sponsored shaman ritual and a cosmological system interpreted by scholarly men. These studies have thus far been received as interesting digressions on the atypical experiences of shamans and diving women or as discourses on esoteric ritual lore. They have not forced Koreanists to rethink prior assumptions; that push has come from another direction.

Social historians now suggest—as Martina Deuchler reminds us in her preface—that our textbook image of Confucian Korea lacked both depth in time and breadth of social impact. Recent studies have shown that there were great differences in the social order at various times in Korea's past. Deuchler (1980) has shown how the founders of the Yi dynasty adopted neo-Confucianism, not merely as a philosophy of reform but as a basis for completely rebuilding the polity, and yet the changes were slow to reach all levels of society. Deuchler's account of the marriage ceremony (1977) is an interesting case in point. The Confucian texts clearly state that the wedding takes place in the groom's home, where the newlyweds will live, but early Yi Koreans were marrying and living in the bride's home. The fifteenth-century Korean elite compromised and established a pattern for the remainder of the dynasty whereby they held part of the ceremony in the bride's home before completing the ceremony and taking up residence in the groom's home.

Lineage genealogies were compiled under Chinese Confucian influence, yet Song (1980) has shown that a daughter's lines of descent were recorded fully in the earliest documents (fifteenth century); abbreviated in later documents (sixteenth century); and limited to her husband and children after the seventeenth century. Several studies have addressed the equilateral inheritance practices of the early Yi (EWU 1972; Choi 1972, Kim 1977; and Lee 1976) and suggest that daughters lost their inheritance rights only in the seventeenth century. Previously, Korean kinship was structurally more bilateral than patrilineal and in principle, more egalitarian than patriarchal. Aristocrats' daughters once inherited land, slaves, and even the right to worship a parent's ancestor tablet. Most of the social patterns we now associate with "traditional Korea" did not take firm root until the sixteenth or seventeenth century, a scant three centuries ago.

Our predecessor volume, Sandra Mattielli's *Virtues in Conflict*, explored the impact of Yi dynasty Confucianism on women's lives and women's responses to trends and ideas that challenged the overwhelming Confucian paradigm. We might ask the opposite question: to what degree did "traditional" Korean society remain distinctly Korean? Why, how, and to what degree did it change? How much of the total picture have we missed by taking Confucian gentlemen at their word and ignoring women? With enthusiastic iconoclasm, historians, anthropologists, and sociologists find that "traditional Korea"'s bare old bones support some surprising corporeal manifestations—daughter inheritance and heirship by concubines' sons a few centuries ago, wife's "ancestors" rising up in shaman rites, matrifocal diving women, and female shamans whose husbands grovel at their feet. Qualifications and elaborations upon "women's roles" suggest a reconsideration of Korean women's potential as social actors. Conversely, women-centered research teases out broader social and historical issues. As Deuchler suggests, women's status is a bellwether for institutional and ideological change, an excellent measure of social process. Like our predecessor volume, we offer few conclusions but much grist for a continuing debate.

Wagner and Peterson describe aspects of native Korean society in the early Yi period, when women held a more prominent role in lineage and social affairs. They also describe aspects of the transition process and show how women lost ground in the onslaught of Confucian practices. Wagner's description of the earliest known genealogy is fascinating, almost shocking when we consider the social and legal status of contemporary Korean women. The documents reveals a society far removed from contemporary Korea, or from late Yi dynasty Korea. A daughter's posterity was recorded in her father's genealogy in as much detail as a son's posterity. If a woman married twice, both husbands were recorded, apparently without embarrassment. Editors of more recent editions of these same genealogies, however, have recorded the two husbands as having married two separate women; an extra sister was invented to give the extra man a bride and cover up this awkward situation.

Peterson measures social change in the sixteenth and seventeenth centuries by examining the status of women. He compares inheritance practices in the early and late Yi, paying particular attention to the status of women who have not produced sons. In the early Yi, a woman brought property into the marriage and passed it on to her sons and daughters. In the later period, she did not bring an inheritance into the household, nor did her daughter receive one.

Harvey also considers kinship and marriage, describing an institution that severed women most irrevocably from their own kin. In *minmyŏnŭri* marriage, a young girl enters her intended husband's home, is raised by her mother-in-law, and consummates her marriage sometime after puberty and perhaps several years after she has left her own kin. As in China, the practice seems to have died out in the 1920s and 1930s; Harvey's paper is an exercise in oral history, yielding some valuable first-hand accounts of *minmyŏnŭri* marriage. The initial sample Harvey presents here is too slim for solid comparison with the analogous practice of minor marriage in China, but we might speculate on possible contrasts. In northern Taiwan, where minor marriage seems to have been the favored form, baby girls were usually given away to their future husbands' homes within the first year of life (Wolf and Huang 1980: 235, passim.) The women in Harvey's study were all given away much later and apparently with some reluctance. Her informants themselves cite the cruelty of taking a child away from her own parents at a tender age as a reason for avoiding the practice or at least for prolonging a girl child's years with her own kin. Dare we suggest that a lingering bilateral tendency in Korean kinship—a desire for affines and for a sustained link with daughters—modifies an otherwise identical marriage practice?

Kendall suggests that in shaman rituals (*kut*), ghosts and ancestors from the wife's as well as the husband's families acknowledge women as crucial links between households, families, and communities. If men's ancestor worship dramatizes Korean men's agnatic worldview, ancestral and ghostly manifestations in women's shaman rituals provide another perspective on significant kin. A woman's natal kin, her deceased married daughters, and her husband's deceased married sisters appear in the possessed shaman along with the "proper" ancestors and ghosts of the husband's house. The souls at a modern-day seance recall old genealogies (cf. Wagner in this volume).

Papers by Cho and Sorensen—each a discussion of village domestic organization, work, and ritual—troll in counterpoint. Sorensen describes a "typical" agricultural community, where men in groups tend the fields, dabble in local politics, and worship common ancestors. Men have access to public power. Women at home are "less valued" and "subordinate." Sorensen probes the domestic division of labor and concludes that women have considerable managerial authority within the home. The discrepancy between men's public and women's more limited private power—"power" defined here as control over economic surplus—is only significant where men have the resources and lineage position to vie for public prominence. Sorensen presents some telling examples of contrasting domestic arrangements within the same village.

We might add that where a man climbs upon prestigious lineage position and achieves social prominence, his wife must also be exemplary. First sons' brides must be industrious and exacting, more so the brides of lineage heirs, since these women prepare ancestral offerings and the trays of food brought to the *sarangbang* to serve the ambitious husband's or father-in-law's guests. A negative sanction, folktales recount how the strand of hair a slatternly cook let slip into the offering rice sparked swift ancestral retribution (Janelli and Janelli n.d.: 6). We note that Han Pyŏlsu, the lineage heir of Sorensen's account, was adopted into this position at the time of his marriage; one suspects that his bride was chosen with great care.

Sorensen raises the intriguing issue of the Korean housewife's managerial dominion. One recalls Gale's turn-of-the-century description of a "Korean Gentleman's" domestic arrangement. "If the truth were told . . . we would know that the little woman in that enclosure is by no means the cypher he pretends her to be; but that she is really mate and skipper of the entire institution, and that no man was ever more thoroughly under petticoat government than this . . . Korean gentleman" (Gale 1898: 189). Underwood describes a woman of her acquaintance who " . . . was the real man in resourcefulness, energy, and ability to manage . . . Many a Korean woman does that, however, and they are quite used to it" (Underwood 1905: 222-23, passim.).

Anthropologists have also been aware of Korean women's considerable sway in the disbursement of grain and cash. According to C. Han, the male household head pays taxes and educational and ritual expenses, while the senior woman:

> has authority over the grain allotted for household consumption and the various things which women may raise or produce for the purpose of getting extra cash. She keeps the money from the sale of these goods and uses it for the welfare of the members of the household as she sees fit. . . . Since there is a general sex dichotomy at work, men and women are separated and consequently the relative authority in economic matters among members of the two sexes is not distinctly observable. The mother, however, often acts as mediator between father and son. If a son is in need of money it is the mother who persuades her husband to give it to him. If unsuccessful, she spares for the son whatever she has at her disposal [Han 1949: 150].

The topic demands more thorough investigation. A systematic study of budgets and disbursements would be valuable, though difficult to make, since finances are a sensitive topic among tax-paying Korean peasants. Women's own stash—from cottage industry, produce marketing, loan associations (*kye*), and private usury—may be an even more sensitive topic. Let us mention in passing that both Wilson (in this volume) and Harvey (1979) describe women who, thrust upon their own resources, turned immediately to petty entrepreneurship and carried their families. Could the knack have come from some prior modest household ventures?

Again, missionary and traveler hint at the existence of some extremely resourceful women in late nineteenth-century Korea. Since tailoring and laundry were, at that time, two tasks which only women could provide, the homeless widow had some slim means of survival (Gale 1898: 232-33) and the wife of the bankrupt *yangban* could acquire the wherewithal to keep up appearances (Bishop 1897: 101-02). Jones relates that ". . . many of the strutting, self-styled aristocrats in large towns are really drummers up of trade, purveyors of washing and needle work, messengers for the real 'men-of the house' who are too busy or too modest to appear on the street" (Jones 1896: 229). In late dynastic times, a woman might, with no loss of "virtue," engage in cottage industry or become a wet-nurse, house maid, inn keeper, match-maker, or shop proprietress, "though she will not appear in person" (Hulbert 1906: 356-58). A woman with some education could become a physician or tutor young girls (ibid.).

On Cheju Island, diving for offshore sea products has been an exclusively female occupation (ibid.: 356). Cho's Yu Island diving women are overtly proud of their financial success. On Yu Island, diving women are the social and economic mainstays of their "matrifocal" families, and Cho finds them far from subordinate. The men are often away working on the mainland, and marriages are unstable. The women accept this and seem to manage on their own with a dignity Cho attributes to their pride in work; the women pity their often idle men. In these villages, as on the mainland, men cite Confucian homilies in support of their sex's superiority. They gather together in fictive kin groups for ancestor worship, ostentatiously performed. But Cho interprets these rites as compensation for the island men's outsider status, rather than a validation of their centrality. Contrasting social realities underlie the kindred ideology and practice of ancestor worship in the villages Cho and Sorensen describe. Sorensen finds considerable variation between households. Village men and women defy easy generalization.

Both the *kisaeng* described by McCann and the shaman (*mudang, mansin*) described by Wilson were women who left the inner room to sing and dance in public. They were, at once, sought after for their skilled performance and reviled as threats to public morality. Trained to sing and match witty verses with her scholar-official patrons, the *kisaeng* was a literatus of the demi-monde. In his essay, McCann plays upon the analogy of the *kisaeng* abandoned by her lover and the official banished from his king; a parallel apparent in their verses of lament. McCann reflects upon the charm of poets elegant at versifying but not—since they were women—sinified.

Some Korean women are still trained in *kisaeng* arts, but the world wherein they delighted poetic scholar-officials has vanished. The shaman, by contrast, maintains a vivid presence in contemporary Korean life. Wilson uses two modern short stories and a shaman informant's life history to illuminate the contrast between popular stereotypes of shamans and one real-life shaman's experience. After much hardship, the shaman Mrs. Cho was given the authority by her gods to turn the tables on a wastrel husband

and demand his reform. Wilson here follows Harvey's (1979) earlier work; the shaman's initiatory illness is a means of breaking the impasse in an intolerable family situation. Wilson argues that the shaman role gives Mrs. Cho prerogatives denied her as an overworked wife. In trance, she becomes a supernatural general and demands her husband's respect.

While the *kisaeng* and the shaman are the most romanticized of public women, other women in traditional outcaste (*ch'ŏnmin*) professions included jugglers, acrobats, contortionists, story-tellers, diviners, and common prostitutes (Hulbert 1906: 358-59; Dallet 1954: 153). Beggar women and women porters—"robust . . . with the strength of men"—enjoyed the protection of professional guilds. The porters' guild, crucial to commerce in preindustrial Korea, was so powerful that "they [could] pretend that even the government dare not interfere with them" (Griffis 1911: 243; Dallet 1954: 15). Women peddlers are described as running "thousands of small stands for merchandise as well as doing a thriving business in the huckster line" (Jones 1896: 229).

"Traditional Korean women," as they have been recorded in the past or observed in present-day rural villages, seem often to confound the Confucian idealization of passive and sequestered womanhood. That image, and the tension between image and reality, is a part of the twentieth-century Korean woman's heritage. Two final papers by Young and Koh deal with contemporary urban women's problems, but from two very different angles. Young presents urban inspirational diviners and their female clients. Her study opens a rare window on urban housewives' anxieties and on the multiplicity of services women find in diviners' consulting rooms. The Korean woman's extensive ritual role bears further consideration; discussions in this volume by Young, Wilson, and Kendall allude to the breadth of women's religious concerns and suggest that a woman's ritual lore buffers her managerial responsibilities.

If diviners help some women cope with domestic crises, Koh's paper illuminates the extent of women's potential misery. Deuchler, in her important essay on women's status in the early Yi dynasty, concludes that just as Confucian reformers attempted a thoroughgoing transformation of a very different social order, so contemporary Koreans struggle with an arduous transition out of the Confucian embrace (Deuchler 1977: 45). Using court and psychiatric case materials, Koh reveals some of the grim contradictions in contemporary Korean law and custom. She probes areas of stress and suggests possible directions of change.

The contributors to this volume all discuss "traditional" aspects of Korean society, if only to question underlying assumptions. We believe that Korean women belong in Korean studies, that they have too long been absent. We would also welcome discussions of contemporary Korean women in households, factories, and politics. We salute "tomorrow's brides."

Notes

[1] These studies include a survey history by Ewha Women's University (Kim 1977), a volume edited by Mattielli (1977), a study of six shaman lives by Harvey (1979), a study of Korean women and the law by Bae (1973), and a volume on Korean immigrant women in the United States edited by Sunoo and Kim (1978). The June 1977 issue of the *Korea Journal* includes several articles on women. Readers of Korean are referred to the Ewha Woman's University three-volume source book on women (EWU 1972). For additional materials, researchers are referred to Koh's bibliographies on family and kinship in Korea (1980) and on Korean and Japanese Women (1982). Much of the source material for this introduction was discovered in an early draft of her Korea bibliography.

Bibliography

Bae Kyung Sook
  1973 *Women and the Law in Korea* (Seoul: Korean League of Women Voters).
Biernatzki, William E.
  1967 *Varieties of Korean Lineage Structure* (Ph.D. dissertation, St. Louis University).
Bishop, Isabella Bird
  1897 *Korea and Her Neighbors* (New York: Fleming H. Revell).
Brandt, Vincent S. R.
  1971 *A Korean Village: Between Farm and Sea* (Cambridge: Harvard University Press).
Cho Haejoang
  1979a *An Ethnographic Study of a Female Diver's Village in Korea: Focused on the Sexual Division of Labor* (Ph.D. dissertation, University of California, Los Angeles).
  1979b "Neither dominance: A study of a female diver's village in Korea," *Korea Journal*, 19, no. 6 (June): 23-34.
Ch'oi Chae-sŏk
  1972 "Chosŏnsidae ŭi sangsok e kwanhan yŏn'gu" [Research on inheritance in the Chosŏn period], *Yŏksa Hakpo*, 53/54: 99-150.

Dallet, Charles
  1954 *Traditional Korea* (New Haven, Human Relations Area Files). (Originally published in French in 1874 as the Introduction to *Histoire de l'Eglise de Coreé*, Paris: Victor Palmé.)

Deuchler, Martina
  1977 "The tradition: Women during the Yi dynasty," in Sandra Mattielli, ed., *Virtues in Conflict: Tradition and the Korean Woman Today* (Seoul: Royal Asiatic Society, Korea Branch): 1-47.
  1980 "Neo-Confucianism: The impulse for social action in early Yi Korea," *Journal of Korean Studies*, 2: 71-112.

Dix, Griffin
  1977 *The East Asian Country of Propriety: Confucianism in a Korean Village* (Ph.D. dissertation, University of California, San Diego).
  1979 "How to do things with ritual: The logic of ancestor worship and other offerings in rural Korea," in D. R. McCann, J. Middleton, and E. J. Shultz, eds., *Studies on Korea in Transition* (Honolulu: Center for Korean Studies, University of Hawaii): 57-88.
  1980 "The place of the almanac in Korean folk religion," *Journal of Korean Studies*, 2: 47-70.

EWU (Ewha Woman's University, Committee for the Compilation of the History of Korean Women)
  1972 *Han'guk Yŏsŏngsa* [The History of Korean Women], 3 vols. (Seoul: Ewha Woman's University Press). (See also Kim Yung-chung 1977.)

Gale, James S.
  1898 *Korean Sketches* (New York: Fleming H. Revell).

Gifford, Daniel L.
  1898 *Everyday Life in Korea: A Collection of Studies and Stories* (New York: Fleming H. Revell).

Griffis, William Elliot
  1911 *Corea, the Hermit Nation* (New York: A.M.S. Press). (First published, 1882, by Charles Scribner's Sons, New York.)

Han Chungmin Choi
  1949 *Social Organization of an Upper Han Hamlet in Korea* (Ph.D. dissertation, University of Michigan).

Han Sang-bok
  1977 *Korean Fishermen: Ecological Adaptation in Three Communities* (Seoul: Seoul National University, Population and Development Studies Center).

Harvey, Youngsook Kim
- 1976 "The Korean *mudang* as a household therapist," in W. P. Lebra, ed., *Culture-Bound Syndromes, Ethnopsychiatry, and Alternate Therapies* (Honolulu: University of Hawaii): 189-98.
- 1979 *Six Korean Women: The Socialization of Shamans* (St. Paul: West Publishing Company).
- 1980 "Possession sickness and women shamans in Korea," in N. A. Falk and R. M. Gross, eds., *Unspoken Worlds: Women's Religious Lives in Non-Western Cultures* (New York: Harper and Row): 41-52.

Hulbert, Homer B.
- 1906 *The Passing of Korea* (New York: Doubleday, Page [reprinted in 1969 by Yonsei University Press, Seoul, in cooperation with the Royal Asiatic Society, Korea Branch]).

Janelli, Roger L.
- 1975 *Korean Rituals of Ancestor Worship: An Ethnography of Folklore Performance* (Ph.D. dissertation, University of Pennsylvania).

Janelli, Roger L., and Dawnhee Yim Janelli
- 1978 "Lineage organization and social differentiation in Korea," *Man* (n.s.), 13: 272-89.
- n.d. *Ancestral Malevolence in a Korean Village* (unpublished MS).

Jones, George Heber
- 1896 "The status of women in Korea," *Korea Repository*, 3: 223-29.
- n.d. *The Korean Woman* (Boston: Women's Foreign Missionary Society, Methodist Episcopal Church).

Kendall, Laurel
- 1977a "Caught between ancestors and spirits: Field report of a Korean *mansin*'s healing *kut*," *Korea Journal*, 17(8): 8-23.
- 1977b "*Mugam*: The dance in shaman's clothing," *Korea Journal*, 17(12): 38-44.
- 1977c "Receiving the *samsin* grandmother: Conception rituals in Korea," *Transactions of the Royal Asiatic Society, Korea Branch*, 52: 55-70.
- 1979 *Restless Spirits: Shaman and Housewife in Korean Ritual Life* (Ph.D. dissertation, Columbia University).

Kim, Helen K.
- 1934 "Methodism and the development of Korean womanhood," in C. A. Sauer, ed., *Within the Gates* (Seoul: Korea Methodist News Service): 77-83.

Kim Taek-kyu
- 1964 *Cultural Structure of a Consanguineous Village: A Survey on the Mode of Life of Hahoe-dong, a Yangban Village* (Ch'ŏng'gu University Press). (In Korean, with English summary.)

Kim Yung-chung, ed. and trans.
- 1977 *Women of Korea: A History from Ancient Times to 1945* (Seoul: Ewha Woman's University Press). (See also EWU 1972.)

Knez, Eugene
- 1959 *Sam Jong Dong: A South Korean Village* (Ph.D. dissertation, Syracuse University).

Koh Hesung Chun
- 1975 "Yi dynasty Korean women in the public domain: A new perspective on social stratification," *Social Science Journal*, 3: 7-19.
- 1980 *Korean Family and Kinship Studies Guide* (New Haven; Human Relations Area Files).
- 1982 *Korean and Japanese Women: An Analytic Bibliographical Guide* (Westport, Conn.: Greenwood Press).

Korea Journal
- 1977 "Special edition on Korean women," *Korea Journal*, 17 (7).

Korea Review
- 1906 "Women's rights in Korea," *Korea Review*, 6: 51-59.

Lee Kwang-gyu
- 1976 "Chosŏnwangjosidae ŭi chaesan sangsok" [Property inheritance in the Chosŏn dynasty], *Han'guk Hakpo*, 2 (2): 58.

Lee Man Gap
- 1960 *Han'guk Nonch'on ŭi Sahoe Kujo* [Social structure of Korean Villages], (Seoul: Han'guk Yŏn'gu Tosŏgwan). (In Korean, with English summary.)

Mattielli, Sandra, ed.
- 1977 *Virtues in Conflict: Tradition and the Korean Woman Today* (Seoul: Royal Asiatic Society, Korea Branch).

Mills, John E., ed.
- 1960 *Ethno-social Reports of Four Korean Villages* (San Francisco: USOM to Korea).

Moose, Robert J.
- 1911 *Village Life in Korea* (Nashville: Methodist Church South, Smith and Lamar, agents).

Osgood, Cornelius
- 1951 *The Koreans and Their Culture* (New York: Ronald Press).

Pak Ku-hyuk and Sidney D. Gamble
- 1975 *The Changing Korean Village* (Seoul: Shin-hang).

Scranton, M. F.
  1897 "Mission work among women of city and country," *Korea Repository*, 4: 294-97.

Song June-ho
  1980 *An Interpretive History of Yangban Family Records in Korea* (Salt Lake City: Genealogical Society of Utah).

Sunoo, Harold Hakwon, and Kong Soo Kim, eds.
  1978 *Korean Women in a Struggle for Humanization* (Memphis: Korean Christian Scholars).

Underwood, Lillias Horton
  1904 *Fifteen Years among the Topknots, or Life in Korea* (Boston: American Tract Society).
  1905 *With Tommy Tompkins in Korea* (New York: Fleming H. Revell).

Wagner, Ellasue
  1908 "Girls and women in Korea," *Korea Mission Field*, 4 (6): 82.

Wolf, Arthur P., and Huang Chieh-shan
  1980 *Marriage and Adoption in China, 1845-1945* (Stanford: Stanford University Press).

Yoon Soon-young
  1977 "Occupation, male housekeeper: Male and female roles on Cheju Island," in Sandra Mattielli, ed., *Virtues in Conflict: Tradition and the Korean Woman Today* (Seoul: Royal Asiatic Society, Korea Branch): 191-208.
  1979 "Women's studies in Korea," *Signs: Journal of Women in Culture and Society*, 4 (Summer): 751-62.

Two Early Genealogies and Women's Status in Early Yi Dynasty Korea

Edward W. Wagner

As other articles in this volume will clearly show, the status of women in early Yi dynasty Korea was markedly different from what it gradually became in the dynasty's later years. A full assessment of the character of this difference is an extraordinarily difficult task, one that would require the marshaling of far more evidence than can be offered here. It also would demand a much higher degree of sophistication about the inner workings of Yi society, both in the early and in later periods, than the present author commands. Nevertheless, important historical materials that shed considerable light on this problem recently have become available. My purpose in this paper, then, is to explain the nature of these materials and to assess their significance for understanding the position of women in family and lineage structure in early Yi Korea.

The materials to which I refer are the genealogies, or *chokpo*, of two major Korean upper-class (*yangban*) clans, both of which were published within 175 years of the founding of the Yi (Chosŏn) dynasty in 1392. The earlier of the two is the first published genealogy of the Andong Kwŏn clan, entitled *Andong Kwŏn-ssi sebo* and dating from 1476. It had long been thought lost, but a copy surfaced in Seoul some fifty years ago, in the late 1920s. The clan organization then decided to reprint it, and this was done in 1929. One copy of the new edition was deposited in the National Central Library in Seoul, where it remained unnoticed until 1978. In the intervening years, the whereabouts of the 1476 original edition was forgotten, and, indeed, not even the Andong Kwŏn clan organization appears to have been aware of the fact that a copy of the 1929 reprint was kept in the National Central Library. In 1980, happily, the owner of the original came forward and donated this valuable document to the Kyujanggak Library at Seoul National University, where it may be seen and used by those interested. This event also made it possible to test the fidelity of the reprint edition, which in the meantime had begun to be used for scholarly purposes, and it turns out to have been reprinted with meticulous concern for accuracy in every detail.

The other early *chokpo* is the 1565 edition of the Munhwa Yu genealogy, apparently the second published edition of the family records of that large and important lineage. It was compiled over a twenty-year period by a member of the clan (Yu Hŭi-jam), who, fortunately for us, was sent into banishment in the purge of the literati in 1545 and so had ample time to collect the incredible amount of data that he presents in this monumental work. The only known copy of this *chokpo*, the formal title of which is the *Munhwa Yu-ssi sebo (Kajŏng p'an)*, is kept in Andong by a descendant of the great sixteenth-century philosopher, T'oegye Yi Hwang. Although its existence was known to some scholars, at first its owner adamantly refused to let it be used or copied. Finally he allowed it to be microfilmed, and in June 1979 a reprint edition made from the film was published by the Munhwa Yu-ssi Chongch'in Hoe in Seoul.

Both these early Yi dynasty *chokpo* were compiled in accordance with a fundamentally different concept of the scope and nature of the clan lineage structure than that which later came to govern *chokpo* compilation. And both can be distinguished from the typical genealogy of later years by the presence or absence of certain kinds of information or according to the way in which certain categories of data are presented. As will be shown below, these features have an important bearing on the different status that women enjoyed and the different role they played in Korean society of the early Yi period.

The first point to be made in regard to the way in which these two genealogies reflect the position of women in the early Yi dynasty concerns the way in which daughters are listed. The briefest glance at the two *chokpo* will reveal that daughters are recorded in the Andong Kwŏn genealogy in a way that is slightly different from those of the Munhwa Yu genealogy and later Yi dynasty genealogies. That is, although the Andong Kwŏn genealogy follows the usual practice of listing daughters by the names of their husbands, it does not simply say, for example, "Yun Kyŏng-yŏn/daughter Sin Suk-chu," but instead it always records a son-in-law with the term "*yŏbu*," i.e. "daughter's husband." This practice, of course, is an entirely precise and accurate description of the actual fact. Surely it is not amiss to suggest that this practice reflects an attitude of higher regard for female children as individuals, an attitude of regarding daughters as being in a more equal position with sons within the family structure, than was the case later in the Yi dynasty. The Munhwa Yu genealogy, published ninety years later, already adopts the practice of prefacing the recording of a son-in-law's name with the single Chinese character for "daughter," not the two characters for "daughter's husband." Should it not be concluded, then, that this change in format reflects a change in attitude toward greater emphasis on the male line of descent?

A more significant feature of these two genealogies is that both record sons and daughters in order of birth, not sons first and daughters last. Actually, it was the usual practice of compilers of genealogies to record children in this way, by order of birth, until some time around the beginning of the eighteenth century. For about one more century after that, one can find considerable evidence that a transitional practice existed. That is, children began to be listed "sons first, daughters last," but some genealogies continued to indicate clearly the actual order of birth. And it is an interesting development that a major traditional *yangban* clan, the Pannam Pak, in compiling its new comprehensive genealogy published in 1981, decided to revert to the old practice of listing children in order of birth, regardless of sex.

The early genealogy practice of recording children by order of birth indicates, once again, that daughters in the early Yi dynasty occupied a more important position within their families, and within society, than they did later, when the process of Confucianization of the Korean value system had been completed. The present-day reversion to the early Yi dynasty practice is not only a welcome restoration of older, purely Korean values but also a sign that women are being accorded a more equal position in modern Korean society.

The fundamental distinguishing feature of both the Andong Kwŏn and the Munhwa Yu genealogies is that they are not merely records of a single clan's male lines of descent, as later Korean genealogies were to become, but instead may be called multiclan genealogies. That is, the lines of descent of daughters as well as those of sons are recorded continuously—through *their* sons and daughters and grandsons and granddaughters—down to the very time of genealogy compilation. This fact itself is a powerful proof that the position of women in the family and clan structure, and probably to some extent in the society in general, was more equal and more important than it soon would become under the impact of Neo-Confucian values.

This process of change toward a strictly patrilineal family and clan structure can be seen quite clearly in these two genealogies by looking at the phenomenon of adoption. Because of my long experience in using genealogies for historical research, I had been aware that adoption to continue the male line of descent was a much more common practice in the later part of the Yi dynasty than in the first century or so. Nevertheless, when I made a thorough examination of the Andong Kwŏn genealogy I was surprised to find not one single indication of adoption. This Andong Kwŏn genealogy consists of three volumes with a total of 182 pages (actually twice that, or 364 pages, since traditional East Asian pages are folded over, with the same page number assigned to both the recto and verso sides), and it records the names of roughly nine thousand men of the late Koryŏ and early Yi periods. And yet there is not a single indication of adoption to be found. Some of these men had only daughters, but they did not adopt sons; some of these men had no children at all and are labeled "*muhu*" ("no descendants"), but still they did not adopt sons. In numerous other cases the Andong Kwŏn genealogy records no children and also fails to note that there were "no descendants," and of course in these cases, too, we can find no indication of adoption.

Ninety years later, however, in the pages of the Munhwa Yu genealogy that was published in 1565, we can see that the practice of adoption has already begun. It is surprising, nevertheless, to see how limited the practice still was 170 years after the founding of the Yi dynasty. The Munhwa Yu genealogy contains the names of perhaps forty-five thousand men, presumably all *yangban*, in its 950 (= 1,900) pages, but there are only 126 instances of adoption (only 7 of these adoption cases are found within the Munhwa Yu lineage itself). And as a clear indication, I think, that the practice of adoption was in a beginning, transitional stage at this time, the method of recording adoptions in this Munhwa Yu genealogy is different from that employed in later genealogies. The usual practice in later genealogies is to list an adopted son under his adoptive father, with an appropriate Chinese character notation indicating that he is an adopted son. Then the adopted son is listed again under his natural father, with a notation indicating that he has gone out to become the adopted successor to another line. In the Munhwa Yu genealogy, however, the adopted son is listed only once (with only 1 exception in the 126 adoption cases), always under his natural father. And if the adoptive father had no daughters as well as no sons of his own, then the Munhwa Yu genealogy typically will record the notation "*muhu*" ("no descendants"), which of course in this case means simply that the adoptive father had no direct blood descendants.

It is of interest to observe that, once adoption became a widespread social practice, a number of retroactive adoptions took place. Using a later edition of the Munhwa Yu genealogy, in a recent article Professor Ch'oe Chae-sŏk, who has published widely on the history of Korean society, compiled statistics of the chronology and frequency of adoption in the Munhwa Yu clan.[1] When his statistics are compared with the adoptions recorded in the 1565 genealogy, it is evident that about two-thirds of the adoptions recorded in the later edition were effected retroactively. The actual statistics are as follows:

Generation	Lived ca.	Adoptions Recorded in the Later Genealogy	Adoptions Recorded in the 1565 Genealogy
15	1455	2	0
16	1480	1	0
17	1505	7	0
18	1530	7	5
19	1555	13	2
		30	7

(I have adjusted the fraction downward to two-thirds, on the supposition that a number of the nineteenth-generation adoptions may have occurred too late for inclusion in the 1565 Munhwa Yu genealogy.)

Accordingly, based on the information of the Munhwa Yu genealogy, we may conclude that adoption rarely occurred before about 1520 or so and still was far from widely practiced even in 1565. Among the 126 adoptions found in the Munhwa Yu genealogy, only 4 occurred among men who are recorded in the seventeenth-generation (from the tenth-century founder of the Munhwa Yu clan) rows of this genealogy; all the remaining 122 adoptions occurred in later generations.

Needless to say, the absence of the practice of adoption as a means of continuing the male line of descent before the early to middle years of the sixteenth century is another definite indication that the position and role of women within the lineage structure were quite different in the early Yi period.

On this point, in addition to the data I have already presented, still other meaningful evidence can be found in these two early genealogies. For example, the use of the "no descendants" notation may be cited. In these two genealogies, the term "no descendants" refers specifically to the person, male or female, under whose name it is written. That is, whenever someone's son-in-law is recorded with the notation "no descendants," it means that the son-in-law's wife, a daughter of the particular lineage then being presented, had no children. Her husband may have married again and produced children by a second or third wife, but it was not considered proper to record such children in a way that would lead to erroneous identification of their mother.

Again, even the fact that few if any illegitimate sons or daughters are recorded in these genealogies, quite contrary to our expectations derived from experience with later genealogies, perhaps may be interpreted as indicating a higher regard for the role of women in the lineage structure. After all, a man's children by a concubine, or secondary wife, do represent a continuation of his own blood line, no matter who the mother may be. But such illegitimate offspring do not in any way represent a continuation of the blood line of their father's legal or primary wife, and the emphasis in these early genealogies is on the line of descent of that wife, rather than more broadly on that of her husband.

The most striking, and perhaps the most unexpected, evidence of the different position of women in the early Yi dynasty is the recording, in both these old genealogies, of second marriages by *yangban* women. Such second marriages are marked by the notation *"hubu"* ("later husband"), and I have found seventeen such cases in the Andong Kwŏn genealogy and eighteen such cases (fourteen of which are also among the seventeen Andong Kwŏn cases) in the Munhwa Yu genealogy. Of course this is a small number, and many of them are late Koryŏ rather than Yi dynasty occurrences. And the fact that the instances of second marriages by *yangban* women are so few, along with the fact that the additional number of instances found in the Munhwa Yu genealogy is only four, must mean that this practice, once more widespread, was already dying out in the early Yi period.

There is other evidence for this, of course. Legislation discriminating against the sons of remarried women was included in the *Kyŏngguk Taejŏn* (the administrative code of the Yi dynasty), promulgated finally in 1474, just two years before the publication of the Andong Kwŏn genealogy. And

I have seen cases of appointments to office in the early 1500s criticized on the ground that the appointee was the son of a remarried woman. These two genealogies themselves provide an interesting piece of evidence that the attitude against remarriage by *yangban* women had changed. The Andong Kwŏn genealogy has no "principles of compilation" (*pŏmnye*), a standard feature of later genealogies, so we cannot tell how the compilers felt about recording such remarriages. But in the "principles of compilation" of the Munhwa Yu genealogy we find an explicit condemnation of the practice—although the compiler could not persuade himself that he should refuse to include such shameful records. This "principle of compilation" reads as follows:

> In the case of remarried women we record the names of both the first and second husbands with no attempt to conceal the fact of remarriage, since these cases are well known to all. Moreover, we feel that openly recording such instances will serve as an admonition to society.[2]

In spite of the hardening attitude against remarriages by *yangban* women, there is no evidence that their children by their second husbands encountered discriminatory treatment. A good illustration of this is the case of a man named Pyŏn Nam-nyong, whose wife had already had children by an earlier marriage. One of her two sons by her first husband passed the highest civil service examination in 1401, while a daughter married a man who achieved the same success in 1399. Both her sons by her second husband, Pyŏn Nam-nyong, also passed the highest civil service examination, in 1414 and in 1419, respectively. This woman, a daughter of the powerful late Koryŏ figure Yŏm Che-sin (1304-82), was herself the child of the second marriage of a remarried woman.[3]

In another case, a granddaughter of the famed scholar-official Chŏng In-ji (1396-1478), the daughter and only child of his eldest son, married a second time; her second husband was the son of Kwŏn Chŏl (1422-?), one of the so-called "Six Loyal Subjects" who protested the usurpation of the throne by King Sejo in 1455, and her descendants from this marriage passed the highest civil service examination in the seventeenth century.[4]

I have not yet done enough research to determine whether these second marriages by *yangban* women were also the second marriages for their second husbands. This probably was true in some cases, but certainly not in all. I also do not know whether these second marriages always took place after the first husband had died, or whether divorce may sometimes have occurred. But the case of a daughter of the high official Hong Cham would seem to clearly indicate that divorce did occasionally take place. Both the Andong Kwŏn genealogy and the Munhwa Yu genealogy say that she was the second of her first husband's three wives. This apparently means that she left her husband, or was divorced by him (she had no children by this man and perhaps was put aside by him for this reason), while he still was alive, since he and she both subsequently married again.[5]

It is interesting and significant to see how these second marriages by *yangban* women are treated in later genealogies. Of course such a practice would never be mentioned in later periods, when the changed value system made it impossible for a *yangban* widow to remarry. In some of the cases that I have been able to investigate in later genealogies, both husbands of the remarried daughter *do* appear, but in these cases another daughter has been created to account for the appearance of two sons-in-law! Should we conclude that this was done deliberately? Or that, understandably, the compilers of the later genealogies could conceive of no other way to explain the existence of an extra son-in-law except by assuming that somehow there had existed, in faraway, early Yi dynasty times, another daughter?

It has been suggested that inferences can be drawn about the strength of patriarchal clan consciousness in the early Yi dynasty on the basis of one unusual feature of the Munhwa Yu genealogy. In his recent study Professor Ch'oe Chae-sŏk explains his point of view in these words:

> As the 1565 Munhwa Yu genealogy indicates to us, 16th century genealogies recorded the surname for both the Munhwa Yu patrilineal line of descent itself and also for the members of the various families related to it by marriage. Later genealogies, however, recorded the surname only for the in-law families but, in contrast, recorded the surname once only for the Munhwa Yu itself—that is, only in the recording of the "first ancestor" of the clan. We may regard this phenomenon to be the consequence of a way of thinking that attached primary value to the clan's patrilineal line of descent. And this practice arose from a desire to differentiate between those descendants having the same surname and clan name—the sons and their male descendants, and those descendants bearing different surnames and clan names—the descendants of daughters.[6]

This is a thoughtful interpretation, but it is of interest to note that the only fifteenth-century genealogy that we have, the Andong Kwŏn genealogy of 1476, uses a quite different approach with respect to recording surnames. The system of the Andong Kwŏn genealogy, in fact, is exactly opposite that of the Munhwa Yu genealogy, since the former records the surname only to indicate into what family a daughter married, but then omits the surname in listing her sons and their male posterity. This is equally true of the Andong Kwŏn lineages and of all the in-law lineages contained in this early genealogy. Certainly this is an impractical idea, causing considerable hardship to the user of the genealogy trying to trace a particular lineage upward and downward over several pages. But what does this practice signify? It seems to me that this practice of the fifteenth-century Andong Kwŏn genealogy directly supports Professor Ch'oe's hypothesis: failure to record the surname for either the main line lineages or the in-law lineages may also be said to constitute proof that patriarchal clan consciousness in the early Yi dynasty was relatively weak, that the *yangban* of that time, in Ch'oe's words, "did not particularly distinguish between same-surname descendants, the main male line of descent, and different-surname descendants, the in-law female line of descent."

It has been asserted repeatedly above that the evidence of two early Yi dynasty genealogies strongly suggests a different and more important role for Korean upper-class women of that period than was the case later in the dynasty. This evidence is to be found most significantly in the fact that these genealogies attempt to record male and female lines of descent with impartial exactness and detail. Other evidence can be adduced from a variety of other unusual features of these genealogies, relating to the kind of data that does, or does not, appear and to the way in which certain information is recorded. Thus the evidence presented in regard to the practice of adoption, the failure to record illegitimate offspring, the occurrence of remarriage by *yangban* women, the use of the "no descendants" notation to indicate the ending of a female line of descent, the listing of children by order of birth, the terminology used to record daughters in the Andong Kwŏn genealogy, and the ways in which the surnames of those included in the two genealogies are recorded—all of these features are thought to be signposts pointing with greater or lesser clarity to the existence of values and practices in early Yi Korea that accorded women a more central role in society than they later enjoyed. But if the nature of these different values and practices is to be delineated with any precision, it must be done by other approaches and through other bodies of data.

Notes

[1] Ch'oe Chae-sŏk, "Chosŏn sidae ŭi chokpo wa tongjok chojik" [Yi dynasty genealogies and clan structure], *Yŏksa hakpo*, 81 (Mar. 1979): 37-79.

[2] *Munhwa Yu-ssi sebo* (1565 edition), Preface, p. 2a.

[3] *Andong Kwŏn-ssi sebo* (1476 edition), v. 1, pp. 5a-5b.

[4] *Andong Kwŏn-ssi sebo* (1476 edition), v. 1, p. 25a; *Munhwa Yu-ssi sebo* (1565 edition), v. 2, p. 98b.

[5] *Andong Kwŏn-ssi sebo* (1476 edition), v. 1, p. 38b; *Munhwa Yu-ssi sebo* (1565 edition), v. 4, p. 82b.

[6] Ch'oe Chae-sŏk, op. cit., p. 57.

Women without Sons: A Measure of Social Change in Yi Dynasty Korea

Mark Peterson

Namjon, yŏbi

Men are honored,
But women are abased.

Perhaps no other expression better describes the position of women in traditional Korean society. Sons are preferred over daughters. Sons inherit the family line, but daughters are "raised for others" and are considered outsiders once they have married. In this paper, we will examine Yi dynasty (1392-1910) society through the lens of women's status within the family, and we will find that the late Yi dynasty, the time described by the above stereotypes, was radically different from the early Yi dynasty. The transformation period, the middle of the Yi dynasty,[1] was marked by a widespread implementation of Confucian practices, and thus we will refer to the transformation as the "Confucianization"[2] of the Yi dynasty social order. Other causes, such as economic and demographic factors, were undoubtedly involved. Korea had exhausted its frontiers, that is, there were virtually no new lands to be brought under cultivation, in the seventeenth century. The causes and dynamics of the transformation are beyond the scope of this paper; herein, we will merely offer one measure of the change. Woman's role in inheritance and succession will be our measure of the Confucianization of traditional Korean society.

After the middle of the Yi dynasty, during the Confucianized period, the predicament of a sonless woman throws the overall position of women into sharp relief. The barren woman (or the woman who had given birth to daughters only) was in a perilous situation. She was liable to be divorced and sent back to her own family and village (perhaps the most shameful thing for a young woman). Confucian ritual texts list the famous "seven offenses" for divorce, the *ch'ilgŏ chi ak*. Listed either first or second in most texts is the offense of not bearing a son. The other offenses include disobeying a parent-in-law, adultery, jealousy, theft, chronic illness, and talkativeness. These were not mere aphorisms: cases of divorce for each of these reasons can be found in the Yi dynasty annals.[3] Women who did not have sons were, in fact (although rarely), divorced for this offense.

In the late Yi dynasty, the sonless woman was not totally vulnerable. Her main protection was the institution of adoption. Adoption as defined by late Yi dynasty Koreans meant taking the son of a brother or cousin to be one's heir. The matter was of concern to a broad category of kinsmen: the adopting father, the biological father, and the lineage elders decided the matter. The son who was to be adopted was also a party to the process. The average age of the son was between twenty and thirty;[4] he was not a baby at the time of adoption. Childlessness became the concern of a large segment of the patrilineage, rather than of the conjugal unit alone, and the responsibility for providing an adopted son for a man who had died without issue was transferred from his widow to representatives of the lineage.

The practice of adoption was extremely widespread in the late Yi dynasty and in the early twentieth century. Around 15 percent of the men who passed the civil service examination in the late Yi dynasty were adopted sons.[5] A similar percentage of adoptions is seen in the genealogies covering the period. Demographically, the percentage of men who had no children, or who had daughters only, is probably around that same percentage. In the late Yi dynasty, apparently all those who could adopt sons did so.

The process of adoption enabled the barren wife to fulfill indirectly her duty of providing a son to carry on the line. The disrupting and unpleasant issue of divorce was avoided. A marriage allied two families and two lineages more than it did two individuals. The breaking up of the marriage therefore affected more than the husband and wife. It strained relationships between large groups of people who generally lived in fairly close proximity to one another. While marriage within the same village was rare, most marriages were contracted between members of two lineages with bases in the same or contiguous counties. Adoption was the means of attaining two important goals of Confucianism: the preservation of the marriage tie and the provision of a son to carry on the commemorative rites for the ancestors.

A woman was an associate member of her husband's patrilineage in the Confucianized society. Having been lost to her natal lineage through marriage, she was recorded in her husband's genealogy and was buried and commemorated in ceremonies with him, in consideration of having served as the instrument for carrying on his line through time. While it is true that a daughter was usually listed in her own lineage's genealogy—in the minimal sense that the Chinese character for "daughter" was written in, and beneath it her husband's name was recorded—nevertheless her children belonged to another lineage. And although a woman's line ended in her own lineage's genealogy, her line did continue in her husband's genealogy, at least in the sense that her sons and male descendants were recorded, and her daughters' marriages were listed. If she had no sons, the adoption of a son was indicated; her surname still appeared as the wife. Her place in the genealogy was protected through adoption.

Since a wife was considered a member of her husband's patrilineage in the late Yi dynasty, she received no share of inheritance from her father. Even if her father did not have a son, rather than give the property to his daughter, he would adopt an heir, who would be charged with carrying out the ancestor ceremonies and be given property in order to do so. The daughter was provided for by her husband's patrilineage. In the late Yi dynasty, if a man had several sons and daughters, the eldest son got the lion's share of the inheritance, the other sons divided up the rest, and the daughters got nothing (except for their dowries, which, however large, were not inheritances). Since daughters did not join in the ancestor ceremonies as ritual participants, they had no entitlement to the ritual land or the property used to finance these ceremonies.

Also as a hallmark of the Confucianized society of the late Yi dynasty, widows were discouraged from remarrying. Since a widow was a member of her husband's patrilineage, her remarriage posed numerous problems. What was to be done with the children? Once remarried, she would become a member of her new husband's lineage, while her children would remain members of her former husband's lineage. The ideal of a virtuous widow who eschewed all thought of remarriage became one of the most important values in Yi Korea. Being a chaste widow was one of the three paramount virtues that warranted the erection of a memorial tablet in the village in which such a woman lived. Even today, one sees the monuments honoring chaste widows (*yŏl*), filial sons (*hyo*), and loyal subjects of the state (*ch'ung*).

To summarize, we can make the following general statements about late Yi dynasty society:

1. Society was organized on the basis of the patrilineal descent group. The patrilineage, as it can be called, is succinctly defined as men related to men through men.
2. The superiority of males and the inferiority of females was assumed: *namjon, yŏbi*. In genealogies, for example, all sons were listed first and daughters listed last, regardless of birth sequence.
3. Only sons received inheritances, with the eldest son receiving the largest share.
4. In the ancestor ceremonies, the first son's line was more important than the other sons' lines. This division of importance in ceremonial position is manifest in the terms *k'ŭnjip* (direct descent line) and *chagŭnjip* (collateral descent line).
5. Intralineage adoption was the means of obtaining a son for the sake of continuing the line. A man who had daughters only was considered to have no children. Matters of adoption were decided by representatives of the patrilineage.
6. The record of a daughter in the lineage genealogy was brief. Lines of daughters seldom extended beyond one or two generations.
7. Remarriage for widows was strongly discouraged.

Confucianism is manifest in all of the above statements. The founding fathers of the Yi dynasty consciously sought the creation of a Confucian state. There were debates in the early Yi dynasty about the propriety of accepting an alien belief system at the expense of the indigenous one,[6] but how long after the founding of the dynasty did it take for the society to achieve a Confucian transformation? By examining the status of women we shall see that the "Confucianization" of the society took place long after the establishment of the political state.

The earliest records of sociological significance show that early Yi dynasty society was radically different from late Yi dynasty society. In fact, of the seven statements listed above that describe the salient features of late Yi society, *not one* is true of early Yi society. In the following section, we will examine some of the early Yi dynasty documents, and by looking at the role of the woman, we will see how much the society has changed.

WOMEN WITHOUT SONS

The documents that best reveal the surprisingly high status of early Yi dynasty women are inheritance documents. Not only do the Yi dynasty codes indicate that daughters should inherit property equally with sons but the actual wills and other inheritance documents also show that, in fact, property was divided equally. Inheritance documents that predate the seventeenth century clearly show that, regardless of the number of sons or daughters in a family, all got equal shares. If there were no sons, the daughters received the property. Whether there were two daughters and no sons[7] or five daughters and no sons,[8] the property was divided among the daughters. Sons were not adopted as they would have been in similar situations in the late Yi dynasty. Some inheritance documents indicated that the ancestor ceremonies should be carried out by all the children, on a rotational basis. Since all siblings had equal shares of the property, all also had equal responsibilities for the ceremonies. In cases where there was no son to carry on the line, daughters were urged to carry on the line and give the property to their children and urge them to carry out the ceremony. This practice is referred to as *oeson pongsa*, ancestor ceremony through the line of an "outside grandson," a grandchild by a daughter. A patrilineal grandson has the same surname as the grandfather, but an "outside grandson" has a different surname.[9] And yet, in the early Yi dynasty, there were numerous cases of people with one surname performing the ceremonies for an ancestor with a different surname.

Although wills and other inheritance documents indicate that property given to daughters was given to them in their husbands' names, this does not mean that it was given to their husbands. Women could own, control, give, and receive property.[10]

Another valuable category of document is the *chokpo*, the lineage genealogy. Early genealogies are rare. The fact that the compilation of genealogies on a really significant scale only got underway around the seventeenth century is in itself evidence of the influence of Confucianization.[11] In examining the oldest extant printed Korean genealogy, the *Andong Kwŏn-ssi sebo* of 1476,[12] one finds information on several interesting aspects of women's status.[13] In the first place, daughters and sons were listed in the order in which they were born, not sons first and daughters last. Second, the daughters' lines are continued in as much detail as are those of the sons. For this reason, people with the surname Kwŏn are in a minority in the *Andong Kwŏn-ssi sebo*. Third, there are numerous cases in which couples have recorded daughters only. In some cases there is only one daughter, in other cases five or six, but in no case is an adoption indicated. In the whole genealogy, there is not one case of adoption! Lest it be thought that this particular lineage was somehow out of the main stream, it must be pointed out that many prominent men, scholar-officials who held high government office, and even queens are listed in the genealogy. The Andong Kwŏn were prominent throughout the Yi dynasty.

Perhaps the most revealing feature of the 1476 *Andong Kwŏn-ssi sebo* is the indication that women remarried, and that they did so without any condemnation or hindrance. There are seventeen cases of women marrying twice in the genealogy. In contrast to the late Yi dynasty, when the Confucian ideal against the remarriage of widows held sway, we see that in the early Yi dynasty, not only did women remarry but they did so with impunity. In one case, the daughter of a woman who had remarried also remarried. The daughter's second husband was the mayor of Seoul.[14] Other husbands, sons, and sons-in-law of remarried women held important government offices. Some of the remarrying women were widowed, and some were divorced; in either case, they had a degree of freedom that the late Yi dynasty Confucianized woman would never have thought possible.

The transition between the pre-Confucian society of the early Yi dynasty and the Confucianized period of the late Yi dynasty seems to have taken place largely in the seventeenth century. One measure of that process can be seen in the adoption documents of the period. The Yejo (Board of Rites) kept a record called the *Register of Adoptions*,[15] in which each request and its approval or rejection were entered. In the *Register of Adoptions*, an abstract of the request, including an indication of who endorsed the action, was recorded. In the case of an unusual request, the justification for approving or denying the adoption was also given. Often the Yi dynasty codes were quoted to justify certain procedures. If a man feared that he might die without an heir, he could ask the government for permission to adopt a nephew; but if the man, himself, was deceased, then his wife, and only his wife, could make the request. In the early period of the register, there are requests made by uncles and cousins who asked special permission of the king for an adoption in cases where a husband and wife had both died. Initially, such requests received a great deal of attention, but as time went by, requests for adoptions initiated by lineage representatives, ignoring the role of the wife, increased in frequency and became routine. The role of the widow became unimportant.

Another tendency seen in the *Register of Adoptions* is a decrease in the role played by the wife's natal lineage in matters of adoption. Throughout the period covered by the register, requests had to be endorsed by representatives of "both families." In the requests dating from the early seventeenth century, those who endorsed the adoption were representatives of the wife's lineage as well as the husband's lineage. After the middle of the seventeenth century, the representatives of the wife's side ceased to be included. The quotation from the codes concerning "both families" continued to be used, but the interpretation was changed, so that it came to mean the two parties within the husband's lineage, the adopting family and the natal family of the son to be adopted. After the seventeenth century, only the names of members of the patrilineage are seen as the endorsers of an adoption. Adoption formalities had become a matter to be decided exclusively by members of the patrilineage.

Further evidence of the transition period is seen in a collection of wills and other inheritance documents of the Puan Kim-ssi lineage.[16] An inheritance document of this lineage dated in the early seventeenth century declared a new policy concerning daughters' inheritances and daughters' responsibilities for ancestor ceremonies. The preface of the document states: "Our family, unlike other families, no longer allows a married daughter to participate in the ancestor ceremonies on a rotational basis. For this reason a daughter will be given only one-third of a share." The Kims of Puan were in the avant garde of the social process we are calling Confucianization.

One final document will be abstracted to show the transition of Korean society from the more egalitarian,[17] indigenous culture of the early Yi to the Confucianized, patrilineal society of the late Yi dynasty. The document is the final disposition in a long series of law suits between a Ma family and a Chin family.[18] At issue was the question of who should inherit the ceremonial property for the merit subject, Ma Chŏn-mok (1358-1431), a man who helped Yi Sŏng-gye found the dynasty. In the first four generations of Ma's descendants, there was only one son in each generation. Then in the fifth generation, there were two sons, and the line divided. The second son had a large posterity, but the first son's line again had only one son for each of four generations. In the third generation after the line divided, there was a daughter, who was also given property of the primary line of Ma Chŏn-mok. This daughter married a man named Chin, and they had three sons, who carried out the ceremonies for Ma Chŏn-mok and his descendants. They performed the *oeson pongsa*, ancestor ceremonies by an "outside grandson." The brother of Mrs. Chin had one son, but there the line ended. The last man in the primary Ma line, and his wife, did not adopt. (See the diagram, below.) In the seventeenth century, adoption was not perceived as mandatory, and furthermore, the Chin brothers, the *oeson*, could carry out the ceremonies; therefore, no adoption was made. If this had occurred in the early Yi dynasty, the *oeson*, in this case the Chin brothers, could have held onto the Ma lineage property and carried out the ceremonies. If this had occurred in the late Yi dynasty, there would undoubtedly have been an adoption. But in the transitional seventeenth century, the solution was not clear. The collateral line petitioned King Sukjong to transfer the rights of the primary line to the collateral line ten years after the last man in the primary line had died. The king so decreed, and the right to perform the ceremonies was transferred, along with the ceremonial property, to the primary heir in the secondary line. The property that had belonged to the last man in the primary line was immediately transferred to the secondary line, but property that was held by the Chin brothers was not transferred. Several years later, after the Ma woman who had married into the Chin family had died, the heir of the secondary line filed suit against the Chin brothers, claiming that they no longer had the right to carry out the ceremonies and no longer needed the property.

The decision of the magistrate originally upheld the position of the woman's descendants, the Chin family, but on appeal, countersuit, and successive appeals, the decision was eventually reversed, and the collateral Ma line was given all the ceremonial property. The first suit was filed in the late seventeenth century, and the final judgment, in favor of the male line, was issued in 1751. One of the statements of the Ma descendant in his successful appeal was that "property of a prominent ancestor should not fall into the hands of an 'almost insignificant *oeson*'." The tenor of the final disposition is supportive of the idea that the male descendant should be the heir, and the impression is given that the Chin family somehow usurped the role of heir. From what we have seen above, however, a more reasonable appraisal is that the Chin brothers would have been legitimate heirs had they lived a few generations earlier. Had they lived a few generations later, they would have not have had any claim on the property. But living, as they did, in the

Diagram of the Ma Lineage

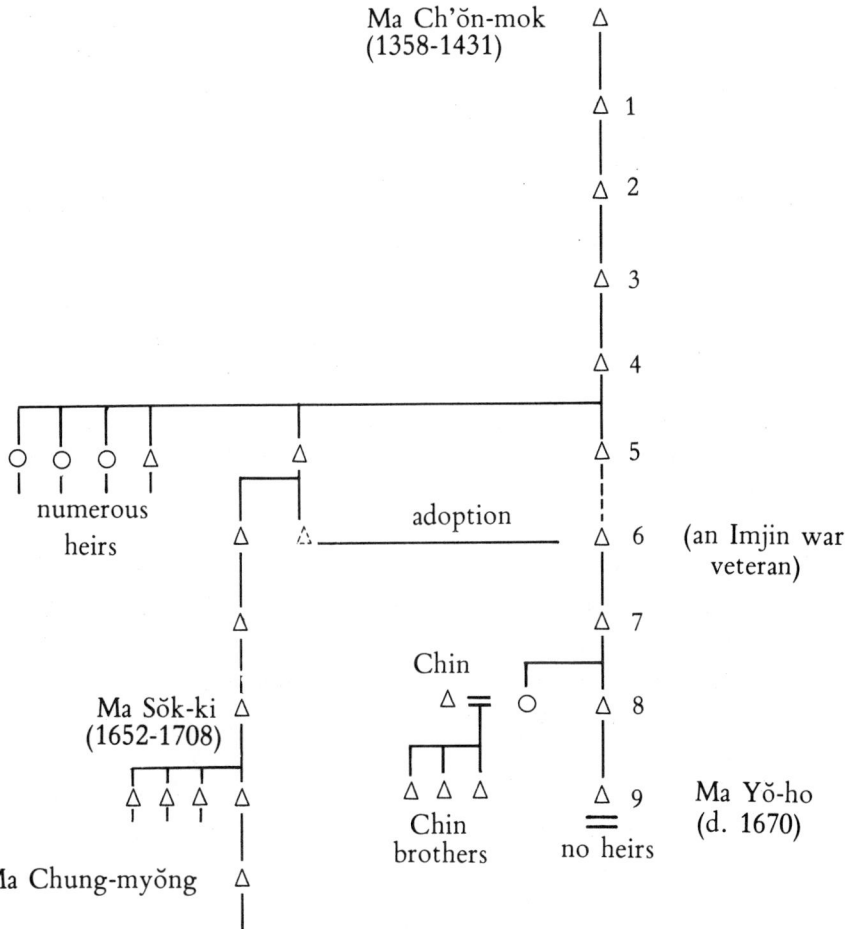

In the fifth generation, there were three sons and three daughters. The first son, the primary heir, did not have a son, but neither did he have a daughter; therefore, he adopted the eldest son of his younger brother. In the next generation, there were one son and one daughter; the son had one son, Yŏ-ho, but he had no children. It was probably due to the fact that Yŏ-ho had an aunt, the woman who married Mr. Chin, that an adoption was not made. The collateral line represented by Ma Sŏk-ki initiated a law suit against the Chin brothers in 1680. Eventually, after numerous countersuits and appeals, Ma Chung-myŏng in 1751 won the suit and gained ownership of the primary line's property, which had been held by the Chin brothers.

seventeenth century, the claim to heirship as an *oeson* weakened, as did a daughter's claim to heirship. By the middle of the eighteenth century, the transition appears to have been completed.

At the beginning of this paper, a list of seven statements describing the salient features of late Yi dynasty society was presented. The basis for generating those statements was an examination of the social position of women, particularly that of the woman who did not bear a son. By focusing on the role of women in early Yi society and by comparing the above statements to what we know about the early Yi, a list of the salient features of Korea's pre-Confucian society can be developed.

>1. The patrilineage was not the basic unit of society. The lineages that did exist were not organized on the principle of "men related to men through men."
>2. *Namjon, yŏbi*, the principle that men were superior to women, did not apply. As an example, daughters were listed with sons in the order of their birth, both in the genealogy and in inheritance documents.
>3. Inheritance was equally divided among sons and daughters. Women held rights to property and could give or receive property on an equal footing with men.
>4. Ancestor ceremonies were not the responsibility of the male children alone. Daughters also had responsibility for the ceremonies and held land to support the ceremonies.
>5. Adoption was seldom practiced. When an adoption took place, representatives of the woman's natal lineage were involved in the decision-making process. It was not a matter for the husband's kinsmen alone.
>6. Female lines were as important as male lines. In record keeping and in recognition of relationships, affinal ties seem to have been as significant as those between lineage members.
>7. Remarriage was not unusual. Prejudices against or limitations on remarried women and their children were minimal in the first century of the dynasty, but hardened thereafter.

The Korean society we often refer to as traditional, or Confucian, developed in the relatively recent past. The Yi dynasty Confucianization process was initiated by the founders of the dynasty at the end of the fourteenth century. The fifteenth century saw the implementation of a completely Confucian government and the beginning of arguments on changing the social order. In the sixteenth century, the acceptability of the alien philosophy was assumed, and the refinement of Korean Confucian commentary reached its high point. But it was not until the seventeenth century that the family and lineage were transformed.

Women in the early Yi dynasty could succeed to their own family lines, provide successors to their husbands' lines through either sons or daughters, and even have successors in their own right. With the complete Confucianization of society, a woman in the late Yi dynasty retained only the right of providing a successor to her husband's line, and that right was forfeited if she did not bear a son.

Notes

1. The seventeenth century is a general demarcation line. Certain aspects of the transition, such as the proscription against women remarrying that was implemented in the late fifteenth century, were realized earlier, while other aspects were realized later. Daughters received equal shares of inheritance in some households well into the eighteenth century.

2. It is possible to speak of the Confucianization of the Silla dynasty or the Confucianization of the Koryŏ dynasty. Each saw an influx and an acceptance of Confucian philosophy. The Confucianism that transformed the Yi dynasty was, of course, that of the Sung dynasty, revived by Chu Hsi, the Cheng brothers, and others, which is generally known as neo-Confucianism. It is recognized that the term "Confucianism" can mean many different kinds of things, as do Christianity, Buddhism, or Socialism. While it may be an oversimplification, the term will be used here for the sake of convenience.

3. For examples, see Lee Tae-yŏng, *Hanguk-ihon-jedo-yŏn'gu* [Studies on Divorce in Korea] (Seoul: Institute of Women's Studies, 1957); and Kim Tu-hŏn, *Hanguk-gajok-jedo-yŏn'gu* [Studies on the Korean Family] (Seoul: Seoul National University Press, 1969).

4. The calculation of the ages of the parties to an adoption is based on a study of the *Register of Adoptions*, used in conjunction with the *Tŏksu Yissi Chokpo*. See my article, "Adoptions in Korean genealogies," *Korea Journal*, Jan. 1974.

5. In the nineteenth century, the percentage of successful examination candidates was generally between 12 percent and 18 percent in any given year. The percentage in the eighteenth century was between 8 percent and 14 percent. The percentage was down to almost 0 in the fifteenth century, and there were very few indicated in the sixteenth century. The percentage increased drastically in the seventeenth century, from a range of 2 percent to 4 percent at the beginning of the century to a 6 percent to 10 percent range at the end of the century. The calculations are based on a survey of *Sama Pangmok* [Examination Rosters for the Secondary Civil Service Examination].

6. The publication of neo-Confucian texts and the promulgation of laws affecting the social order as well as other aspects of Confucianization are covered by Martina Deuchler in "The tradition: Women during the Yi

dynasty," in *Virtues in Conflict*, Sandra Mattielli, editor (Seoul: Royal Asiatic Society, Korea Branch, 1977); and in "Neo-Confucianism: The impulse for social action in early Yi Korea," *Journal of Korean Studies*, 2 (1980): 71-111.

7   Such a case is illustrated in a document in the *Kyujanggak*; a photocopy is included in *Komunsso-jipchŏn* [A Collection of Photocopies of Ancient Documents] (Seoul: National University Library, 1972): p. 202.

8   This case is described in a document in the museum at Ojukhŏn, the shrine to Yulgok, near Kangnŭng; a photocopy is included in Lee Tong-uk, *Komunsŏjipchin* [A Collection of Photocopies of Ancient Documents] (Seoul: Humanities Research Center, Yonsei University 1972): p. 62.

9   Conceivably a man and his *oeson* could have the same surname, but they would belong to different lineages. Two people with the same surname but with different lineage origins (*pon'gwan*) have different surnames for all intents and purposes.

10 The following document shows that property rights were held by women independently of their husbands. The document is a deed to five slaves given by a mother-in-law to a daughter-in-law. Since the groom was twenty and the bride was nineteen, the presentation could have been on the occasion of the wedding. In late Yi dynasty Korea, it would have been unthinkable for the wife of one man to give property to the wife of that man's son, for all the property was held by the men.

> The thirty-third year of the reign of Kanghsi (1694), June 3.
> A special allocation to Mde. Hong, the wife of my son, Ch'u.
>
> Fortune has been bad; I have lost my husband and have only one son. All my life I have wanted an illustrious daughter-in-law on whom I could rely to carry out the ancestor ceremonies. Now when I behold your visage and observe your deportment, I realize that you are all that I have ever hoped for. I am overcome by joy. Therefore, I have set aside these five servants and all of their posterity for you.
> Ongnye, a female slave, age 37
> Sang-ŏp, a female slave, age 9, first child of Ongnye
> Mungsil, a male slave, age 4, second child of Ongnye
> Mŏnsoe, a female slave, age 19, third child of Kyewŏl
> Maksoe, a male slave, age 10, fourth child of Kyewŏl
> They should "collect your edibles, fetch your water," and perform errands for you forever.
> Seal affixed by the property owner, Mde. Park, wife of Yi Sŏng-bu
> Scribed and attested by Yi Il-bu, cousin (*sach'on*) of Yi Sŏng-bu
>
> [Source: A quotation from an obscure Chinese text.]

11 The *chokpo* was used to keep track of the birth and death dates of ancestors, dates on which Confucian ancestor ceremonies were held. In the Confucian world view, society was hierarchical, and having a *chokpo* was primary evidence that one belonged in the upper stratum.

12 A copy of the 1929 reprint of the 1476 edition is in the National Center Library. An original recently emerged and has been loaned to the Kyujanggak for the purpose of printing another edition.

13 For more details, see Wagner's paper in this volume.

14 This individual was Pyŏn Nam-nyong, of whom Wagner also made note (see page 29).

15 The *Register of Adoptions* [*Kychu-dŭngnok*] survives today in the *Kyujanggak* collection of the Seoul National University library. The first volume is missing, but the second volume dates from 1618, and subsequent volumes cover virtually the remainder of the dynasty.

16 This collection is in the possession of the family, but photocopies are available at the Chŏnbuk National University Museum.

17 Society on the whole was strictly hierarchical, both before and after the transformation, with slave holders on top and slaves on the bottom of the social order. Within each class, however, society was more egalitarian in regard to the way women were treated.

18 This document is in the *Kyujanggak*, catalog no. 11981.

Minmyŏnuri: The Daughter-in-Law Who Comes of Age in Her Mother-in-Law's Household*

YOUNGSOOK KIM HARVEY

Introduction

> When my father died, . . . Our situation got worse with each passing year, and my mother had to give me in *minmyŏnuri* marriage when I was not quite twelve years old. . . . I was just told that on such-and-such a day I would be taken to my future husband's house. . . . I was so very young. . . . I didn't know enough to be even scared. So, carrying the *katsangja* [a hat box for the traditional hat worn by married men], I followed my elder uncle to my husband's house. . . . [Harvey 1979: 140].

Continuing, this *minmyŏnuri* recalled that seven years later, when she was almost nineteen,[1] she was married in a brief ceremony held in her mother-in-law's household.

> My mother-in-law and sisters-in-law prepared a small feast and invited some relatives and neighbors. They then put my hair up in a *tchok*, dressed me in the finest silk I had ever worn, and made me bow to my husband. I was married [Harvey 1979: 142].

She lamented half in jest that she had never ridden in a bridal palanquin [*kama*], but that is scarcely the most conspicuous distinction between *minmyŏnuri* and daughters-in-law married in the dominant form of marriage. Literally translated, *minmyŏnuri* means a daughter-in-law without a *tchok*, that traditional hairdo of long braided hair coiled at the nape and held in place by a long rod called a *pinyŏ*. The *tchok* was the most unmistakable diacritical mark proclaiming the status of a married woman. Symbolically

---

* The research upon which this paper is based was made possible in part by a grant from the National Institute of Mental Health.

more to the point, a woman married in the conventional way had her hair put up in a *tchok*, underwent the wedding ceremony at her natal household, and entered the household of her husband as a socially acknowledged adult. Not so the *minmyŏnuri*. She entered the house as a child, her hair in a single braid down her back, and ritually came of age upon marriage to one of the sons. Ideally, the *minmyŏnuri* about to be married was sent back to her natal home, there to have her hair put up in a *tchok* and to be fetched back by her husband to his household, but this procedure was apparently rarely practiced.

Many Koreans who have lived in China, Manchuria, or in the Korean provinces bordering China add a curious note of pride to their apologies for the institution of *minmyŏnuri* marriage. They say that while some Koreans, like the Chinese they have observed, bring in young girls to rear as future daughters-in-law, the Koreans wait at least until the girls are six or seven years old. The Chinese, they say, with a show of contempt, take these young girls away from their natural mothers in their infancy. Their remarks reveal that these Koreans were not particularly proud of the custom, although *minmyŏnuri* marriage was probably fairly common in Korea well into the first third of the twentieth century. Their attitude may also provide a clue to the relative paucity of information on the subject in Korean sources.

Today, young people in middle and high school speak of *minmyŏnuri* marriage with the detached familiarity of those who have learned about it from textbooks—as indeed they have.[2] People in their thirties and forties speak of the custom with much feeling and sometimes with horrified excitement at their narrow escape—by barely a generation—from the possibility of such a marriage. Most of their knowledge comes from a two-volume novel entitled *Minmyŏnuri*, which became a best seller at some time between 1945 and 1950.[3] Some Koreans in their forties and fifties have childhood memories of *minmyŏnuri*, usually of members of their parents' generation who came into their kin groups and/or villages.

Many Koreans of age sixty or more—about half of the people I interviewed—have intimate, detailed, personal recollections of specific brides or grooms who made *minmyŏnuri* marriages. Moreover, some of these women had been *minmyŏnuri* themselves; I found four. None could talk of her *minmyŏnuri*-hood without crying, though for one of them the event had taken place some seventy years prior to the interview, in 1903, when she was ten years old.

From all indications, the custom is vanishing, which makes it imperative to record such information about the institution as can still be gathered.

Collection and Sources of Data

In collecting data, I focused on the following issues:
1. Who became *minmyŏnuri*?
2. Who took a *minmyŏnuri*?
3. How old were they when taken to the households of their future husbands?
4. Were they ever adopted, even in the most informal way?
5. How were they treated? Were they treated like the natural daughters of the household?
6. How old were they when they had their hair put up in *tchok* and were pronounced married?
7. In what other ways did *minmyŏnuri* marriage differ from the dominant form of marriage?
8. How did *minmyŏnuri* marriages fare?

For this last question, asked only of informants who claimed personal knowledge of *minmyŏnuri*, I requested: "Tell me the tenderest story you know about a *minmyŏnuri* you knew. Tell me the cruelest story you know about a *minmyŏnuri* you knew." When interviewing *minmyŏnuri* themselves, I modified and elaborated the request further: "Tell me the cruelest experience you ever had because you were a *minmyŏnuri*. Tell me the tenderest experience you ever had as a *minmyŏnuri*." I then invited them to comment upon the common stereotype.

Reconstruction of the Custom of Minmyŏnuri Marriage

Some evidence suggests that the institution of *minmyŏnuri* marriage existed as long ago as the Three Kingdoms period (37 B.C. to 677 A.D.). In the Koryŏ dynasty (917-1392 A.D.), the officials of the Board of Rites entered numerous complaints about children being forced into marriage at an early age. This recurrent complaint echoed throughout the Yi dynasty (1392-1910 A.D.), with specific references to the abuse of *minmyŏnuri*. The

Yi dynasty government saw the custom of *minmyŏnuri*—widely practiced among the commoners, but also found among impoverished nobility—as a disguised form of slavery. The government attempted to ban the practice by establishing an absolute minimum age for marriage at twelve. Such official efforts apparently went unheeded, and the practice continued more or less unabated, since references to the evils of *minmyŏnuri* marriage appear regularly in official records (Deuchler 1977: 11-13). We know from both missionary and Korean accounts that the custom was prevalent in the late nineteenth century and the early twentieth century (cf. Moose 1911).

Kim Ku, a national hero of the Independence Movement, defends his unfilial disobedience to his mother in an impassioned passage of his autobiography. He had refused a *minmyŏnuri* marriage that his mother had arranged for him. He likened the institution of *minmyŏnuri* marriage to the forced Japanese annexation of Korea and vowed in a letter to his mother that he would resist such a marriage as he was already resisting the colonial rule of Korea by Japan (Kim 1947).

The novel *Minmyŏnuri*—if my memory serves—centers on the psychological conflicts of a man torn between his good will for and devotion to the woman his family reared to become his wife and his love for a radically different, modern woman, whom he ultimately marries. The dilemma of the triad is resolved, at least structurally, by the life-long sacrifice and devotion of the *minmyŏnuri*, who remains unmarried and dedicated to the welfare of the man, his wife, and their children.

The informants I have interviewed confirm the negative view of *minmyŏnuri* marriage that is implied in this brief review of the literature. Like *sim-pua* marriage, its Chinese counterpart, *minmyŏnuri* marriage was a despised form of marriage, practiced only by impoverished families out of economic necessity.[4] Also like *sim-pua* marriage, *minmyŏnuri* marriage was a social humiliation for the families involved. To minimize the shame, a family compelled to arrange a *minmyŏnuri* marriage could approximate the dominant form of marriage by exchanging gifts and sending the *minmyŏnuri* back to her natal home to be fetched back by her husband, her hair in a *tchok*, but it was apparently rarely economically possible to do so.

Like the Chinese *sim-pua*, the Korean *minmyŏnuri* marriage involved the transfer of the prospective bride from her natal household to the household of her future husband while she was a mere child, occasionally in infancy, but usually when she reached the age of six or seven. A *minmyŏnuri* candidate's desirability increased with age, whereas the groom's desirability diminished with increasing age. Even so, a big age gap between husband and wife was a conspicuous feature of *minmyŏnuri* marriage; it was possible for the husband to be as much as thirty years older than his wife. Apparently, a groom's parents considered *minmyŏnuri* marriage as a last resort, when it seemed the only means of obtaining a daughter-in-law.

Like the Chinese, the Koreans saw the advantage of training a future daughter-in-law "in the way of absolute obedience to a mother-in-law" (Moose 1911: 76) as the outstanding advantage of *minmyŏnuri* marriage over the dominant form of marriage; still, they were reluctant to enter into *minmyŏnuri* marriage except when economically necessary. It appears that the Koreans, unlike the Chinese, very consciously wanted to avoid the possibility of a mother-in-law abusing her defenseless *minmyŏnuri*.

Unlike the Chinese, the Koreans never confused the transfer and placement of *minmyŏnuri* in the households of their future husbands with adoption, not even as a euphemism. Female children brought in as *minmyŏnuri* were addressed and referred to as "the *minmyŏnuri* of such-and-such a household" by the villagers and were easy targets for the mercilous teasing of village children, as were their intended husbands. Within the household, the terms of address and reference used by a *minmyŏnuri* and in reference to a *minmyŏnuri* were those of a daughter-in-law. The only exception was that the *minmyŏnuri* observed an avoidance relationship with her future husband. The Koreans I interviewed dismissed as absurd the suggestion that *minmyŏnuri* might have developed emotionally intimate childhood or sibling associations with their intended husbands, as the Wolfs suggest for the Chinese *sim-pua*. My informants acknowledged that *minmyŏnuri* and their intended husbands were necessarily familiar with each other insofar as they were long-term coresidents in a single household.[5]

The quality of a *minmyŏnuri*'s daily life depended almost entirely on the disposition of her mother-in-law and sometimes of her sisters-in-law, the unmarried sisters of her future husband. Like the Chinese *sim-pua*, the *minmyŏnuri* was often badly treated. She learned her proper place in the household hierarchy from the different treatments that she and her sisters-in-law received.

A family that gave its daughter away in *minmyŏnuri* marriage was stripped of any claim to social advocacy and alliance. Thus, a *minmyŏnuri* might be a de facto slave in the household in which, much later in her life cycle, she would reign as mistress.

The *minmyŏnuri* was usually married soon after menarche in a ceremony before the family ancestral altar. She appeared with her hair done up in a *tchok*. Depending upon the family's economic circumstances, the occasion might be celebrated with a special meal of wedding noodles, to which neighbors and relatives were invited.

If, after several years of coresidence, culminated by a perfunctory wedding ceremony, either the bride or the groom or both objected to consummating the marriage, such objections are not reflectd in any of the culturally stereotyped references to *minmyŏnuri* marriage. It was not a problem with any of the four *minmyŏnuri* informants I interviewed. (Parenthetically, it may be of interest that many couples married in the dominant form of marriage report failure to consummate marriage on their wedding night because either one or both parties felt inhibited by shyness or frank disinclination.) Instead, the majority of my informants made recurring references to the continuing day-to-day hardships of *minmyŏnuri* even after the marriage ceremony. Without exception, informants added that *terilsawi*, the rare Korean uxorilocal marriage, was equally difficult for the husband. The two forms of marriage were seen as mirror images of each other, equally undesirable because of the extreme asymmetry of the spouse's power relationship to the affinal household. The informants themselves can best illustrate the kinds of problems that arose.

A sixty-seven-year-old informant[6] attributes his humanism to an incident involving a *minmyŏnuri*. The informant was the close friend of a Mr. Shin, who, almost immediately after his involuntary wedding to a *minmyŏnuri*, took a concubine and earned his mother's public and permanent wrath. When his mother died some years later, Mr. Shin sought my informant's help in arranging a "marriage" for his *minmyŏnuri* wife. Mr. Shin knew of a kindly old man of means, who agreed to take her as a concubine. Mr. Shin confessed to my informant that he had never consummated his marriage to his *minmyŏnuri*, explaining that he simply could not bear to have as a wife a woman so cruelly abused by his own mother and kin.

Another informant, an eighty-year-old woman (in 1980), related the following accounts, one from her natal village and the second from the village into which she had married.

MINMYŎNURI

When my informant was a young girl, she would visit a *minmyŏnuri* in her village. She recalled that she used to like visiting this woman, a bit younger than her own mother, because her whole household was warm and hospitable to neighbors, even young girls. One day, in a rush of good feelings for this lady, my informant spoke up: "Even though you are a *minmyŏnuri*, I think you have the most joyous life of all in our village. When I grow up and marry, I want to live like you, too."

"Is that so?" the lady said, adding, "Shall I tell you an old story?" She then proceeded to tell the following story:

> When I first came to this village as a *minmyŏnuri*, I was younger even than you; must have been all of seven. . . . Whenever I had a free spell, I used to sit huddled against the outside wall of the house by the chimney and cry. I wanted to go home to my mother. They fed me well enough here and kept me in warm clothes in the winter, but they worked me hard. Fetching water from the well in the winter was the bitterest thing I had to do. I was so cold that I used to cry, and that made it worse. One day when I was teetering toward the inner quarters [*anch'ae*] under the weight of my water jug that kept sloshing cold water over me, I heard someone hissing, "pss, pss!" It came from the kitchen of the male quarters [*sarang-bang*]. It was our Kolsu's father [her future husband]. "Come," he said, motioning me, "there are no elders at home." I was scared; I walked hesitantly toward him. He came forward and, lifting the water jug off my head, said: "You're cold, aren't you? Here, thaw your hands a little." He turned around to give me his back and told me: "Put your hands on my back, way up, under the jacket." My fingers were stiff and purple from the cold, but I just stood there. "Quick," he said, "do as I say." My hands melted in no time at all, next to his skin. After a bit, he said, "Have they thawed a little? Well, you'd better go now before the elders return." After that, I wasn't so scared any more and I stopped crying so much.

The next incident is from my informant's husband's village, and while it is no less touching, it is terribly cruel.

In this village, about a fourth of the households had brought in *minmyŏnuri*, so that discriminatory treatment of these young girls was commonplace, but one household was particularly notorious for mistreating the *minmyŏnuri*. The widowed mother and her son sometimes punished the child *minmyŏnuri* by hanging her by the wrists and burning the soles of her feet. The villagers were concerned for the girl's welfare, but they felt reluctant to intervene. Then one day, the girl was found missing. The villagers searched everywhere, including the well, often a place where unhappy women drowned themselves.

On the evening of the second day of the young girl's disappearance, my informant's husband was clearing the fire-hold (*agung*), reaching way into the flue with a long stick to get the ashes out before he started to cook cow fodder, when he felt a tug at the other end of the long stick. "Uncle," the missing girl called out from inside the flue, "don't start the fire. It's me; I'm hiding in here." Pulled out of her hiding place she said she could not take being burned on the soles of her feet any longer and had run away.

Thoroughly outraged, the villagers went to the home of her tormentors and grabbed the son. The village men gave him a public flogging. The mother was forced to witness her son's flogging, and both were told that continued abuse of their *minmyŏnuri* would not be tolerated. The next morning, the shocked villagers discovered that the mother and son had fled, apparently with the *minmyŏnuri* in tow. They were never heard from again.

It is clear that the Koreans, like the Chinese, have developed a cultural stereotype of *minmyŏnuri* based on actual incidences of cruel treatment and/or marital difficulties. The Koreans differ from the Chinese in the explanation they offer for the cultural stereotype. The Koreans point to the trauma of abandonment by their own kin and the abusive treatment that *minmyŏnuri* endured in childhood as the primary causes of marital distress. They do not attribute marital difficulties to sexual aversion resulting from childhood familiarity; nor do they assume the institution of *minmyŏnuri* marriage to be anything like incest.

Although a number of informants in their sixties and older have told me that about a quarter of the households in an average village used to have *minmyŏnuri*, I lack demographic verification. I do not know whether *minmyŏnuri* marriage was ever as commonplace in any part of Korea at any period as *sim-pua* marriage was in Hai-shan, Taiwan, where it was actually the predominant form of marriage. My impression is that it was not. In any case, *minmyŏnuri* marriage seems to have come to an abrupt decline around 1930, curiously enough about the same time that *sim-pua* marriage came to a noticeable decline in Taiwan (A. Wolf 1975).

Case Histories

The first *minmyŏnuri* I interviewed was born in 1893 in an isolated mountain village as one of the five daughters of impoverished parents. When she was ten years old, the family could no longer eke out a living in the village and headed for Seoul to seek work as laborers. En route, they stopped in the village where she now resides to visit an acquaintance from their village. A few days later, her parents and her infant sister—the other sisters were already married—left to continue their journey, leaving her in a stranger's household. She was to remain there, with a widow and her son, until her father returned for her. She was terrified, but, not knowing what else to do, she obeyed. Every day, as soon as the day's chores were done, she went to a spot overlooking the road where she had last seen her family, hoping for a sight of her father. After a month of it, the widow, her future mother-in-law, forbade this vigil. Now she hid among the soy sauce crocks and wept until she fell asleep. No one explained to her that she had been left as a *minmyŏnuri*. She cannot recall how she discovered it, but when she spoke to me of this period, some seventy years earlier, she wept. About three years later, she had her hair put up in *tchok* and was declared married in a family ceremony. Her husband, the only son of an impoverished widow, was eleven years her senior. She learned later that an earlier *minmyŏnuri* had died before she was old enough for a wedding ceremony.

Asked how she felt about marrying a man she had lived with in the same house for three years, she laughed like a shy young girl and said: "Such affairs have their own way of working out by and by." She gave birth to three sons and five daughters; two sons and two daughters are still living. Her first child was not born until she was nineteen, almost six years after her wedding.

She was "deathly afraid" of her mother-in-law, both before and after the wedding, and always knew that she was different from other village girls her own age.

When she was about fifteen and again when she was about seventeen, her father came to visit, but her mother-in-law would not allow them a meeting. The girl could only steal a look at her father from a distance and choke back her burning wish to ask about her mother and sister. On his final visit, when she was nineteen, he came with her younger sister, and her mother-in-law allowed them a brief meeting, then took her outside. There she said, "Your mother is dead. You must wail," and pulled out her *pinyŏ*, letting her hair fall loose and signaling permission to mourn her mother's death. Her father wanted to leave her younger sister with her, but her mother-in-law refused. Years later, she heard from an itinerant peddler that her younger sister was a *minmyŏnuri* in a village not far away; but she died shortly afterward.

Although they lived in the same house, she never spoke to her future husband directly until they were married. She never interacted with him, although of course she did his laundry and prepared his food. When asked if she had ever felt like a sister to her husband, either before or after the wedding, she thought the question absurd. According to her, it was simply not possible to confuse the premarital relationship of a *minmyŏnuri* and her intended husband with the relationship of a brother and a sister. She added, however, that she trusted him more than if she had come to him as a stranger, for she had had opportunities to observe him. She has much kinder memories of her husband, now twenty years dead, than of her mother-in-law. She recalled with joy that her husband tried to please her in small and often secretive ways, lest he anger his mother. Their marriage, she said, was "blessed," and they prospered. Her sons and grandsons are now among the more prosperous farmers in the village. Today villagers sympathize with her past hardships and love her for her hardworking and kindly nature.

The second *minmyŏnuri* was born in 1913 and orphaned by the time she was three years old. She was sent to live with her uncle and aunt in the village where she now resides. When she was about ten, she was given in *minmyŏnuri* marriage to the bachelor next door, a man long past marriageable age. Since she had lived next door for seven years, and since her aunt was still nearby, she did not suffer the *minmyŏnuri*'s sense of abandonment. Anxiety arose, instead, from the extreme poverty of her husband's household. They sometimes subsisted on pumpkin vine alone. Her aunt considered the marriage a good match nonetheless, because an orphan could not expect to marry a younger husband or a more prosperous one. In addition to her parents-in-law, there were three brothers-in-law and a sister-in-law, all younger than her husband. Having grown up next door, they were all very kind to her. The whole family pooled their resources to purchase some rice paddies of their own.

Her husband, she says, was kind to her. Three years after moving into her husband's household, she had her hair put up in a *tchok* and was pronounced married. She was thirteen. She claims she and her husband never quarreled, they were as happy as could be; and their neighbors agree with her claim. They had a total of ten children, three of whom are still living. Indeed, surrounded by their numerous grandchildren and great-grandchildren in one of the most prosperous houses in the village, she and her husband are the very picture of contented senescence. Recalling the earlier years of their life together, the informant says that with each additional increase in their lands, their self-confidence increased, and as they prospered and as time passed, they were able to forget the pain of their earlier grinding poverty.

The third *minmyŏnuri* I interviewed was born in 1919, the youngest of six children and the only daughter. She was cherished by her parents, who named her Kwinyŏ, precious girl. But because her father was blind, her family was unspeakably poor, and she was given away at six as the future bride of a widower's then fourteen-year-old son. She was carried piggy-back style by her future father-in-law from her home to the village where she now resides and immediately began to keep house for him and her future husband. In this case, the informant and her intended husband were referred to as "the children of our house" [*uri-chip aedŭl*] by the father-in-law, who himself had to instruct her on housekeeping tasks, since there was no mother-in-law. Still, the informant says that she never thought of her future husband as a brother or even like a brother. Certainly, she never addressed or referred to him as one. Her father-in-law was a kindly man, who raised her as if she were a true daughter. When he brought her firewood, he made sure that there were no thorns and cut it to just the right size so that she need not do it herself.

When she reached the age of sixteen, her father-in-law had her hair put up in a *tchok* and married her to his son in a family ceremony. The groom was twenty-four. When asked about marital sex, she says: "I slept at one end of the room and he, at the opposite end." Then, with a wry smile so fleeting as to be doubted, she adds: "Children are meant to be born." She gave birth to her first child when she was eighteen and eventually gave birth to eleven more children. Five are still living.

This informant felt that her case was atypical not only for *minmyŏnuri* but for any bride, since she had had neither a mother-in-law nor a sister-in-law in the household to contend with. But a neighbor woman who remembers the informant's arrival in the village added that it was immediately apparent that the informant was an extremely intelligent girl of cheerful disposition. Everyone, she said, "took to her": they were impressed by her determination to carry out her responsibility and were pleased by the warmth and cheer she seemed to bring into the household which had been without a woman for a long time. The family prospered after she came into it. Until the father-in-law died in 1968, four generations lived together in the largest house in the village.

My fourth *minmyŏnuri* is a shaman. Born in 1921, she was given away in *minmyŏnuri* marriage at age eleven, following her father's death. The fifth of seven daughters born to a well-to-do farmer whose land was taken away by his brothers on his death, she was sent to an equally prosperous farm household to become the wife of the eldest son, who was about fifteen years her senior and a widower with a two-year-old daughter. In addition to them, there were his parents, his two younger brothers and their wives, and their children. It was a busy household, where her primary responsibility was looking after her two-year-old stepdaughter-to-be. Her mother-in-law and two sisters-in-law were tolerant and easy-going people who gauged their demands on her according to her ability and maturity. She was always aware of the man who was to become her husband, but she had little direct interaction with him, as she did not interact with any of the male members of the household. She was raised like a prenuptial daughter by her in-laws and had her hair put up in a *tchok* when she was sixteen.

The most notable change in her life after marriage was that her husband, who continued to sleep in the men's quarters [*sarang-bang*], now periodically visited her at night. Until the Korean War uprooted the family, she had a very comfortable life as a whole, living harmoniously with her husband. She gave birth to seven children, all of them alive today.

MINMYŎNURI

Summary

For most Koreans below the age of sixty, knowledge of *minmyŏnuri* marriage comes from secondary sources, though some have childhood memories of *minmyŏnuri*. Even though a few *minmyŏnuri* informants can still be found, systematic data gathering is almost impossible, making the reconstruction of the institution necessarily a cautious matter. As a result, the description of the institution of *minmyŏnuri* marriage presented here is tentative and partial. Moreover, at least three of the cases reported here are not at all typical of the Korean cultural stereotype of *minmyŏnuri* marriages.

The available evidence indicates clearly that *minmyŏnuri* marriage was an undesirable form of marriage, most often a consequence of dire economic necessity in both contracting families or of poverty in the bride's family, matched by some equally compelling social disadvantage in the groom's family or personal disadvantage of the groom. The fourth informant's parents-in-law were sufficiently well-to-do to have negotiated a second marriage in the dominant form for their widowed son. Instead, they chose to bring in a *minmyŏnuri*, thereby averting potential conflicts between the new eldest daughter-in-law and the two secondary daughters-in-law already well established in the household, the mother-in-law, and the stepchild. In effect, the family opted to mould a future daughter-in-law, sister-in-law, and stepmother in patterns of behavior and temperament already established by the women of the household. There is no suggestion in the data presented here that the Korean mother-in-law used *minmyŏnuri* marriage to defend her uterine[7] family against the daughter-in-law's conflicting claim on a son's loyalty, as seems to be the case for the Chinese *sim-pua* marriage (Wolf and Huang 1980: 290).

Although three of the four cases presented above might give a contrary impression, the informants' general comments on the institution of *minmyŏnuri* marriage suggest that *minmyŏnuri* were usually badly treated, rather like second-class daughters in the Cinderella tradition, and were sometimes cruelly abused. Again, *minmyŏnuri* marriage was under no circumstances the preferred form of marriage for anyone able to negotiate marriage in the dominant form; it was a marriage option for families negotiating on the basis of mutual disadvantage. This option nevertheless gave a definite edge to the groom and his family, insofar as the bride's family relinquished all claim once the girl entered the groom's household. A *minmyŏnuri* forfeited even the hope of intervention by her natal family, were she to suffer abuse in her husband's household.

The emic perception of *teril-sawi* [uxorilocal] marriage as an exact mirror image also signifies that the chief difference between these options and the dominant form of marriage was the relative powerlessness of the incoming spouse. Recurring official references to the abuse and to the de facto slave status of *minmyŏnuri*, echoed in the cultural stereotype today and verified by actual first-hand accounts, all converge to single out the cruel oppression of the *minmyŏnuri* as the institution's most conspicuous attribute. In addition, informants spontaneously explained that the fundamental cause of the stereotypic marital difficulties associated with *minmyŏnuri* marriage lay in *minmyŏnuri* abuse. In contrast to the Chinese, who point to sexual aversion resulting from childhood familiarity as the primary cause of *sim-pua* marital difficulties, no Korean informant mentioned this as a factor. When asked explicitly to consider sexual aversion as an alternative or accompanying explanation, Korean informants considered the very suggestion absurd.

The four *minmyŏnuri* informants presented above ranged in age from six to eleven at the time they were transferred to their future husbands' households. The information elicited from other informants and secondary sources suggests that these four women were not exceptionally old at the time of their transfers. It appears that *minmyŏnuri* usually spent their early childhood—until the age of six or so—in their natal homes, an important contrast to the Chinese *sim-pua*.

Minmyŏnuri were apparently transferred to their husbands' households without any institutionalized ritual. The incorporation of the *minmyŏnuri* into the husband's household on arrival was equally unmarked by ceremony. This process of transfer was in no way perceived as a form of adoption, in contrast to the analogous process in China and Taiwan. The Korean kinship terms of address and reference used by and for the *minmyŏnuri* make explicit her status as a wife-to-be.

Following her transfer to the groom's house, the socially and personally powerless *minmyŏnuri* was socialized by her future mother-in-law and/or sisters-in-law to take her proper place in the household and to govern her behavior in accord with her subordinate status. When she came of age, the *minmyŏnuri* was married in a wedding ceremony that ideally replicated as much of the proper wedding ritual as possible, but that in reality might be little more than putting her hair up in a *tchok*.

In conclusion, it is not surprising to find that Koreans have held *minmyŏnuri* marriage in contempt. *Minmyŏnuri* were abused and, as a consequence, these marriages were notoriously unsatisfactory by Korean standards. The four *minmyŏnuri* I have described here are atypical: they matched or excelled those who married in the dominant form in approximating Korean ideals of marital success—family harmony, prosperity, health, and children—and at least three of them had unusually positive premarital socialization experiences in their husbands' households. The fourth woman's cruel treatment by her mother-in-law was amply compensated by her husband's kindness. These women's experiences—their kind treatment as *minmyŏnuri* and their subsequent successful marriages—support the emic hypothesis that abuse of *minmyŏnuri*, especially in childhood, was the primary cause of unsatisfactory *minmyŏnuri* marriages. It might be worthwhile to reconsider Wolf's sexual aversion hypothesis for similarly unsatisfactory *sim-pua* marriages in Taiwan. In Korea, at least, where *minmyŏnuri* spent their early to midchildhood in their natal homes, their particular socialization experiences as *minmyŏnuri* seem to provide more appropriate explanations of their subsequent marital histories than the sexual aversion hypothesis.[8] In any event, it is indisputably clear that Koreans are relieved to see no more of *minmyŏnuri* marriage as an institution.

Notes

[1] Koreans consider a child a year old at birth. Thereafter, everyone gets a year older on New Year's Day. As a result, there can be a difference of as much as two years between what Koreans have come to call "Korean age" and age computed by the anniversary of one's birth. In this paper, I use the Korean system.

[2] See, for example, *Middle School Social Studies, Vol. II*, by Sŏng-kŭn Kim, T'ae-rim Yun, and Chi-ho Yi, 1972: 18, for typical coverage of the subject in school texts.

[3] I myself read this novel when it was first published, but I have been unsuccessful in my efforts to procure a copy of it, although I have been searching since 1972.

[4] Margery Wolf (1968 and 1972) and Arthur Wolf (1966, 1968, 1970, 1975) have reported extensively on this practice for Taiwan. In his 1975 publication and in the more recently published work (1980) coauthored with Huang, Arthur Wolf reports that the *sim-pua* marriage was the preferred form of marriage in certain areas, even when it was economically unnecessary.

5 Some informants cited the Confucian concept of *namyŏ-ch'ilse-pudongsŏk* — the prohibition on males and females sitting together after age seven, which resulted in strict observance of spatial segregation by sex even in poor households — to explain the improbability of the suggestion. Some informants explained that intimacy between brothers and sisters was difficult even for natural siblings.

6 Some of the interviews were collected between 1971 and 1973 and others in 1980.

7 Margery Wolf (1972) defines the uterine family as the small, cohesive unit within the household created by a mother's relationship with her own children, particularly her sons. Her sons' wives are the greatest threat to the solidarity of the uterine family, because a daughter-in-law has the potential power to alienate her husband from his mother.

8 For a more complete treatment of the explanatory possibility suggested here, see Harvey and Lebra, 1978.

References

Deuchler, Martina
  1977   "The tradition: Women during the Yi dynasty," in Sandra Mattielli, ed., *Virtues in Conflict: Tradition and the Korean Woman Today* (Seoul: Royal Asiatic Society, Korea Branch): 1-47.

Harvey, Youngsook Kim
  1979   *Six Korean Women: The Socialization of Shamans*, American Ethnological Society Monograph #65 (St. Paul: West Publishing Co.).

Harvey, Youngsook Kim, and William P. Lebra
  1978   *The Minmyŏnuri Marriage in Korea: Incest or Daughter-in-Law at a Bargain?* Paper Presented at the Annual Meeting of the American Anthropological Association, Los Angeles, November 1978.

Kim Ku
  1947   Kim Ku Autobiography: *Paekpŏm Ilchi* (Seoul: Kukt'o-wŏn, in Korean).

Moose, J. Robert
  1911   *Village Life in Korea* (Nashville, Tenn.: Publishing House of the M.E. Church, South).

Wolf, Arthur P.
1966 "Childhood association, sexual attraction, and the incest taboo: A Chinese case," *American Anthropologist*, 68 (4): 883-98.
1968 "Adopt a daughter-in-law, marry a sister: A Chinese solution to the problem of the incest taboo," *American Anthropologist*, 70 (5): 864-74.
1970 "Childhood association and sexual attraction: A further test of the Westermarck hypothesis," *American Anthropologist*, 72 (3): 503-15.
1975 "The women of Hai-Shan: A demographic portrait," in Margery Wolf and Roxane Witke, eds., *Women in Chinese Society* (Stanford: Stanford University Press): 89-110.

Wolf, Arthur P., and Chieh-shan Huang
1980 *Marriage and Adoption in China, 1845-1945* (Stanford: Stanford University Press).

Wolf, Margery
1968 *The House of Lim: A Study of a Chinese Farm Family* (New York: Appleton-Century-Crofts).
1972 *Women and the Family in Rural Taiwan* (Stanford: Stanford University Press).

Women, Men; Inside, Outside:
The Division of Labor in Rural Central Korea

CLARK SORENSEN

Introduction

The public social structure of traditional agricultural villages in central Korea might be characterized as peasant, patrilineal, patriarchal, and Confucian. In spite of South Korea's industrial development since the mid-1960s, many social institutions developed during the more than five hundred years of the Yi dynasty persist with some modifications to accommodate a modern economy.

The villages are socially stratified, with a portion of the economic surplus going to the central government in the form of taxes. The household is the basic unit of both production and consumption. Apart from the government administrative structure, the lineage (*munjung*) is the most important social institution that links and organizes the households within the village. Membership in the lineage and eligibility to succeed to the house headship is reckoned patrilineally: Only direct descent in the male line from the founder of the lineage or household qualifies one for these social roles.[1] Most positions of authority in the household, in the lineage, and in the larger society are in the hands of males, and women must defer to males of the same or higher social class in most situations. The mode through which these social relations are formally expressed is based on standards of behavior taken from the Chinese Confucian classics.

In these villages, moreover, one observes a culturally-determined male/female division of labor. Women, in general, are confined to the domestic domain, running the household and taking care of the children; while the men take care of most affairs in the public domain. Politics are in male hands: Positions of authority requiring direct interaction with the government bureaucracy and rural or urban elites are invariably occupied by men. It is the (usually male) house head who represents the family in village assemblies or lineage councils. These bodies decide such important issues as who shall be adopted to succeed to a sonless house headship.

In the ancestral sacrifices, the most conspicuous rituals in which the relationship between households is expressed, only men make offerings; women must watch from the sidelines. In traditional villages, public social mixing of unrelated males and females is frowned on. Men work and socialize with men; women work and socialize with women. Male/female interaction thus takes place largely in the domestic domain—where the man's superior status is obvious and unequivocal. At meals, for example, women serve the men first, in sequence by status and seniority within the family. Often, the men eat in a special separate room. Only after the men have been served the best food do the women retire to a ritually less important part of the house—either the unheated half of the Inner Room (*unmok*) or the kitchen—to partake of the remains from the men's meal.

Under these conditions, a woman is marginal in two respects: Her tie to the household where she lives most of her life and raises her children is only by virtue of marriage rather than descent, and her tie to the institutions of the formal social structure is based on her husband's genealogical position and activity rather than her own.

In her natal home, a girl may be referred to as a "*ch'ulga oein*": "an outsider who will leave the household." Following patrilineal kinship, the typical Korean marriage in agricultural villages of the central region is patrilocal. The bride leaves her natal home to live in her husband's home (*sijip*), but she is not immediately integrated into her new household. Even though a married woman cannot participate significantly in the legal and ritual activities of her natal family or lineage, she retains her natal surname and clan seat (*sŏng* and *pon*) throughout her life. In contrast to her husband, who was typically born and raised in the household in which he resides as a married adult,[2] the woman is conceptually an outsider, brought into the household to provide services that cannot be provided by "true" family members.

According to standards based on formal and public institutions of kinship and social status, women's position is precarious: Women are confined to the domestic sphere; they have little formal authority; and they have a marginal status both in their natal and in their marital households. By confining our analysis to the formal and public institutions of village society, however, we get a distorted picture. The portrait of village society that has been painted so far is based primarily on the view of male informants. Public religious, social, and political action do not exhaust the possibilities of village behavior. In fact, they do not even exhaust the possibilities of *necessary* behavior. Other activities that are vital to the organization of village life must take place outside the public domain for the village to continue over time. Children must be born and raised; old people must hand their tasks over to the young; and, amidst it all, the household must produce enough food for everyone.

Males often seem to take for granted activities in the domestic domain, and the intimate details of everyday life are not the object of public display. Informants who can conceptualize the intricacies of lineage structure as an abstract system do not usually think of the structure of domestic life in an organized, systematic way. Still, the organization of domestic life has an important influence on the relative power of the sexes, despite an ideology that denies important public roles to women. In a large number of households in traditional, central Korean agricultural villages, women's position is far less subordinate than one would expect, given the preceding description of village social structure.

There is little variation from house to house in the culturally-determined division of labor between males and females; everybody agrees upon the work that is appropriate for males and for females. As one might expect in a stratified peasant society, however, the concrete socioeconomic circumstances of the various households are not all the same. Some households have a great deal of land, while others have none; some households have a shortage of labor, while others have a labor surplus; some households are embedded in powerful local lineages, while others are almost totally isolated from agnatic kin. Because of these variations in the social and economic positions of village households, the females' relative contributions to the households' incomes, the relative weight of labor and resources controlled by females, and the importance of male activity in the public domain also vary. These variables, in turn, affect the social and economic position of a household in village society. By this scheme, although females may appear to be marginal and powerless, in the domestic sphere they can attain positions of power comparable to or greater than those of their husbands.

My analysis of the domestic organization of Eight Peaks Village, where I lived and researched for eleven months in 1977,[3] reveals that (1) the social structure of village society allows women certain kinds of power, despite social norms that seem to deny them any; and (2) variations in the social and economic circumstances of village households cause variations in the relative power of males and females in those households.

Village Social Structure

The upland extension of the Han River Basin into the western part of Kangwŏn Province in South Korea is known as the Yŏngsŏ Region. Although the villages of the Yŏngsŏ Region are not as rich as their counterparts in the more favorably situated Han River plain around Seoul, the life of the inhabitants differs little in its essentials from that of their richer, lowland brethren. Except for the extreme highland areas of the T'aebaek Range, most of the area drained by the Han River (Kyŏnggi Province and Western Kangwŏn Province) belongs to a culture area that can be defined by three characteristics: an agricultural economy centering on the cultivation of single-cropped, irrigated rice (Bartz 1972: 69); the use of one of the central group of Korean dialects (Ogura 1944), and the construction of the L-shaped farmhouse (Ima 1924). Eight Peaks Village is an example of a village in this central culture region. It is made up of several named hamlets, which range in size from 3 or 4 households to more than 40 households, with a total population in 1977 of 608 persons in 114 households.

Two of the main sociological units in Eight Peaks Village are the household (*chip*) and the local lineage (*munjung*). Both units are organized along agnatic principles, but they have distinct functions. The lineage is a corporation of men, all of whom are descended in the male line from the same ancestor. Although every male, since he is the descendant in the male line of *someone*, potentially belongs to a lineage, not all of the theoretically possible lineages actually come to be organized. A potential lineage becomes an actuality when some paddy is set aside and rented out to finance annual tombside sacrifices to the lineage ancestors (*sihygangje*). The descendants of these ancestors found an organization with officers who manage the property, arrange the ancestral sacrifices, and keep the lineage genealogy up to date. The lineage is not primarily an economic unit. Although tracts of land are owned by the lineage, the income from each tract serves primarily to finance the ancestral sacrifices; it is usually not used for subsistence. Villagers depend upon neighbors, whether they belong to the same lineage or not, for cooperation in agricultural activity.

The right to participate in lineage ancestor ceremonies and the genealogical order of precedence observed in these rites are ritual expressions of the status of each of the lineage members vis-à-vis one another. Since the status of the household follows the status of the house head, and since it is the house head who represents the household in lineage rites, lineage relationships structure the hierarchical relationship between lineage households in the village. The lineages usually try to operate as unified political units. Lineage elders try to promote lineage interests by encouraging united voting in elections and by fraternizing with the bureaucrats who are responsible for local administration. High-status lineage elders usually have relatively free access to such local bureaucrats as the township head (*myŏnjang*) or village head (*ijang*). Although the economic functions of the lineage are few, the political functions are extremely important.

A man who holds a prominent genealogical position in a lineage may exploit this position by acting as host in the *sarangbang*. The *sarangbang*—a separate room in a separate wing of the household—is the preserve of senior household males. It is the only room of the household that can be directly entered from the outside. The *sarangbang* of prominent men become gathering places where, of an evening, issues of village concern are discussed. Because of the ethic of respect for elders and genealogical seniors, the men who host these gatherings often exert a disproportionate amount of influence on discussions and become informal leaders in village opinion making.

The household, in contrast to the lineage, is primarily an economic unit. An on-going economic corporation under the legal control of the house head (*hoju*), it exists independently of its membership at any given point in time, though, of course, it must have *some* members at all times. Rules of marriage, legitimacy, divorce, succession, and adoption determine which members can be added to, or subtracted from, the household and insure the continuity of the corporation despite changes in personnel.

In its ideal form, a household is made up of the house head, his unmarried siblings, his wife, his eldest son, his eldest son's wife and children, his other unmarried children, and all his other direct descendants in the senior male line, together with their wives and children, as well as direct male ascendants up to the fifth generation and their wives. The household is thus equivalent to the patrilineal stem family. With succession, these households theoretically could continue eternally. As a practical matter, however, households come and go. A new household is established when a younger brother splits off from his natal home at marriage (*pun'ga*), or an old household may die out if there is no male issue, either biological or adopted. Households usually die out only if there is no inheritance to motivate an adoption.

The household is the basic socioeconomic unit of the village, because the fundamental tasks that are most basic to human survival are all performed within the confines of the household. The house head, as the representative of the household, should ideally have under his control all the resources in land and capital that are necessary for the family to support itself through its own agricultural labor. Households are thus the basic units of both production and consumption. For the household to function over time, members must produce, store, and process food; build and maintain a homestead; prepare and serve meals; procure, wash, and mend clothes; and bear and raise children. For all of these tasks, there is a clear division of labor between male and female household members.

The bulk of household income comes from the major field crops—primarily grain (rice, barley, wheat, sesame, and maize) and beans (soy, red, and kidney). Although women on occasion do all agricultural tasks except those involving the use of animal or mechanical power (such as plowing or threshing), males provide most of the skill and the labor used in producing these crops. In addition, males provide labor for the construction and maintenance of houses, dikes, and agricultural tools. Males usually gather the fuel for heating and cooking. Most of this work is done outside the house and is known generically as *pakkannil* (outside work).

Labor requirements and labor organization for wet-rice agriculture in central Korea are such that no household is totally self-sufficient in animal and labor power. Households exchange or hire labor (*p'um*) to meet peak period demands. They also may join other households in cow exchange (*sokkyŏri*), irrigation, and cooperative crop marketing. To operate advantageously in this system, men must constantly socialize and exchange information among themselves. Since the quality and amount of each man's interaction among the other men are conditioned by his position in the political system, a man's concern with village social structure forms an integral part of his economic role in the agricultural system.

If it is the males who provide the house and the major part of the income necessary for the maintenance of family life, it is the females who run and organize domestic life. They grow vegetables for cooking and process the foodstuffs that are provided by the men. Although rice is commercially milled, females in the more remote rural areas still do such primary processing as making bean curd (*tubu*) out of soybeans and grinding grain into flour. Women prepare and serve meals, do the laundry, clean the house, and—most important of all—bear and raise children. Women's work is usually done in or near the house and is generically known as *annil* (inside work).

By dividing the necessary household labor into two components—inside work and outside work—and assigning one component to the females and one to the males, the residents of Eight Peaks Village have developed an efficient system for expediting their work. Working in or near the house, the women combine such time-consuming daily tasks as food preparation with other less regular but equally important tasks—food processing, tending the vegetable plot, and doing the laundry—all in a context where they can care for young children, without the added burden of transporting them long distances. At the same time, the men can count on smoothly-run households and hot food awaiting their return from work that is done at a distance from the house—field labor, gathering firewood, and dealing with the bureaucracy. Agricultural tasks, while highly seasonal, require in their season a dawn-to-dusk commitment in a place far from the household. In addition, some of these tasks—like plowing or repairing dikes—require a fair amount of physical strength.

This division of labor between males and females is reflected in the organization of space in the Eight Peaks farmhouse. In Eight Peaks, the well-developed house is usually divided into two L-shaped wings, almost enclosing a courtyard. One, the Inner Wing, is completely surrounded, either by the homesite fence or by the other wing. The Inner Wing holds the Inner Room (*anbang*). This wing is the place of work and residence for the house mistress, her children, and her daughter-in-law, if she has one. The other wing, known as the Outer Wing, is located on one edge of the housesite so that the main gate to the homestead bisects it. This wing holds the *sarangbang* (house head's room) and is the place of work and residence for the house head and other unmarried adult household members. Other rooms in the Outer Wing are used to store agricultural equipment and to shelter domestic animals.

If we look at the male/female division of labor and at the arrangement of the Korean house, it is easy to see that an inside/outside theme is present. The house mistress lives in the Inner Room (*anbang*) of the Inner Wing (*anch'ae*) and takes care of the inside labor (*annil*); while the house master lives in the *sarangbang* of the Outer Wing (*pakkatch'ae*) and takes care of the outside labor (*pakkannil*). Moreover, the house mistress, although formally known as *chubu*, can colloquially be called the "inside master" (*an chuin*); while the house head, formally known as *hoju*, can colloquially be known as the "outside master" (*pakkat chuin*).

This use of the native Korean words for inside and outside to designate the chief male and female members of the rural household reflects the actual physical location of each person's work and residence. The woman's work *is* mostly done inside the house, and she *does* live in a wing located inside the fence that marks the house site. Similarly, the man's work *is* mostly done outside the household, and he *does* live in a wing that is on the outer edge of the house site. The use of these metaphors goes beyond mere location, however, and reflects the sociological positions of the house master and house mistress within the household. The family in Eight Peaks is normatively patriarchal; most authority—the socially sanctioned right to make decisions binding upon others—lies in the hands of the house head, who is by law the senior male of the household. But the economic division of labor and the social interplay of males and females in a typical household leave the house mistress with a great deal of de facto power. The house head is not competent to control the day-to-day economy of the household, both because he is outside the house most of the time and also because he does not have the knowledge or skills necessary to do the work. A man leaves the allocation of those resources necessary for the day-to-day running of the household to his wife. The house master retains the ultimate authority, so that, for example, if he wants something to eat, he has the right to direct one of the women of the household to provide it for him, but that authority is only indirect, since he does not actually go into the kitchen to procure this food for himself. In Eight Peaks, if no woman was in the house at the moment when the man wanted to eat, the usual solution was to get some other woman, perhaps a neighboring kinswoman, to prepare the food (of which she herself could also partake), or obtain the food from the local winehouse, or go to the house of a kinsman, where food would not be begrudged him. In Eight Peaks, men very rarely and only under unusual circumstances actually tried to cook for themselves.

The control of money yields a similar pattern. Traditionally, the house head controlled the money and did the marketing. This pattern has changed, however, since the end of World War II. Women now take a larger role in money management, and ordinary marketing at the periodic markets is done almost entirely by women. This change in men's and women's activities is still consistent with the inside/outside, male/female division of labor. Until only recently, women needed little money to manage the household from day to day. Most households were almost entirely self-sufficient in foodstuffs. With the gradual commercialization of the rural economy, more and more ordinary items—noodles, canned fish, ramen, candy—are purchased at the periodic markets scattered around rural Korea, and, consequently, markets are now patronized by women rather than men. Although men control the money for major purchases, the small amounts of cash that the women need to do their marketing usually come from their own housekeeping money. This money, if not taken from a hiding place to which both husband and wife have access, comes to a woman in any of several ways: She may take small amounts of grain to market to sell for the cash she needs, or she may earn a little egg money from her chickens—a limited option in remote villages like Eight Peaks. A woman's responsibility is to run the household efficiently however she sees fit, and a man has no reason to probe into the details of that management unless something goes wrong.

Since the house mistress has relatively independent control over the allocation of the resources that are associated with the inside labor, the house head, who normatively is supposed to control all household activities, only indirectly controls the resources associated with the day-to-day running of the household. If the family is poor, moreover, there may be virtually no surplus left after the subsistence needs of the household have been met. Here the house head can control his household only by exerting his authority over his wife. Thus, the actual dimensions of the house head's power over the house mistress depend upon the relative contributions of the husband and wife to the household economy and on their own personalities. There is no set balance of power that holds for the relationships between all the house heads and house mistresses in Eight Peaks Village, but rather a range of possibilities, conditioned by the socioeconomic circumstances of each individual family. The extent of this variation can be illustrated with a few examples of village households.

(1) Forty-one-year-old Paek Pujok is the youngest of four sons in one of the more prosperous segments of the village's dominant lineage. His eldest brother refused to divide the inheritance.[4] Therefore, up until last year, the three younger brothers lived together in an undivided household under the headship of the second brother and made their living by tenant farming. Last year, the three brothers split up. One brother went to a neighboring village, and each of the other two brothers found a house in one of the hamlets of Eight Peaks itself. As a tenant farmer, Paek Pujok is economically in the lowest fifth of the village, but, since he has many patrikin in the village, he can always count on finding land to rent. As a supplement to his meager income from farming, both he and his wife do day labor for wages (*p'ump'ari*) when the opportunity arises in his own or in neighboring villages where he also has patrikin. Male labor is in demand more often than female.

Like other villagers at his economic level, Paek lives in a thatched house, consisting of a single wing of three rooms—the kitchen, the Inner Room, and the Upper Room—lined up to form a rectangle. He has not added the verandah and the Opposite Room that would make his house the typical L-shaped central Korean farmhouse, because his eldest son, who normally would marry and live with his wife in the Opposite Room, is only seventeen and unmarried, and has gone to Seoul to find a job. He will probably not come back to Eight Peaks even after his marriage. Since the family is short of land instead of labor, it would be even more difficult for them to make ends meet as a stem family than as a nuclear family.

Membership in an important and powerful local lineage is a great advantage to a person like Paek Pujok. His many patrikinsmen will rent out land to a kinsman in preference to a non-kinsman. This gives Paek Pujok an advantage over the majority of tenant farmers, who do not have such connections. In other respects, however, his position in the lineage is marginal. Formally he is classified as a branch house (*chagŭnjip*) of his eldest brother (*k'ŭnjip*). Household ancester worship is carried on, in Eight Peaks, only at the home of the eldest sons or grandsons (*chongson*). At the tombside ancestor worship ceremonies (*sije*), the heads of these main households of the senior lines (*k'ŭnjip*) play the most important roles. Thus Paek is in a poor position, both economically and genealogically, to exploit activity in the public domain for the benefit of his household.

His wife is known as a woman of strong will and sharp temper. Paek cannot control her in the least. In fact, she makes most of the household decisions. Paek is so afraid of her that once, when he went to a neighboring village to do wage labor and lost his wages on the way home, he was afraid to come home for two days, much to the disgust and amusement of the other village men.

(2) Kang Hanso's father died young, so that he had to start working in the fields when he was only ten years old. Although he is the second of two sons, his elder brother granted him some land, and, by raising cattle, he earned enough money to buy his brother out when he moved to town. Now Kang Hanso is one of the richest farmers in the village and has a new house with a tile roof, the second largest in the main hamlet of Eight Peaks. This house, although large, consists of a single Inner Wing, but with two spare rooms rather than the more usual single one; the rooms are larger than the rooms in most village houses.

Although Kang has patrikin in the village, they are only distantly related to him, and there is little solidarity among them. In any case, since Kang is the younger of the two brothers, he participates in ancestor worship at his brother's home in town, rather than in the village. He is less tradition-bound than many of his fellow villagers, and he is less inclined to try to consolidate his position through kinship or run a *sarangbang*.

Although he could use one of his spare rooms as a *sarangbang*, he prefers to invest his capital in economic ventures, which is one reason for his present prosperity. His son is presently at an agricultural high school and will probably return to the village to occupy an empty room and form a stem family. With a great deal of land and only one son, Kang is short of labor, even though he has several daughters. His wife does an unusual amount of field labor for a woman in such a wealthy household, while Kang Hanso helps with silk raising, normally a woman's task. Kang and his wife are relatively equal. Both of them make their own decisions in their own spheres, and they consult with each other on major decisions.

(3) Han Pyŏlsu's economic level is approximately equal to that of Kang Hanso. He was born the eldest son of a branch house of an important village lineage segment. The headship of the segment should have been passed to

the son of Han's senior uncle, but this uncle died without male issue. Han, as the seniormost grandson, was thus raised under the watchful eye of his grandfather and was eventually adopted to succeed to the line of his deceased senior uncle. When Han Pyŏlsu married, he was brought into his grandfather's household, where he now lives as house head. This house exhibits all of the features of the ideal traditional homestead—it has both Inner and Outer Wings developed into the full L shape, and it has an active *sarangbang*. Upon the death of his grandfather, Han succeeded to the house headship, inherited the household property, and moved into the *sarangbang* from the spare room in the Inner Wing, where he had been living up until that time. The three other lineage households that are ritually dependent upon Han are economically independent, but their ritual dependence puts Han in a strong position in the village kinship network. As head of the main household of the local lineage, he plays a major role in all lineage-related rituals. He spends considerable amounts of money in conspicuous consumption related to this ritual and in providing hospitality to patrikin who visit the village. A constant stream of visitors, both from the village and from the area within about twenty-five kilometers of his house, fills his *sarangbang*. Publicly, he is an important figure, and for a number of years he was village head.

Han's wife is hard working, and has considerable responsibility in running such a large household. Nevertheless, Han wields considerably more power than she does. He uses a large portion of the household resources to uphold his image in the public domain. Han, as befits his important public position, lives in the *sarangbang*, where he spends a great deal of time interacting with visitors and transacting public business. Food is usually brought to him there by members of the household. He spends a great deal of his time in the township seat or in the provincial seat transacting business with government bureaucrats, maintaining contact with important patrikin, and settling more mundane matters. His wife, on the other hand, does not participate in these high status activities or manage the large sums of money that are not used in day-to-day subsistence.

In these three examples of domestic relations, taken from the more than 100 households of Eight Peaks Village, we see a wide spectrum of behavior, ranging from a husband under the control of his wife, to a couple with a relatively equal power relationship who cooperate in decision-making, to a couple with sharply differentiated roles and with the male clearly in a more powerful and prestigious position than the female.

Because of Paek Pujok's poverty, the differentiation between the roles of husband and wife is minimal. Both the husband and the wife make important contributions to the household income, and there is little income surplus for male public activities to raise the household's position in the community. Almost all of the income goes into running the household, which is the female's responsibility. In such cases, the man's control over the allocation of household resources depends upon his ability to wield his formally recognized authority over his wife. With the wife in the strategic position, the de facto division of power between husband and wife depends largely on the forcefulness of personalities of the two people. A strong-willed woman may gain effective control of the family, though in most cases a fairly equal cooperative relationship between husband and wife develops.

In the case of Kang Hanso, the relative equality of husband and wife rests not so much on the lack of an economic surplus but rather on the effects of a "capitalistic" investment strategy. Because of his genealogically unfavorable position in the lineage—albeit a poorly developed lineage—Kang would gain little by investing his resources in conspicuous consumption related to ancestor rituals and lineage affairs. He would always have to play second fiddle to his older brother no matter how great his investment. Economic investments give a good return nowadays, not only in monetary gain but also in social status. Having large amounts of land and only a nuclear family, Kang is short of labor. His wife does more field labor than is usual for families in Kang's economic position. Since Kang does not participate much in the public activities that exclude women, and there is no marked distinction between inside and outside labor in his household, Kang and his wife remain on fairly equal terms.

Only in the case of Han Pyŏlsu do we see the full economic and social development of the differentiation between male and female roles. Because of his wealth and his pivotal position in the kinship system, Han is able to invest his economic surplus and time in the rituals that enhance his social status and in the political activity that increases his power. He presides at the semipublic ancestor worship ceremonies for the ancestors of his sublineage and he serves as the village representative of his local lineage. Each of these activities enhances his status but excludes his wife. As a concomitant of these activities he has received enough traditional Chinese-style education to read ritual manuals written in *hanmun*[5] and to be somewhat of an expert in traditional ritual. Within the village, Han draws on his sublineage for political support. Outside the village, politically useful contacts with nonresident patrikin allow him to operate as a broker between the less sophisticated villagers and the outside world of business, schools, and bureaucrats.

Han Pyŏlsu has the economic resources, the genealogical position, and the motivation to operate within the traditional lineage system. These activities maximize the differentiation between his and his wife's responsibilities. He has little time or inclination to concern himself with "trifling" household matters, though he controls a great deal of the household economic surplus, investing it in activities which enhance his status. His activities in the public sphere take him physically away from the family much of the time, and this allows him to acquire a sophistication and knowledge about outside affairs which his wife cannot match. The qualities required of one who plays these high prestige roles—education, proper behavior, command of standard and formal Korean, sophistication in dealing with urbanites— are in themselves highly valued, and make his wife, who shows considerable ability in managing a complex household, seem ignorant by comparison.

Conclusion

In the social structure of Eight Peaks Village, two spheres of activity—the domestic and the public—are dominated by two different institutions, with totally different functions. In the domestic sphere, the *household* functions to provide the basic subsistence needs of the villagers. It is formally structured by patrilineal principles, so that the patrilineal stem family, with authority vested in the senior male, is the ideal. The inside/outside division of labor, however, leaves the house mistress in de facto control of those resources necessary for the day-to-day running of the household, so that marked differentiation between the amount of power held by the husband or wife is not a necessary consequence of household organization per se. In the public sphere, the *lineage* functions to link, rank, and organize households within the village and the local area. Structured by principles of patrilineal descent and the restriction of public activity to males, lineage activities in principle and in fact exclude women almost entirely.

Although the woman of Eight Peaks comes into the patrilineal household as an outsider with a marginal position, as she gives birth to children she becomes the "inside master," the one who controls most of the purely domestic household resources. In a poor household, or in a household with no important patrikin, both males and females must make significant contributions to the household's income, and there is little surplus left for the male's exclusive control after the household's day-to-day needs have been met. Under these conditions, marked differences in status and power between males and females do not usually develop. It is only when the household can produce an economic surplus for investment in status-enhancing activity in the public sphere, and when the household's genealogical position in the lineage is prominent enough to merit such investment, that the inside/outside division of labor allows the house head to attain a great deal more power in the public sphere while his wife remains at home.

Notes

[1] There are two main circumstances in which a woman may become a legal house head: When the household has no male members and when a uxorilocal marriage (*ippuhon*) has been contracted in the absence of a male heir. In the former case, the household is on the path to extinction, since no heir has been provided. The latter institution, uxorilocal marriage, is seldom resorted to, and there were no cases of it in Eight Peaks Village.

[2] The case described is that of the eldest son. Subsequent sons will form new households at or shortly after their marriages.

[3] Research for this paper was done with the financial assistance of a Fulbright-Hays predoctoral grant from the United States Department of Health, Education, and Welfare and a Stout Grant from the University of Washington, Seattle.

[4] This was made possible by a peculiarity of the inheritance law during the colonial period (1910-1945) in which, although a younger brother had the right to demand a portion of his father's land if he had already split from the parent household (*pun'ga*), he needed permission from the house head of that household to split off in the first place. By denying permission to split off, the eldest brother, head of the main house, could effectively prevent the younger brothers from claiming their share of the household property (Kim 1975, pp. 277, 486).

[5] *Hanmun* means classical Chinese, which was the literary language of Korea up until the twentieth century.

Bibliography

Bartz, Patricia. *South Korea* (Oxford: Oxford University Press, 1972).

Brandt, Vincent S. R. *A Korean Village: Between Farm and Sea* (Cambridge: Harvard University Press, 1971).

Ima Kazujiro. *Chōsen buraku chōsa tokobetsu hōkoku, Daiichi setsu* (Minka) [Korean Village Special Survey Special Report, vol. 1, (houses)] (Keijō: Toto Shoseki, 1924).

Kim Chu-su. *Ch'inch'ŏk Sangsok Pŏp* [Family Inheritance Law] (Seoul: Pŏp Mun Sa, 1975).

Ogura Shmpei. *Chōsengo hōgen no kenkyū* [A study of Korean Dialects] (Tokyo: Iwanami Shoten, 1944).

A Fully Elaborated Eight Peaks Farmhouse

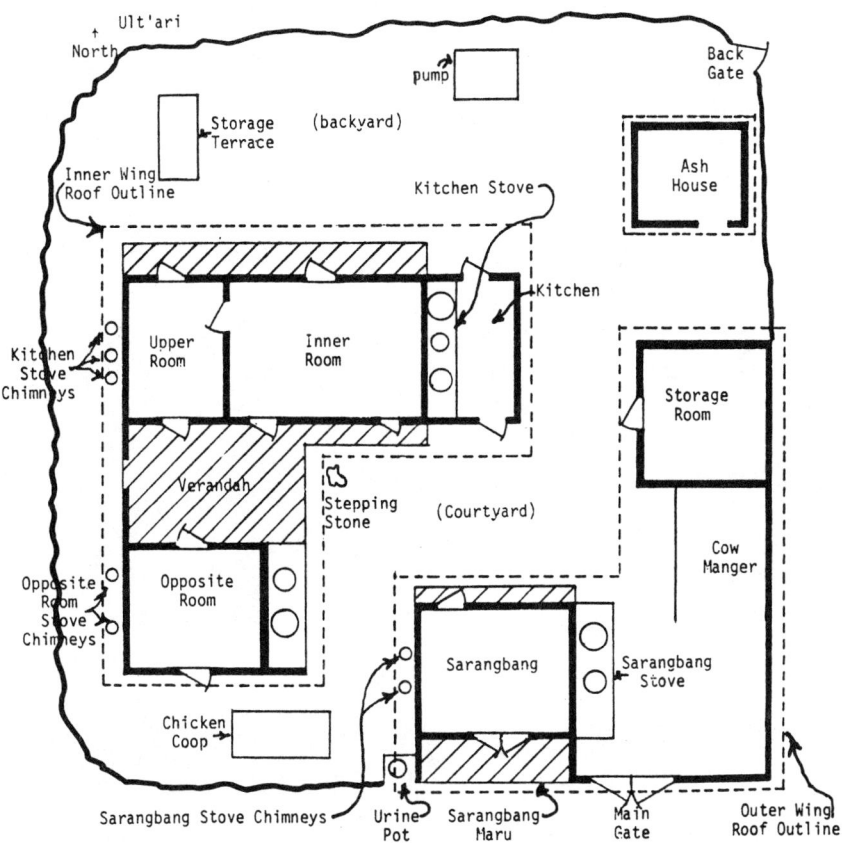

© Copyright by
Clark Wesley Sorensen
1981

The Autonomous Women: Divers on Cheju Island[1]

HAEJOANG CHO

Introduction

On a sunny day in October 1976, in a village house with a view of the ocean, a geomancer from the mainland consulted with the village elders. I was there with several other women when the geomancer explained: "The land formation in this village indicates that women are destined to call and men to follow." No one contradicted his insightful remark.

I will describe life in this female divers' village on the island of Udo, off Cheju Island. In this village, sex roles and responsibilities pose a dramatic contrast to patriarchal communities on the Korean mainland. Observations come from two field trips to Udo, one in 1976, the other in 1978. In this study, I will use feminist theoretical perspectives to highlight the "separate realities" of women and men.

Strathern (1976) has argued that wherever women dwell in a different social world than that of their men, and engage in different tasks, they have different vantage points, different interests, and even different "models" of social reality. A recognition of this separation and of the oppositional and complementary nature of the two worlds is crucial to an analysis of such women's lives.

Sexual Division of Labor

DIVING. Yong Dong,[2] my major field site, is one of eleven villages on Udo, a small island off the eastern tip of Cheju Island. In 1976, the population of Yong Dong was 346, in sixty-six households. Diving and farming are the major economic activities. *Chesa*, ancestral memorial services, serve as the focal point for most organized kinship activities and as the village's main socioreligious events.

Diving yields cash income and is an exclusively female activity. Women dive for top-shells, abalone, lobster, octopus, and various kinds of seaweed. The divers call themselves "*henyŏ*," or "women of the sea," and consider themselves career women. There are ninety-two active divers in Yong Dong, virtually all of the women in the village over fifteen years of age. Women dive all year round, for four to eight hours a day, on an average of fifteen days a month. They dive during their menstrual periods and even when they are pregnant. A woman may dive up to the very date of her delivery and resume diving one or two weeks after the delivery.

Women acquire the right to dive in the village site through residence, and all village divers are members of the Women's Association. They hold their meetings on the beach while they change their clothes. Divers discuss ocean conditions and the proper timing of the seaweed harvest. At least one diver from each household joins the Fishing Cooperative Union. Members can sell their diving produce through the Union and can also borrow money from this group.

Diving is skilled labor, requiring a long training period. Women start diving around the age of seven, become professional divers at about eighteen, and retire in their sixties. A young girl starts to play in the water when she is about five years old. Within a few years, she will have taught herself to swim and to dive for game under water. Even among children, skillful swimming and diving are sources of pride.

By the time she goes to middle school, a girl is ready to ask her mother for diving equipment—a small float, a mask, a game bag, and perhaps a new swimming suit. She dives with her friends in a protected area. Her mother teaches her how to use her arms and hands to plunge, and how to cut plants from their roots without killing the plants. From her summer diving, a girl earns her own school tuition and pocket money.

After middle school graduation, when she is about fifteen years old, she starts diving seriously and becomes a member of the Women's Association. Now, her mother provides her with an adult woman's float, mask, wet suit, hood, fins, and abalone knife. The young woman now dives with the regular divers. She learns underwater geography and ocean currents. She learns to plot her diving strategy by the moon's movement, and she knows where to look for game. In a year or two, she begins to join extended migratory diving trips to the mainland coast and to other islands. By the age of twenty, and after several of these trips, a woman is finally considered a regular diver. By the time she reaches twenty-five, she will have saved enough money to start a family, and many women stop making diving trips after marriage.

A diver's prime years are between ages twenty-five and forty-five, and she stops deep diving after fifty-five. Although one is supposed to stop diving completely at around sixty, many older women were still diving when I was in the field. Financially self-sufficient, they went to the water because "there's not much else to do in this good weather."

The women normally dive at depths of five to seven meters and hold their breath for thirty-five to forty seconds for each jump. "Top-level" divers (*sang'gun*) can dive to as many as twenty meters and can catch sea products most effectively. They are also well versed in underwater geography and current movements. An experienced scuba diver and not a bad skin diver by U.S. standards, I myself was not, by the diving women's high standards, considered even "shitty level" (*tong'gun*). All I got from my diving was one top-shell. Much amused, the divers suggested that I mail the top-shell to my parents in Seoul, since it was something I finally got after such a long trial.

Companionship is very important in diving. Divers spend what may seem to be an unnecessarily long time changing their clothes, but it is a joyful time, when they can exchange information, talk about their family problems, joke, and sometimes sing. A sixty-six-year-old woman who no longer dove said: "After my friends are gone, I feel so bored and lonesome. I'll go down to the beach tomorrow to joke, laugh, and be with my friends."

Most divers enjoy diving. When they could not go diving for several days, due to inclement weather, they said they had body-aches and wanted to dive as soon as possible. Only a few divers said they preferred farming to diving, because of the danger in diving. When a forty-five-year-old diver expressed a preference for farming over diving, a younger woman remarked: "It's because you are greedy. You try too hard to catch game. Catching abalones, talking with others, and swimming around . . . think about the fun we have." Another woman talked about her daughter-in-law, who was unable to dive while recovering from a hysterectomy:

> She would cry, all alone, leaning on the wall, down by the beach, in the kitchen. It hurt me to watch her; she was so anxious to go diving. Now she is diving again. Her smile has come back. She jokes and laughs. I feel relieved.

A girl in middle school wrote me this essay on her "future aspirations":

> I want to be a *henyŏ* in the future. How happy I will be, working and laughing together with my friends. When I think about the danger we may have in the sea, I become scared. But we will cooperate and guide one another for safe and enjoyable diving.

In sum, diving is skilled labor and highly valued work, since it is the major source of cash income. Moreover, diving is not drudgery. Village women enjoy their diving and their comradeship with other diving women.

FARMING. The land on Cheju, a volcanic island, is not suitable for irrigation. The crops grown around Yong Dong are drought-resistant: barley, kaoliang, and sweet potatoes. Women's contribution to the work of farming is time-consuming and requires endurance and stamina—weeding, cutting, flattening the land, seeding, and slicing and drying sweet potatoes. Most of the men's farm work can be done in a standing position—carrying, plowing, driving motorized or horse carts, and using motorized slicing machines. Plowing is considered to be men's work, although I did observe one woman plowing. Weeding is exclusively women's work—one man said that men's knees are too stiff for weeding.

Men work when they feel like working, and their contributions depend on personal inclination. Although village men gave "farming" as their occupation, women are the major farm workers. During the busy harvest, Sonna's mother, a thirty-five-year-old woman, found her husband sitting with me and a group of men friends. Since she had been looking for him for quite a while, she shouted at him: "Damn you! What have you been doing all day? Don't you dare spend time like this. Come along at once, you son-of-a-bitch." She left. Sonna's father was embarrassed, since this scene took place in my presence. He grumbled and stayed a little longer before he went out to the field.

Another man commented on a poor harvest in his own field: "It's such a relief! I don't have to work hard harvesting and drying potatoes, since we had a poor harvest this year."

Drying sliced sweet potatoes is painstaking work. When Yang-mi's aunt announced that it was raining, Yang-mi's mother jumped up instantly and went out to cover a heap of sliced sweet potatoes. She was swift, a contrast to her husband, who took some time to find his raincoat and flashlight, then went slowly out to help.

Husband and wife discuss harvesting and planting decisions, but it is usually the wife who takes the initiative and carries out the work on schedule. She asks or coaxes her husband to help her, and sometimes has to remind him several times to plow a field.

Since she can hire men for plowing and threshing, a woman can farm by herself. Widows and some other village women successfully cultivate crops without the aid of husbands, although no men farm without their wives. Women work cooperatively, usually with their close relatives. Women who lack close relatives form cooperative labor teams (*su-notta*). They say: "Working together makes the work fun, and we can work faster that way."

Ninety percent of the land in Yong Dong was registered in men's names. Men have more claim on the income from farming than on that from diving, since they "own" the land and they "help" farm it. The men collect reimbursement for produce from the Union and can borrow money from the Union. I noted that gambling had a burst of popularity whenever the Farming Cooperative Union made its payments.

CHESA. Performing Confucian rituals for the ancestors is the most important male activity in Yong Dong. Men spend a great deal of their time performing and attending rituals. Between 10 and 20 percent of the family budget is spent on the mutual aid allowance (*pujo*) for funerals (*changnye*) and ancestral memorial ceremonies (*chesa*). A village elder said proudly: "I've been in many places, and I now know that Cheju people perform *changnye* more properly and elaborately than any other people in Korea."

Preparations for *chesa* are indeed elaborate. The night before, the man or his wife goes shopping in the city. On the following morning, women who are closely related to the memorialized person come to the house to help the hostess. All the food except meat dishes are prepared by women.

The men perform the ceremony at midnight. After the ceremony, the host and the other men serve up the sacrificial food with rice and soup from the kitchen. Elderly men are served first. Once all the men are fed, the boys get their share and, last, the women and little children.

A man attends several *chesa* a month. Men do not consider *chesa* an absolutely sacred occasion—"just an occasion for memorializing ancestors." But they do consider *chesa* more than just an excuse to eat and drink well. A man is highly esteemed if he holds many *chesa* and performs them properly.

A woman attends *chesa* only for her close relatives. A woman who goes often to "eat *chesa* rice" is not considered quite proper.[3] *Chesa* is a man's ritual. In a sense, women are excluded from *chesa* as long as they live, but after death, women are memorialized as men's equals.

OTHER ACTIVITIES. Cooking, cleaning, and washing are considered women's work, but, depending on the situation, these tasks are shared. During the diving season, the husbands or children of divers prepare meals, wash dishes and clothes, and clean house.

Child-care is a shared activity, and baby-care during the day is mostly a man's job. After the women have gone to dive, the village seems quiet and empty. Men with their babies visit each other, talk, and drink. They may discuss international affairs, national policies, and local politics, but they also talk about the difficulties of baby-care. A forty-five-year-old man said: "Baby-care looks like an easy job. But it is one of the most difficult jobs. You will realize it when you actually take care of a baby." Village men are fond of children, especially little children and babies. They take good care of them, and their women recognize and appreciate this effort.

Villagers raise domestic animals: horses, cows, pigs, and fowl. Tending horses and cattle is said to be a man's job, but many women and children tend animals, and the women generally tend the pigs.

The village leaders are all men. Village elders, who know Confucian ethics and rituals and can read classic Chinese books, influence decision-making in village affairs. On occasions such as funerals and weddings, they are invited to supervise the ceremonies. They also act as consultants to the villagers, especially to women whose husbands have died or gone away. Modernization has undermined the elders' traditional leadership to some extent, however.

The villagers elect a village manager every year. He mediates between villagers, government organizations, and unions as the head of the Village Association, and he supervises most extradomestic activities, such as voting or mending the road. He gets a little pay for his services from the villagers.

Social Organization

Yong Dong is a kinship-oriented society, based on the principle of patrilineal descent. A person is identified as a member of his or her patrilineage. Household headships, property, names, and the responsibility of performing *chesa* are all inherited through the patrilineal line.

Village exogamy and lineage exogamy are marriage rules on the Korean mainland. In Yong Dong, however, lineage exogamy is strictly practiced, but village exogamy is not. The villagers, especially the women, prefer village-endogamous marriages. Economic advantages and emotional closeness make mothers and daughters prefer marriages within the same village.

Virilocality (the practice whereby a married couple settles in the domicile of the husband's family) is the principal rule of residence, but people in the village can choose between virilocality and uxorilocality (the practice whereby a married couple settles in the domicile of the wife's family). When there are no practical advantages to living in the husband's village, the couple may decide to settle in the wife's village instead. If a man has not inherited any property from his parents, for example, newly-weds may profit by settling in a wife's village where underwater resources are abundant.

Mutual assistance through the kinship network is an important form of collaboration in village life. Especially, brothers and patrilineal male relatives up to eight *ch'on*[4] cooperate in performing *chesa*. They cooperate mostly by participating in the rituals, rather than by making financial contributions. Men who do not have brothers usually build fictive kin relations to one another as sworn brothers. Commonly, sworn brothers participate in each others' *chesa*.

Wives of brothers and sisters who have married into the same village form intimate collaboration groups, helping one another prepare *chesa*, weed and harvest farmland, and market. Women who have few relatives to depend on establish fictive kin relations as sworn sisters. Like real sisters, sworn sisters support one another emotionally as well as economically. They are of great assistance to one another, particularly at weddings and funerals.

Yong Dong families are "matrifocal"; the mother is ideologically and structurally central (Tanner 1974: 133). Yong Dong mothers are dedicated and responsible breadwinners, who do their best to insure comfortable lives for the members of their families and to finance their children's formal education. These mothers also prepare *chesa*, plan house construction, arrange marriages for their children, and save money to send their sons to high school and college. Weddings and funerals, the biggest celebrations in the village, are all managed by the mothers.

A Yong Dong mother also provides emotional support. To her son, she is always available; he can turn to his mother for money, for comfort, or whenever he is in trouble. To her daughter, a mother is the best companion and teacher.

A woman's illness is a serious family problem. For example, a husband sold his farm plot to pay for his wife's medical treatment, saying: "If you are sick, what is the use of the farm plot?" Since a mother's illness disrupts her entire family, most women are very careful about their health. If exhausted or ill, women go on quiet retreats to Buddhist temples.

Widows tend to remain single, and it is considered perfectly normal for a woman to live alone. Significantly, most of the female-headed households belong to the higher income group in the village. Young widowers, on the other hand, do not remain long alone. Relatives usually arrange a marriage right after a wife's funeral. An older widower moves into his eldest son's house, while an older widow may choose either to stay alone in her own house or to move in with a favorite son. Most widows prefer to live alone, saying that living alone is more comfortable and less restrictive.

If a husband is dissatisfied with his wife, he usually leaves his family instead of getting a divorce. Since the husband's presence is not vital to the household's survival, men leave home rather casually. A man may go to an island city or to the mainland to find work, and he may take a second wife there. "Most men have had at least one second wife," a village woman told me.

Polygyny is not legal according to Korean family law, but it is socially accepted and common in Yong Dong. All the "little wives" (common parlance for second wives) are either widows with few children or divorcées. Men have the same social responsibilities to their "little wives" as they have to their first wives. They are expected to be lovers to the women and genealogical fathers of their children. But women expect no economic support from the men. The Yong Dong saying, "Two wives mean two purses," reveals the role of the "little wife." She does not get anything economically from her husband; she provides instead.

Some anthropologists claim that polygyny adversely affects the status of women and forces competition among the co-wives for the husband's economic resources (D'Andrade 1966; Martin and Voorhies 1975). In Yong Dong, polygyny stems from the man's insecure status in the matrifocal family. Psychologically, it helps men cope with marital conflict and their wives' dominance. Structurally, it provides a way out of marital problems without divorce.

In sum, the Yong Dong social organization provides a buffer for male egos, with male-exclusive *chesa*, polygyny, and the first son's responsibility for the older male parent. Maximum female cooperation is institutionalized in village endogamy, uxorilocality, and the matrifocal family.

Village Life, for Women and Men

Since men and women experience the social environment differently, they develop different personalities. Let us now consider how individuals develop gender personality.

Divers' songs, sung while the divers rowed their boats, acknowledge the women's responsibility as breadwinners:[5]

> Leaving behind a crying baby,
> Leaving behind a loving husband,
> I've come here to dive
> Since money makes a better life.
> Working hard and making money
> To support children [Lee 1974: 363-64].

Although the women lament their hard lives, they also show pride as independent income earners. For diving women, hard work is not drudgery. A sixty-five-year-old diver mocked the mainland women, who "play and do little work." Women's perception of work was well expressed in a statement made by a fifty-three-year-old woman: "How frustrated and restless one may be who plays with all one's might! A lucky one doesn't play."

Both mainland and Cheju men recognize the Cheju women's independence. A man from the mainland who had lived in Cheju for six years said he would not marry a Cheju woman, because: "Women here are too independent. If they do not like something, they ask for a divorce right there, and often marry again. I cannot take such a woman."

A civil servant at the provincial court commented on the low divorce rate among divers: "Cheju *henyŏ* rarely seek a divorce, since they are self-supporting." A diving woman is essentially independent and psychologically self-sufficient, and therefore even when she does not get much joy and satisfaction from her marital life, she does not need to divorce her husband. She simply withdraws her emotional involvement from him, becomes even more self-sufficient, and draws joy and gratification from her work, her children, and her friendships with other women. Believing that she cannot expect much from any man, she does not see much point in bothering to divorce her husband.

Yong Dong women manage their married lives for themselves. Once married, they try not to rely on anyone, even their parents. Autonomy is their highest value, and they resist any form of dependence or dominance. The women's cooperativeness and egalitarianism also stem from their economic abilities. Women help one another in difficult situations and run village life in a spirit of cooperation.

Compared with the hard-working—often overworked—women, the men in Yong Dong lead what can be called "idle" lives. Some do baby-sitting, housekeeping, or cattle-tending or try to help their wives farm or process sea-weed. Others spend their days talking, drinking, and taking naps. In this village, men eat only half the amount of food consumed by women. As one old woman said: "How can they have a taste for food when they work so little?" Laziness in men is not considered a vice, however. The men's ideology holds that doing nothing is better than working hard for a living: A noble man does not work.[6] One young man said: "Women are too busy to be reflective. They do not think." He implied that the lazy and philosophical men are superior to the hard-working and practical women.

The men's financial and psychological dependence on their women allows them to remain a leisure class. Men consider their female relatives and wives—indeed all women—as a source of stability, on which they can depend and to which they can turn as needed. Women, on the other hand, are indulgent of their dependent husbands.

Although Yong Dong men lead leisurely and privileged lives, the Thematic Apperception Test (T.A.T.) stories[7] uncovered their basic loneliness and frustration. The loneliness of their fathers was often expressed in the children's writings. The frustration and sense of inadequacy of the village men may stem from a conflict between reality and ideology.

Confucian ideology assumes male-dominance: a man is the head of his family. In Yong Dong, men demand formal deference, but in reality, they are not the masters of their families. They may be treated well, but as guests of the household, not as masters with paternal authority. Village men are peripheral members of their families, and they have to cope with this contradiction.

The men of Yong Dong lack significant roles. Some wish they had been born as women, so that they could lead hard-working, active lives. The men try to cope with their frustrations in several ways. Some try to be hard-working farmers or village leaders. But heavy drinking, frequent trips, gambling, getting second wives, and day-dreaming are more common means of escape. As dependent and indulged individuals, the men are generally other-oriented, sensitive, and self-centered. They make unreasonable demands, presume upon other people—especially women—and lack motivation and will power. Insecure about their positions in their families and the community, village men are generally defensive and argumentative toward outsiders. They consider life to be meaningless and illusory. Pessimism and passivity prevail among them. The women, on the other hand, dwell in an ordered society, where life's problems are real and can be solved by making an effort. For the women, life is meaningful, continuous, and rewarding.

The Autonomous Women

What does this divers' village tell us about power relations between men and women? This is not a community of equals, wherein women have the same opportunities as men. But neither is it a "male-dominant" society. In fact, neither group dominates.

On the Korean mainland, rice cultivation was, until recently, the major economic activity. Irrigation farming in rice paddies demanded solidarity and cooperation among men, social relationships reinforced by the hierarchical and male-dominant ideology of Confucianism. *Chesa*, an expression of filial piety and a statement of patrilineal continuity, gave ritual reinforcement to the social solidarity of men.

Yong Dong villagers have made only a selective adaptation of Confucianism. Confucian ethics seem incompatible with a social system in which women, not men, are the primary economic actors, and female solidarity is the most essential basis of cooperation. Yet Yong Dong villagers seem to perform *chesa* more faithfully and extravagantly than the members of many mainland communities. I was struck, in the first few weeks of my field work, by the villagers' overt display of Confucian ritual. Later, I began to notice that they regularly ignored or violated Confucian rules of conduct. Men of the same surname have little sense of solidarity and cooperation. Younger villagers do not defer to older people. Women rarely defer to men. Whenever a woman wants to speak, she does so. Despite the Confucian dictum that a woman should not talk in public, village women often do, and even use strong language.

The nuclear family system belies filial piety. Grown children do not support aged parents. Mothers-in-law have little power over their daughters-in-law. A young woman at the peak of productivity has the strongest voice among the women.

While the Yong Dong villagers ignore Confucianism's ethical code, the men claim superiority and self-esteem through their exclusive control of Confucian ritual. They cite Confucian scholarly values—contempt for manual labor and respect for knowledge and nobility—to devalue their working women. But beneath this thin veneer, a very different picture emerges. Women in this village seem content, successfully pursuing their own life goals. They are competent and dedicated social actors, full of self-respect. The real "social adults," the women, support their families and run the village economy.

Village men experience internal conflict and frustration. In reality, they are of less consequence than their wives. When a man is away, his household and his community take small note of the fact. But when a woman falls sick or dies, the whole village expresses concern. As one woman said: "A motherless child is pitiful, while a fatherless child is not. A mother makes money and sends her children to schools. Men's presence does not really matter."

Male domination of the symbolic realm serves as a buffer for the men's weakness and insecurity. Akin to male secret societies among New Guineans (Langness 1974), Trobrianders (Weiner 1976), Mundurucu (Murphy 1959), and Kofyar (Netting 1969), Confucian ritual serves in this village as a sort of "collective fetishism" (cf. Murphy and Murphy 1974: 232). Like the Mundurucu men, who use the prerogatives of the men's house to "conceal the fragility of their own superiority" (Murphy and Murphy 1974: 229), the status of Yong Dong men is based on illusion and is therefore vulnerable.

A diving woman's autonomy comes from economic independence, but for diving women, work means something more than labor. Work means self-importance and enjoyment. It is a "career,"[8] a life-long activity promising personal satisfaction and achievement. Although the men publicly denigrate the importance of women's activities, the women clearly recognize the importance of their own work. Diving women sometimes complain about being overburdened, but, as career women, they claim that they have someone to care for and work for—their children. As one woman said: "While young, a husband may be valuable, . . . but once you get old, the children are all you need. Even if your husband fools around with other women, you wouldn't care much."

Yong Dong men, by contrast, lead dependent lives, wrestling with meaninglessness and insecurity. They lack purposeful work through which they can explore their potentials and actualize themselves. They ostentatiously insist on an ideology of male superiority and on the importance of male ritual, but theirs is a poor weapon against female autonomy.

This case study suggests that both women's and men's liberation demand meaningful, life-long careers for all.

Notes

[1] This is the revised version of a part of the author's Ph.D. dissertation, which was submitted to the University of California, Los Angeles, in 1979. The dissertation research was supported by the American Association of University Women and by a Departmental Grant from the Department of Anthropology at U.C.L.A.

[2] Yong Dong is a fictitious name. I have changed all the proper nouns, in order to protect the privacy of the people in the field site.

[3] When a villager is asked where he or she is going, on the way to participate in *chesa*, the answer would be: "I am going to the house of *chesa*" or "I am going to eat *chesa*." The latter expression is more popularly used in the village.

[4]*Ch'on* is a unit used to calculate the distance between consanguineally related kin in Korea. The distance between parents and their offspring is one *ch'on*, and the distance between siblings is two *ch'on*. The distance between first cousins is four *ch'on*, since each one is a parent's (one *ch'on*) sibling's (two *ch'on*) offspring (one *ch'on*).

[5] Until motor boats were introduced, divers rowed boats by themselves to the diving sites during their migratory trips. Since the 1950s, however, motor boats have been in use, and divers' songs are no longer sung. Most young girls do not know these songs.

[6] There is a legend about the origins of the diving women of Cheju Island: When some court nobles were expelled from the capital city and were sent to the island in exile, their women retainers began diving to support their noble lords. An implication of this legend is that men are the nobles and women are their servants.

[7] For T.A.T. analyses, cards 2, 3, 4, 6M, 7M, 9, 11, 12F, 13, 18, and J22 were used. The Korean version of the Murray Standard Edition was drawn by Ms. Kyŏng-ja Song, a Korean artist. Japanese and Chinese versions were consulted. For results of the T.A.T. analyses, see Cho 1979.

[8] W. Goldschmidt introduced and elaborated on the concept of "career" at the seminar on "Problems in Cultural Anthropology" that was offered in 1977 at U.C.L.A. The focus of his theorization of "career" lies in the relationship between humans as goal-oriented actors and their ecological adaptation. In this paper, I use the concept in a more general sense. "Career" is meant to be a life-long task through which a person can fulfill his or her life. A career person is not just carrying out an assigned role, but is highly motivated to develop his or her abilities fully, positively pursuing self-satisfaction within the context of culturally-defined values.

References

Ardener, Shirley
    1975   "Introduction," in S. Ardener, ed., *Perceiving Women* (London: Malaby Press): vii-xxiii.

Boserup, Ester
    1970   *Women's Role in Economic Development* (New York: St. Martin's Press).

Cho Haejoang
    1979   *An Ethnographic Study of a Female Diver's Village in Korea: Focused on the Sexual Division of Labor* (Ph.D. dissertation, University of California, Los Angeles).

D'Andrade, R. G.
    1966   "Sex differences and cultural institutions," in E. E. Maccoby, ed., *The Development of Sex Differences* (Stanford: Stanford University Press): 173-203.

Friedl, Ernestine
    1975   *Women and Men: An Anthropologist's View* (New York: Holt, Rinehart and Winston).

Geertz, Clifford
    1973   *The Interpretation of Cultures* (New York: Basic Books).

Langness, L. L.
    1974   "Ritual, power, and male dominance," *Ethos*, 2(3): 182-212.

Lee Chi-soon
1974 *Han'guk Minsok Chonghap Chosa Pogosŏ* [General Report of the Studies on Korean Folk Culture], 5: Cheju Do (Seoul, Ministry of Culture and Information).

Martin, M. Kay, and Barbara Voorhies
1975 *Female of the Species* (New York: Columbia University Press).

McCune, G. M., and E. O. Reischauer
1939 *The Romanization of the Korean Language* (Seoul: Royal Asiatic Society, Korea Branch).

Murphy, R. F.
1959 "Social structure and sex antagonism," *Southwestern Journal of Anthropology*, 15: 89-98.

Murphy, Y., and R. F. Murphy
1974 *Women of the Forest* (New York: Columbia University Press).

Netting, Robert M.
1969 "Women's weapon: The politics of domesticity among the Kofyer," *American Anthropologist*, 71 (6): 1037-46.

Sanday, Peggy R.
1974 "Female status in the public domain," in M. Rosaldo and L. Lamphere, eds., *Woman, Culture and Society* (Stanford: Stanford University Press): 186-206.

Strathern, Marilyn
1976 "An anthropological perspective," in B. Lloyd and J. Archer, eds., *Exploring Sex Differences* (New York: Academic Press).

Tanner, Nancy
1974 "Matrifocality in Indonesia and Africa and among Black Americans," in M. Rosaldo and L. Lamphere, eds., *Woman, Culture, and Society* (Stanford: Stanford University Press): 129-56.

Weiner, Annette B.
1976 *Women of Value, Men of Renown* (Austin: University of Texas Press).

Yoon Soon Young S.
1975 *Occupation: Male Housekeeper (Male-Female Roles on Cheju Island, Korea)*, paper presented at the Annual Meeting of the American Anthropological Association, San Francisco. (Reprinted in Sandra Mattielli, ed., *Virtues in Conflict: Tradition and the Korean Woman Today* [Seoul: Royal Asiatic Society, Korea Branch, 1977]: 191-207.)

Korean Ancestors: From the Woman's Side

Laurel Kendall

> The father's sister is a restless ancestor;
> the mother's sister is a restless ancestor.
> Kyŏnggi Shaman Chant

The Korean shaman's *kut* is a dramatic ritual evocation of the spirits of the house. Perhaps the most poignant segment of a *kut* is the *chosang-gŏri*, the ancestors' sequence, when the ancestors of the house appear in the person of the possessed shaman. Manifesting a sobbing ancestor, the shaman clutches at the shoulders of a child, grandchild, sibling, or spouse and laments death and separation. Tears course down the cheeks of both shaman and client, while less overwhelmed spectators shout to the ghostly presence, "Take your travel money and go!"

Although Korean ancestor worship, *chesa*, is a male rite par excellence, the care and feeding of the familial dead is not solely the concern of Korean men. Restless ancestors and ghosts are a common concern in female-centered shaman rites (*kut,* or *p'udak-kŏri*), but are the "ancestors" of *kut* the same "ancestors" that the men of the household acknowledge when they make offerings?

The Korean family, the *chip*, is a patrilineal, patrilocal unit. Male rites honor the *chosang*, the ancestors of the *chip*. In the ideal, men are born, live, and die among their close consanguinal kin. The first son eventually becomes an ancestor in the direct line of his natal *chip* (*k'ŭnjip*); other sons become ancestors as the founders of related minor *chip* (*chagŭnjip*). The ancestors of the *chip* are thus fathers and grandfathers, ascending generations of male-linked kin who are honored in ancestor worship by their sons and grandsons. A woman cannot become a proper ancestor in her natal *chip*. As the mother of a son, she becomes an ancestor and receives offerings in her husband's *chip*.[1] Familial ideology holds that the out-marrying woman is severed from her natal kin. As an oft-cited aphorism tells it, the daughter is a "*ch'ulga oein*: once married out, a stranger." Ties through women do not figure in the organizational principles of the *chip*.

Women assume the appropriateness of patrilineal principles demarcating an exclusive group of ancestors for worship in *chesa*. When they consult shamans, however, the women accept that all manner of "ancestors" who would never qualify for positions of honor at the household ancestors' table might yet influence the family fortunes. A woman assumes that ancestors and ghosts from her natal home will affect the health, wealth, and well-being of members of her affinal *chip*. So, too, might a married daughter return to her natal household after death. When and why do these ethereal entities appear? Does their presence imply another view of significant kin, one predicated on the life experience of the Korean woman as she passes from her natal to her affinal home?

The Household and the Shaman

My understanding of Korean women and Korean shamans is based on a year of fieldwork in northern Kyŏnggi Province, Republic of Korea, in 1977 and 1978 and on several follow-up visits in the months after I left the village.[2] The material I present here comes from the localized context of my observations. While ritual manuals have gone a long way toward standardizing male ancestor worship, women's rituals and shaman lore are learned through observation and oral transmission, and there is some variation from place to place.[3] But, as we shall see, shaman rituals reflect organizational principles basic to Korean society, not random assortments of "superstitious" practices.

In this part of Korea, the shaman is politely addressed as *mansin* and derogatorily referred to as *mudang*. In contrast to hereditary shaman families found further south, the *mansin* receives her calling through inspirational possession. Most *mansin* are female, but several *paksu*, male shamans who wear feminine garments under their costumes when they perform, are also active in the Seoul region. Whether the shaman is male or female, those who consult the shaman and hire him or her to perform rituals are almost exclusively female, and women are the most numerous and enthusiastic participants at shaman ceremonies.

A woman's participation in shaman ceremonies is an extension of her ritual responsibilities in the home. While the men serve the ancestors of the family with rice and wine offerings, the women give *kosa*—offerings of wine, water, and rice cake—to the household gods.[4] Some women may also make periodic offerings at the *mansin*'s shrine (*hoengsumegi, ch'ilsŏngmaji*) on behalf of the members of the *chip*. If the household gods (*sin, sillyŏng*) are affronted by neglect or pollution (*pujŏng*), they drop their defense of the family and vent their own wrath. Then all manner of misfortune may arise. Thus, when the household is beset by ill luck, persistent illness, or financial loss, the women consult a *mansin*, who divines the nature of the offended, and thus offending, deity. The *mansin* prescribes appropriate ritual action to patch up the relations between human and spirit and restore the integrity of the house.

For ancestral or ghostly affliction, the *mansin* is likely to prescribe a minor exorcism (*p'udak-kŏri*) or a *kut*. A *kut* is the most elaborate ritual of the *mansin*. Throughout the night and much of the next day, the *mansin* portrays the spirits and ancestors of the house with dance, song, pantomime, and humorous dialogue.

Restless Ancestors and Ghosts

The *mansin* assumes that when the household gods drop their protective guard, the ancestors and ghosts become restless, active (*paltonghada*). When the dead become an active presence among the living, it bodes no good, for, as the *mansin* tells it, the "hand of the dead is a hand of nettles" (*chugŭn sonŭn, kasi sonida*); it cannot touch living flesh without inflicting injury. Weakened spiritual defenses produce disaster. Deaths yield more ancestors and ghosts, who, if not ritually sent along the road to the Lotus Paradise (*kungnak*), will hover ominously about the family, perpetuating a vicious cycle of misfortune.[5] The following two cases illustrate this process of supernatural causation:

Case 1: Sŏng family kut. The married eldest son of the junior *chip* of the Sŏng family had complained of severe headaches for several months. Treatment at local hospitals was of no avail. According to the *mansin* who eventually organized the healing *kut*, an ancestral grandmother of the Sŏng family was a great shaman (*k'ŭn mudang*). Through her influence, the "Great Spirit" in the Sŏng family pantheon was particularly strong. The family's "Spirit

Official" was also strong. A *chip* with such potent deities should do a *kut* once every three years to feast and amuse them, but the Sŏngs had not done a *kut* for over five years.

The year before, the second son of the main *chip*, a bachelor, had drowned. And now the ancestors and ghosts of the Sŏng family, the drowned bachelor foremost among them, had gathered about the eldest son of the junior *chip*, causing his illness. If the Sŏngs had done a *kut* earlier, the *mansin* maintained, both the drowning and the illness could have been avoided.

Case 2: Pae family kut. An unmarried daughter of the Pae family died with her lover on the night before the young man was to report for duty at his military assignment. The couple died of carbon monoxide poisoning from the faulty heating system in the floor of the room where they had taken lodging for the night.[6]

Since the daughter had died young, unmarried, away from home, and through a sudden accident, she fit all of the qualifications of a dangerously restless ghost. The family was advised to swiftly send her soul, together with the soul of her lover, along the road to the Lotus Paradise and avert further misfortune. When the *mansin* divined for the dead girl's mother, she determined that the mother had inherited the influence of a strong "Monk Deity" (Chung-bulsa) from the household pantheon of her natal home. The Monk Deity is found in the household pantheons of families who worship at Buddhist temples. This unpropitiated Monk Deity, followed by restless ancestors from the natal home, exerted a negative influence on the fate of the Pae household. As landless laborers, the Paes had known extreme poverty, and a son had drowned some years before the daughter's death.

Neither the son of the Sŏng family nor the daughter of the Pae family qualifies as an ancestor, since both died unmarried and without issue. It is appropriate to consider here the basis for my use of the terms "ancestor," "restless ancestor," and "ghost," or, more precisely, the *mansin*'s conceptualization of *chosang, chosang malmyŏng,* and *yŏngsan*.

Chosang, or "ancestors," are those who have produced male issue and are thus entitled to receive *chesa* from sons and grandsons. *Yŏngsan*, or "ghosts," are those who died unmarried, without issue, often violently or suddenly when far away from home. A *mansin*'s chant acknowledges: "*yŏngsan* who drowned, *yŏngsan* who were shot, *yŏngsan* who died of carbon monoxide poisoning, maiden *yŏngsan*, bachelor *yŏngsan*," and many more. Because they are not entitled to *chesa* food, the *yŏngsan* are perpetually hungry. They gather wherever feast food has been prepared, but they are most likely to hover about their own families.

Chosang are far more fortunate than *yŏngsan*. They were married and had children when they died, often at a ripe old age and in the bosom of their families. Yet even the *chosang* may express resentment stemming from unfulfilled desires (*han*). When they appear in the person of the *mansin*, they cry for what they have missed. A man who toiled to provide for his family expresses frustration at dying before he could enjoy himself. A first wife who knew poverty in her married life is bitter when she sees her husband's present wife living comfortably. Grandparents rejoice at the birth of a grandchild but regret dying before they could see the baby in life. An old woman who went to her grave craving a fancy rice cake will carry this hunger through eternity. In terms of Korean social expectations, these were all legitimate desires, thwarted by fate.

Emotional attachments draw the dead to the living with no malevolent intent, yet their presence has a negative effect: A mother pities her married daughter's poverty and touches her, driving the daughter temporarily insane. A grandmother fondly strokes her infant grandchild, causing the baby to sicken. A son-in-law's illness is attributed to the presence of his deceased father-in-law, who is grateful because the young man married into the family as an adopted son-in-law, taking the hunchback daughter as a bride.

When the family's spiritual defenses are weak, when the gods of the household pantheon drop their guard, any of these ancestors may grow restless and consequently dangerous. *Mansin* use the terms *chosang*, *malmyŏng*, or *chosang malmyŏng* only when indicating ancestors in this restless, active state.[7]

As a more general phenomenon, the ancestors of the *chip* grow resentful when the family enjoys food and material comforts without giving the dead their due in shaman rites. According to the *mansin*, a run of misfortune indicates that the "ancestors are hungry and the gods want to play," in other words, the family should hold a *kut*.

Ancestors and Ghosts in Kut

When the *mansin* perform the ancestors' sequence in *kut*, they must include deceased relatives of the *chip* up to four ascendant generations (*sadaebongsa*) and deceased male relatives and their wives within four degrees of relationship—the senior and junior *chip* of one's own, one's father's, and one's grandfather's generations. Superficially, these basic ancestors resemble the patrilineal ancestors of ancestor worship, but there are important differences. Ancestors of the main *chip* and the husband's and father's younger brothers appear in *kut*. A man would not do *chesa* in his own *chip*. for ancestors who receive *chesa* at the main *chip*. Neither would his *chip* normally offer *chesa* to his younger brothers or to his father's younger brothers.

The appearance of these kindred spirits in *kut* does not reflect the hierarchical relationship between *chip* so much as the inclusive solidarity of related *chip*. The living members of related *chip* appear when a *chip* celebrates *chesa*, weddings, funerals, and birthdays. In like manner, the ancestors of related *chip* gather to feast and play at a *kut*. In the *mansin*'s diagnosis, otherworldly influences pass freely between major and minor *chip*. Thus, related *chip* often contribute to the joint sponsorship of a *kut* for their mutual benefit. In Case 1, above, the son of a minor Sŏng *chip*'s illness was attributed, in part, to the dead son of the main Sŏng *chip*, his cousin. The main *chip*, although considerably poorer than the minor *chip*, contributed money to send off the dead bachelor's soul at the conclusion of the *kut*. The Pae family, in Case 2, sent several ancestors from the main and minor *chip* to the Lotus Paradise with their dead daughter. Three related Pae *chip* contributed to this *kut*.

Ancestors in *kut* are not exclusively the sons and spouses of male-defined *chip*. While the *mansin* is obliged to invoke certain categories of ancestors, she claims that other *chosang* and *yŏngsan* appear before her eyes in the course of the ancestors' sequence. These visitors, too, are given voice by the sobbing *mansin*.

Dead children are *yŏngsan*, not *chosang*, but they were born into the *chip*. Sons, daughters, nieces, and nephews appear in the ancestors' sequence inside the house, although, as *yŏngsan*, their place is outside the gate. They are not entitled to offerings prepared inside for the ancestors. Instead, the family's kindred *yŏngsan* are fed outside the gate with the other wandering *yŏngsan* who crowd around, anticipating handouts from the feast.

More surprising is the appearance of the husband's deceased sisters, both married and unmarried, sometimes accompanied by their husbands. Patrilineal familial ideology implies that married sisters cease to belong to the *chip* on their wedding days, yet they return. In similar fashion, deceased married daughters are drawn back to their natal homes by the ancestors' sequence. For the *mansin*, their appearance is quite logical: "When a married daughter is alive, she goes back to visit her natal home; after death, it's the same thing." Now, however, she is tainted by death, and her presence may bring illness to her natal home. She should be sent to the Lotus Paradise and urged to stop visiting her own kin.

Married daughters and husbands' sisters are children of the *chip*. Although legally and ritually they cease to be members of the *chip* when they marry, they retain ties with their natal homes throughout their lives. Married daughters visit their natal homes at least on their parents' birthdays or death anniversaries, if distance and/or propriety permit no more frequent visits. Many women deliver their first children in their natal homes or attended by their own mothers. It is not unusual for a married daughter to turn to her own kin in time of adversity; if father and siblings begrudge her aid, her mother provides rice or cash on the sly. And when a mother or a brother's wife holds a *kut*, the married daughters of the *chip* often return for the feasting and holiday atmosphere.

A married daughter's recourse to her natal home and her enduring attachment beyond death are revealed in the following case:

> An old woman from the next village consulted with the neighborhood *mansin* because her husband was suffering from a lingering cold. During the divination, the *mansin* detected the presence of a "restless ancestor" or *malmyŏng*, "someone who went back to the natal home and died young."
>
> The old woman immediately acknowledged that this would be her own daughter. The daughter had married and gone to live with her husband in Seoul. During the war, while her husband was away, the daughter lived in a bomb shelter with an old woman of her husband's family. When her first confinement approached, the daughter asked permission to return to her natal

home. Carrying her possessions in a heavy bundle, she walked all the way to the provincial town where her parents were then living, a day-long journey. When she reached her parents' home, she complained of pains. Her mother thought that she was weakened by wartime hardship and the journey. The mother purchased body-building medicine but the family lacked funds to continue the treatment. The daughter's labor was long and difficult. Her parents sent for a midwife. In desperation, the mother went to a *mansin* for an exorcism (*p'udak-kŏri*). All was of no avail; the daughter delivered her child and died.

The *mansin* was satisfied that this was the restless ancestor of her divination.

Daughters marry out, but, living or dead, they are not strangers. Conversely, women accept that the walls of the affinal *chip* are not impervious to ancestral and ghostly influences from the wife's natal home. A woman's own parents and, less frequently, her grandparents may appear in the ancestors' sequence. A woman's dead siblings, both married and unmarried, frequently appear. A woman's marital misfortunes are often attributed to the ghostly influence of unmarried or childless siblings. A married sister who died pregnant or in childbirth (*haesan'gi*) is particularly threatening, because she would have a great sense of unfulfillment. Dead children, *tongja*, follow the brightly colored marriage quilt and, with the capriciousness of youth, stir up turmoil in their married sister's new home. *Yŏt'am*,[8] offerings made to the ancestors and ghosts of the bride's family on the eve of the wedding, keep these rambunctious ghosts in place.

On the *mansin*'s advice, mothers offer *yŏt'am* that their daughters will be "clean," purified of negative supernatural influences, when they marry. This rite may be taken as part of the ritual process severing the bride from her natal *chip* in the course of her wedding. But *yŏt'am*, as an optional rite, carries the implication that family ghosts and ancestors are inclined to follow the bride. Many find their dead siblings sighted in the *mansin*'s divinations, years after marriage, as the source of their domestic strife.

If ghosts and ancestors from the wife's natal home are everywhere considered a negative influence, their appearance in shaman ritual might merely reinforce male-centered values: married women must be severed from their own kin. Enduring ties are dangerous. It is my impression, however, that ancestral and ghostly influences from the wife's side are no more significantly negative than ancestral and ghostly influences from the husband's side. Close contact with the dead is dangerous; the principle applies to husband's and wife's kin alike. Properly propitiated dead from either side may exert a positive influence on their kin. The *mansin* divines that a dead mother follows and helps her married daughter; a dead sister, like the daughter of the Pae family in Case 2, helps a favorite sibling succeed in school.

Where the woman has lost her natal kin, their appearance in the ancestors' sequence may evoke a cathartic expression of grief. After one ancestors' sequence, a young housewife spoke of the loss of her mother, father, brother, and sister-in-law, all in the space of a few years. Her eyes were brimming over when she claimed to have heard her own dead kin call her by her childhood name as they reached out to touch her in the *chosang-gŏri*. The *mansin* remarked afterward that the wife's ancestors were a far stronger presence in that house than the husband's ancestors.

The death of the mother is considered particularly grievous. While the mother is alive, the married daughter is always welcome at home. A stepmother or brother's wife might not be so generous. Elsewhere (Kendall 1977), I have described the tribulations of a woman who received considerable support from her own kin throughout her impoverished and grief-ridden married life. The final death rites for the woman's mother triggered a temporary fit of insanity, partially attributed to possession by the pitying mother, who expressed concern for her daughter from beyond the grave.

While women and *mansin* thus acknowledge the enduring influence of a woman's own kin, the concept of "ancestor" in *kut* is not pronouncedly matrilateral nor even strictly bilateral. Both in gross numbers of manifestations and in the range and variety of kinship categories represented, ancestral and ghostly manifestations are skewed in favor of male-linked kin (see Appendix I). In general, appearances from the wife's side are restricted to the immediate members of her natal household: parents, grandparents, and siblings.[9] Ties to the wife's natal home are of necessity generationally shallow. Korean women become ancestors in their husbands' homes. A mother's natal kin are not likely to be included in a daughter's conceptualization of her own kin. This patrilateral bias is to be expected, since in their daily lives women have most contact with members of their husbands' and related *chip*. *Kut* reflect social reality.

Kut and the Living

While dramatically acknowledging a woman's affective ties to her own dead kin, a *kut* also reaffirms bonds between a woman and her living kin. Like natal ancestors, living mothers, sisters, brothers, and brothers' wives may be present when a woman holds a *kut* in her own home. A woman's own kin may contribute to the expenses of a *kut*, particularly if their ancestors or ghosts are among those sent along the road to the Lotus Paradise. The pattern of participation by living and dead in the two *kut* described below reveals a chain of households linked by out-marrying women.

Case 3: An family kut. The An family held a *kut* on the initiative of the senior wife of the household, nee Pak.[10] The Ans held this *kut* because the family store was not making money, the son's present employment held no prospects for advancement, and the daughter-in-law, nee Kim, was perennially weak and tired easily. Restorative medicines had little effect on the daughter-in-law's condition.

A joint sponsor of this *kut* was the widow of the Pak woman's brother, nee Yi. The brother had died in a factory fire, leaving his widow with three small children. A wife and a married daughter from the main *chip* of the An grandfather's generation were also present at the *kut* but did not contribute as cosponsors.

Parents of the An family and the Pak woman's own brother would be sent along the road to the Lotus Paradise. The *mansin* would also placate an unfulfilled ghost from the daughter-in-law's family, a brother who had died in his youth of an unspecified illness. The daughter-in-law's father also appeared in the ancestors' sequence. The ancestors and ghosts of primary concern in this *kut* thus represent three separate *chip* linked through women: Pak, An, and Kim (see chart, Appendix II).

Case 4: Yu family kut. The Yu family held a *kut* because Mr. Yu and his wife, nee Im, had both been ill, off and on, for several months. The wife's own mother helped sponsor the *kut*, bringing an unmarried daughter with her to the Yu house.

Yu family ancestors—the father, grandfather, and grandfather's two wives—were sent along the road to the Lotus Paradise. The Im woman's elder sister, who had married but died of a miscarriage, was also sent off along the road with a set of spirit clothes. Technically, this dead woman was two households removed from her sister's husband's home, yet mother and sister collaborated in sending off her soul (see chart, Appendix II).

Conclusion: Women, Ancestors, and Natal Kin

For my purposes here, I have dealt only with the two general categories of "ancestor" and "ghost," most particularly ancestors and ghosts in *kut*. I have neglected to discuss those women, like the wife of the Pae family, who are susceptible to the influence of household gods from their natal household pantheons.

This limited discussion should be sufficient to suggest that ties through women are given dramatic ritual validation when the ancestors descend into the possessed *mansin*. As Werbner (1964) has noted in another cultural context, the out-marrying woman is an axle between two kin groups. Woman-centered rituals are one means of accentuating this tie.

Some would consider the appearance of women's natal ancestors in shaman ritual a "survival" from an earlier, more "matriarchal" Korea (Akiba 1957: 105). Conversely, others might argue that the social and supernatural significance accorded the wife's kin reflects a watering down of traditional patriarchal ideology. Recent research does suggest that Korean society was most likely uxorilocal — not matrilocal — until fairly recent times (Deuchler 1977), and any community study contains ample evidence for the breakdown of traditional patterns. Allowing for systematic variation over time and space, I would explain the presence of these unlikely ghosts and ancestors quite simply, on their own terms.

Marriages establish affinal ties. Women are intimately involved with the kin of two related households. Contradictory ideas of "ancestor" reflect complementary principles of social organization. The ancestors of men's *chesa* and women's *kut* reflect two contrasting but essential notions of family. The exclusive patrilineal family concentrates resources and loyalties within itself. Wives who marry in and sisters and daughters who marry out make the family a matrix for a variety of relationships with a bilateral kindred. The kindred are a store of potential aid, but they are also a potential drain on one's own resources. Relationships with the kindred, like dealings with the dead, are ambivalent and potentially dangerous. Both the kindred and the dead must be dealt with gingerly, brought together periodically in acknowledgment of a bond, given their due, implored for assistance, but when necessary, distanced.[11]

Let me conclude by suggesting that our understanding of Korean society could well profit from increased attention to the role of affines and to the unique position of the married woman who mediates between the living and the dead of two patrilineal *chip*.

APPENDIX I

Ancestors Appearing in Kut

Given the somewhat chaotic circumstances of *kut*, I cannot claim to provide a complete survey of all ancestors and ghosts appearing in each ritual observed. And given the small size of my sample (25 *kut*), indications of the relative frequency with which various categories of ancestors appear are, at best, tentative. While my sample indicates the breadth of categories of kin appearing in the *kut* I witnessed, additional categories of kin may conceivably appear in other *kut*.

Husband's kin	Wife's kin
hufafa's generation: 20	wifafa's generation: 4
grandfather 8	grandfather 2
grandfather's first wife 10	grandmother 2
grandfather's second wife 2	
hufa's generation: 22	wifa's generation: 12
father 18	father 6
father's first wife 1	stepfather 1
mother's first husband 1	mother 5
adoptive father 1	
adoptive mother 1	
husband's generation: 24	wife's generation: 10
husband 4	sister 5
husband's first wife 7	brother 4
husband's sister 6	brother's wife 1
husband's elder brother 2	
husband's younger brother 3	
husband's sister's husband 2	
children: 9	children: 1
son 3	niece 1
daughter 3	
nephew 1	
niece 2	
TOTAL: 87	TOTAL: 27

relatives of senior line of husband's, husband's father's, or husband's grandfather's generation (*k'ŭnjip*) 7

relatives of minor line of husband's, husband's father's, or husband's grandfather's generation (*chagŭnjip*) 9

Miscellaneous no count:
grandparents of third and fourth generation — frequent
relatives of third and fourth degree of relationship (mentioned in passing) — frequent
relatives up to eighth degree of relationship — one mention by my count
relatives of senior line of wife's father's generation — one mention by my count

APPENDIX II

Ties through Women Manifested in Kut

⚎ ancestor or ghost appearing in *kut*

● sponsor

Case 3 - An family *kut*

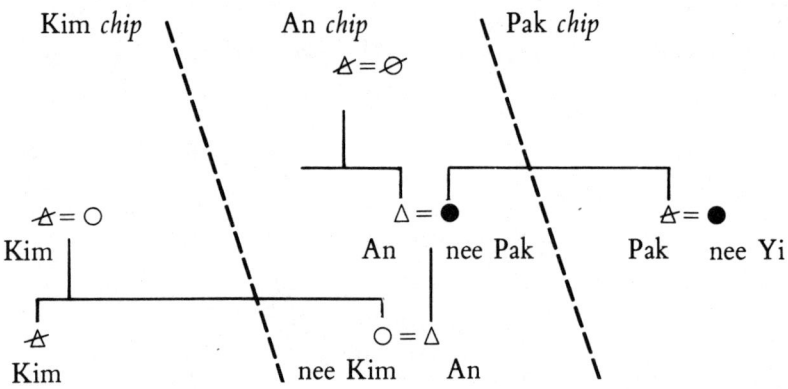

Case 4 - Yu family *kut*

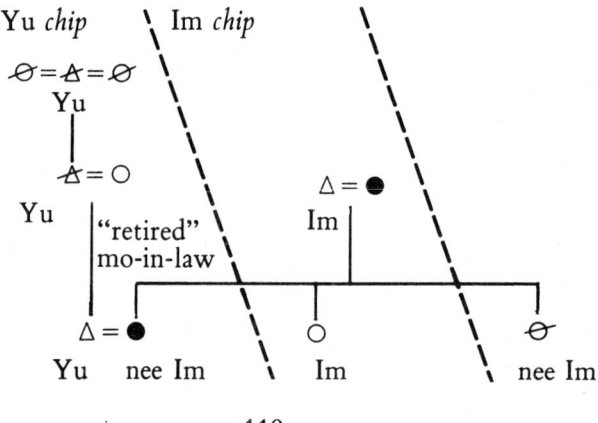

Notes

[1] This is a most cursory account of kinship principles implicit in *chip* membership and the performance of *chesa* rights. For more detailed treatments, see Brandt (1971) and Janelli (1975).

[2] Research was made possible by a Fulbright dissertation fellowship, a Social Science Research Council Foreign Area Fellowship, and a dissertation research grant from the National Science Foundation. I would like to thank Roger L. Janelli, Dawnhee Yim Janelli, Martina Deuchler, Myron Cohen, and Sandra Mattielli for their comments on an early version of this paper. All blunders are, of course, my own.

[3] For a more general introduction to Korean shamanism see Yim (1970), and Chang (1974). See Chŏe and Chang (1967) for a description of shamanism in Kyŏnggi Province, near the village in which I conducted my own study.

[4] While the conceptualization of household gods is fairly consistent throughout Korea, there is considerable variation in the names of particular spirits and in the mode of worship. For descriptions of this cult of the household, see Chang (1974: 163-70), Jones (1902), and Lee (1975).

[5] The dead are sent off in a special ritual (*siyang* or *chinogi*) at the end of a household *kut*. A *mansin* portrays the progress of the soul along the road out of hell and into the Lotus Paradise.

[6] The traditional Korean home is heated by burning coal bricks, *yŏnt'an*, below a clay or cement floor. In a cold and fuel-poor country, the hot floor is a cheap and efficient source of heat, but cases of carbon monoxide poisoning are fairly common, common enough for "those who died of *yŏnt'an* gas" to be among the wandering ghosts commonly invoked in the *mansin*'s chants.

[7] According to my *mansin* informant, there are two categories of *malmyŏng*: *chosang malmyŏng* and *taesin malmyŏng*. The latter are dead shamans who become deities, *taesin*, in the household pantheon after death. The *taesin* leads the spirits of the family dead to *kut*. J. Lee (1977: 7) probably refers to the *taesin malmyŏng* when he glosses *malmyŏng* as: "female spirit of the dead."

[8] *Yŏt'am* may also be offered in the home of the groom, and some families offer *yŏt'am* before a sixty-first birthday feast. Some of the feast food and spirit clothing and a gauzy "handkerchief" are offered to the family dead. Women claim that they offer *yŏt'am* at the shaman's shrine out of ritual propriety: the ancestors, as senior members of the *chip*, should be invited to partake of the feast food before anyone else. The *mansin* shares this view but stresses her belief that without *yŏt'am*, dead siblings will follow the bride and disrupt the marriage. In the course of *yŏt'am*, the *mansin* manifest dead children of the *chip*, along with the ancestors.

[9] I witnessed one *kut* in which the senior line of the wife's natal home did appear. The entire senior *chip* had been executed during the war. The wife sent her unfortunate kin to the Lotus Paradise, since they lacked direct descendants to perform this task.

[10] A Korean wife retains her maiden name.

[11] I owe this insight to Myron Cohen.

Bibliography

Akiba Takashi
    1957 "A study of Korean folkways," *Folklore Studies* (Tokyo), 16 (1): 1-106.

Brandt, Vincent S. R.
    1971 *A Korean Village: Between Farm and Sea* (Cambridge: Harvard University Press).

Chang Chu-gŭn
    1974 *"Mingan sinang"* [Popular beliefs], in D. H. Lee, C. G. Chang, and K. K. Lee, eds., *Han'guk Minsokhak Kaesŏl* [Introduction to Korean Folklore] (Seoul, Minjung Sŏgwan): 128-95 (in Korean).

Ch'oe Kil-sŏng
    1967 *Kyŏnggido Ch'iyŏk Musok* [Shaman Practices of Kyŏnggi Province] (Seoul: Ministry of Culture, in Korean).

Deuchler, Martina
    1977 "The tradition: Women during the Yi dynasty," in Sandra Mattielli, ed., *Virtues in Conflict: Tradition and the Korean Woman Today* (Seoul: Royal Asiatic Society, Korea Branch): 1-47.

Janelli, Roger L.
    1975 *Korean Rituals of Ancestor Worship: An Ethnography of Folklore Performance* (Ph.D. dissertation, University of Pennsylvania).

Janelli, Roger L., and Dawnhee Yim Janelli
    n.d. *Ancestral Malevolence in a Korean Village* (unpublished manuscript).

Jones, George Heber
    1902 "The spirit worship of the Koreans," *Transactions of the Korea Branch of the Royal Asiatic Society*, 2: 37-58.

Kendall, Laurel
    1977 "Caught between ancestors and spirits: Field report of a Korean *mansin*'s healing *kut*," *Korea Journal*, 17 (8): 8-23.

Lee Jung Young
    1975 "Shamanistic thought and traditional Korean homes," *Korea Journal*, 15 (11): 43-51.
    1977 "Mudang's song of Pujŏng," *Korea Journal*, 17 (8): 4-7½

Werbner, Richard P.
    1964 "Atonement ritual and guardian-spirit possession among the Kalanga," *Africa*, 23: 206-22.

Yim Sŏk-chae
    1970 "Han'guk Musok Yŏn'gu Sŏsŏl" [Introduction to Korean Shamanism], in *Asea Yŏsŏng* [Asian Women] (in Korean, with English summary).

The Korean Shaman: Image and Reality

Brian Wilson

Two modern Korean short stories reveal the shaman, or *mudang*, as a formidable presence in Korean society. The two stories are "Chom-Nye," by Choe Chong-hi,[1] and "The Tableau of a Shaman Sorceress," by Kim Tong-ni.[2] While both are excellent short stories, each represents an essentially negative portrayal of the character and role of the *mudang*, and this negativism is an expression of widely-shared Korean attitudes.

"Chom-Nye" is a story of poverty, ignorance, superstition, and cruelty. It concerns a fourteen-year-old girl whose tenant-farmer parents work for a rich landowner. In an effort to lighten their economic burden, the parents betroth Chom-Nye to a young man who has a menial job in an alehouse. With his meager earnings the young man buys some cloth, a mirror, and some powder for the wedding. His aunt provides two chickens, and it is this gift of chickens that leads to disaster.

One of the chickens strays into the garden of the rich landlord, who captures it and ties it to the tip of a long pole. Chom-Nye wants to rescue the chicken but is afraid of arousing the landlord's wrath. Finally she can endure the chicken's screams no longer. She sneaks into the garden to untie the chicken. She is discovered by the landlord, who throws a rock and wounds her in the forehead. The wound becomes infected, and in her delirium Chom-Nye talks about her chicken. Thus, when she dies, the villagers believe that she was possessed by the spirit of the chicken.

The family brings in a *mudang*, who performs a ritual to pacify the troubled spirit of Chom-Nye and send her on her way to the land of the dead. The *mudang* calls on the soul of Chom-Nye, who possesses her and speaks through her, expressing sadness at leaving her family and anger at the chicken for trespassing on the landlord's property. The author regards the behavior of the *mudang* with contempt: "Thus the nonsense of the witch continues in the name of Chom-Nye."[3]

The *mudang*, speaking as Chom-Nye, tells the bereaved mother to give away all of her daughter's meager possessions, including her chickens. The *mudang* and her assistant even take the rice that was used during the ritual, leaving the impoverished family nothing but forlorn hopes for their departed daughter's well-being.

In the second story, "The Tableau of a Shaman Sorceress," the author focuses on the relationship between a *mudang* and the *mudang*'s son and daughter. It is a Gothic tale, set in a decayed and crumbling ruin, where the eerie and uncanny become almost tangible in the bizarre behavior of the "shaman-sorceress."

The description of the *mudang*'s house cues the reader that this is a tale of the supernatural:

> The house was like a haunted den long deserted by human inhabitants — deserted perhaps over scores or even hundreds of years.
>
> In this old, crumbling house that looked like a haunted cavern, there lived Mohwa the sorceress and her daughter Nang-i.[4]

As the story unfolds, we learn that Mohwa the sorceress is fond of drinking and spends most of her time in wineshops. She has had lovers, and both of her children were born out of wedlock. Her daughter is a shy, pale mute, who loves to paint. Both mother and daughter have created their own private fantasy worlds: the mother in shamanism and the daughter in painting.

Mohwa sends her son to a Buddhist temple as a novice, but he runs away to become a Christian. The new Christian religion confronts the old shaman faith, and mother and son lock themselves in a fatal embrace. As the conflict intensifies, the son's understanding of Christian demonology is revealed to be almost an exact replica of his mother's beliefs. Yet neither the shaman mother nor the Christian son perceives nor understands their affinity. The mother-*mudang*'s antagonist is Jesus Christ, in her eyes, the Western "devil" who is afflicting her son. In a crazed attempt to destroy this Western devil, the mother stabs her son. He dies a Christian martyr, and a church is built to commemorate the strength of his faith.

Mohwa, the mother, becomes even more reclusive; the villagers now consider her completely mad. Nevertheless, she is engaged to perform an exorcism for the soul of a girl who had committed suicide by drowning. Rumors spread that Mohwa will also exorcise the demons that have deprived her daughter of speech. Mohwa says, "We shall see which is the more veritable being, the devil Jesus or my divinity."[5]

Mohwa performs the ritual beside the pond where the girl drowned. As she invokes the spirit of the deceased she wades into the pond and is herself swallowed up by the dark and mysterious waters. Thus, both mother and son, shaman and Christian, are destroyed in the service of conflicting ideologies. Never had they really touched each other.

These two stories are, of course, fiction, and were not meant to be read as sociological treatises on the character and behavior of shamans in Korean society. Nevertheless, they depend for their effectiveness upon the shared attitudes of their readers, and these attitudes are sustained by an unexamined acceptance of stereotypes passed down for so many generations that they have come to be accepted as self-evident truths.

One of these unexamined stereotypes is that *mudang* are insane, "crazy," *mich'ida*. They must be crazy, for why else would they do the things they do: dancing in the road, beating drums, chanting, dressing in antique male costumes, and fighting the spirits they alone can see? The *mudang* Mohwa, in "The Tableau of the Shaman Sorceress," is not a "normal" person. Her behavior is bizarre in the extreme. The decadence of her environs reflects her own moral and spiritual decay. She is a drunkard, she is promiscuous, and, finally, she is the murderess of her own son. She is, in short, the very antithesis of what the normative Korean woman should be.

The sanity of the *mudang* in "Chom-Nye" is not in question. Rather, she is described as a greedy, calculating charlatan, who callously exploits the sufferings of her clients and manipulates their credulity and trust for her own selfish gain.

During the seven years that I lived in Korea, I found these negative assessments of the character and role of the *mudang* to be quite common and rarely, if ever, challenged. Why is this so? What has the *mudang* done to deserve all of this contempt, ridicule, and social ostracism?

The answer may be found in the personal history of a living, as opposed to a fictional, *mudang*. I am indebted to my *mansin* informant-friend for providing me with the following autobiographical data. I also owe a special debt of thanks to Mr. Y. N. Kim, who helped me record and translate this material. The research was made possible by a Fulbright-Hays Training

Grant, and by the logistical and moral support of Mrs. Sookhi Chun and Mr. Jae Ho Han.

The *mudang*, or *mansin* (*mansin* is the polite term, but *mudang* is more common) whose story I will present is a woman I have come to know well over the past year. I will call her Mrs. Cho, although that is not her real name. She and her husband run a small doughnut shop in Chungju and live with their children behind the shop. Mrs. Cho was born forty-six years ago in a village in Kyŏnggi Province. Her father, a farmer, died when she was three years old. She had two elder sisters and an elder brother. Her mother, now eighty-four years old, lives with Mrs. Cho's elder brother, a farmer. Mrs. Cho's story is best told in her own words:

> At the time I was born there were a lot of floods and drought and people were just barely surviving. Our father was sick when I was born. Because of his illness, our mother supported the four kids. She had to go to work at rich people's houses whenever the people there had celebrations. For her work, she received grain to feed the children and husband. She also spun homespun cotton and took it to the market to barter for food. After three years of this our father died. We had no money, so our mother had to borrow money for the funeral. All of the relatives gathered to bury our father.
>
> My eldest sister was given to a family when she was nine years old and grew up in that house. When she was grown she became the daughter-in-law of that family — we call it *minmyŏnuri* — given to a house to reduce the number of mouths to feed. The other family needs a hand. She must work hard and if she is suitable they match her up with their son. They told her to have many sons, and she gave birth to seven sons. Now four of them are married, and my sister is the richest woman in the village.
>
> When I was eight or nine the Japanese surrendered to the Americans. My second sister was twelve then. I tied straw and my second sister would weave it into *kamani*, straw mats, and sell them in exchange for rice.
>
> My older brother was drafted by the Japanese and sent to a mine in Japan. He returned home after the Liberation and he was

about twenty years old then. He had never gone to school. Neither had anyone else in my family.

When I was fifteen I went to Seoul to work as a housemaid. I stayed at that job for two years. One day, my brother came and brought me back to our house to get married. He said, "Now your hardship is over, you can stay with me until you get married." I wanted to stay in Seoul because I could save more money there, but he was my elder brother, so I had to obey him.

One of our relatives found a suitable mate for me. I was seventeen, and he was twenty-two. I said, "I don't want to get married," but I knew I would have to. I was afraid of married life. If the husband's family didn't like me they could kick me out. But I knew I would have to go through with it.

Even though I didn't like it, the matchmaker came one day and my mother persuaded me to meet the groom and his family. The groom had decided not to marry me until he had seen me. After seeing me he decided to marry me. I only glanced at him so I didn't know whether I liked him or not. I didn't feel anything at all.

The *mansin* described the traditional Korean wedding and the gifts that she received. The narrative continues:

After the wedding, I was carried to my husband's house in a sedan chair borne by four men. I found that my husband had no father but lived with his mother in a rented room. One year later, the Korean War started. My husband was wounded in the fighting; he had pieces of shrapnel in his skull, shoulder, side, and foot. He was operated on, but they left the shrapnel in his skull and only removed it later. He was in a supply detachment and they were forced to march to Pusan in retreat. My husband, brother-in-law, and brother were all gone for seven months.

I had to peddle rice cakes to survive. I would make the cakes at night and sell them in the daytime. My husband came back and we started a small store, but then the North Koreans came again. We fled to the mountains and stayed there until the Communists were gone. When we returned, our house was gone, burned down. We lived in a small shack and started to sell things.

For the women it was one disaster after another, because the men were all drafted and gone for a full five years. In our one little room we had mother-in-law, our nephew's children, brother-in-law, and sister-in-law. I couldn't live in that house without my husband, so I went to live on the mountain in a dugout bomb shelter. I got permission from the owner of the mountain to make myself a heated floor with stones from a demolished house. I put a woven mat on the hot stones and lay down there with my baby. I was about twenty years old. My husband had left to join the army when our first son was born. The baby was born in the house I shared with the family, then I moved to the bomb shelter.

Now I had a place to sleep but no means of support, so I had to work in a small inn in town. I had to carry the baby on my back while I was working. I was paid about twenty dollars a month. I worked two months but couldn't go on. With the money I earned, I bought a big basket for peddling. I sold fish, soap, matches, candles, and such. I went around with the basket on my head and the baby on my back, peddling. I didn't get cash for what I sold, just rice.

I realized that there was a good market for bootleg liquor, so I begged a man to teach me how to brew. He finally agreed and I bought one *mal* (18 litres) of rice and made rice wine (*yakju*) out of it in a jar hidden in the cellar. There was good profit in it and, for the first time since I was married, I was happy.

When my husband left the army we were in good financial shape and were able to rent a small room. We had enough capital to buy a cart to carry goods to peddle in the villages around the countryside. Then we would buy vegetables in the countryside, and sell them in town.

While we were doing this vending business we had our second child, a daughter who died of measles when she was three years old. We were doing pretty well with the vegetable business, but it was hard with my husband pulling and me behind pushing the cart. When we had enough money we decided to get a small shop. I was twenty-five or twenty-six at the time.

We were able to save some money and, compared to when we started, we were well off. But my husband started a love affair with another woman who later became his concubine. It went on for about a year before I found out about it. My husband would give money to his girl friend and the business got worse. We almost went bankrupt. We had violent quarrels about it. Because of the quarrels, the customers stopped coming in. So finally we sold the shop and left town to come to Chungju. I hoped that moving would end my husband's affair. I was about twenty-nine then.

While we were moving to Chungju I had my third child, a daughter, the one who is now baking and selling food in our store. Since she was sucking the breast, my husband brought our household goods on a cart, and I came by bus with the two children. We rented a small room; the four of us couldn't sleep well because it was so crowded.

We started a business selling rice cakes. My husband peddled rice cakes piled on a cart, and I sold them spread out on a wooden box on the bridge, a little farther down the street from where we are now. But we weren't satisfied just selling the rice cakes, we wanted to bake them too. So my husband signed a contract with a shipper to supply him with the necessary materials.

We saved enough money to rent the shop we are in now. But now we had enough money to sell wholesale to other vendors. My husband stayed at the shop making rice cakes for the vendors, and I went to outlying towns like Kangneung, Sokcho, Wonju, and Chechon to sell rice cakes for extra income.

When we had saved some money the landlord of the house wanted us to deposit "key" money [advanced rent in a lump sum], but the amount was so large that we had to go into debt to pay it. Two years later, the landlord said he wanted to sell the house. We decided to buy it but didn't have enough money, so we went to relatives to raise the money. It took us years to repay the relatives. I was around thirty-eight years old when we bought this house.

When I was out selling, I used to hold back some of the money to save without letting my husband know. Sometimes I would be short and we would quarrel. My husband would say, "Give me the money you are hiding," and I would say, "What money?" My husband knew, because he knew the price and quantity of goods I took out, but I hid the money anyway.

One morning, after a quarrel with my husband, I went out without preparing breakfast. At that moment, Kaju Bosal (a Buddhist-style diviner) dropped in on her way back from a *kut* to rest in our shop. I knew of her, not personally, but had heard of her. I asked her to tell my fortune (*chŏm*) and tell me if I should leave my husband. Kaju Bosal said I couldn't leave because it would bring bad luck. Instead of running away, she advised me to have a *taegam kut* [honoring an important spirit official, or *taegam*]. I should honor the *taegam*, because my will power is strong, stronger than my husband's; I would never yield to him. She also claimed that our house site was full of potent geomantic forces (*t'ŏga seda*). She said that my mother-in-law's spirit was present here, and if I honored my mother-in-law and had a *kut*, then my mother-in-law would help me.

Kaju Bosal told me to choose a date for a *taegam kut*. Ordinarily, the Kaju Bosal would choose the date herself, but because I had such strong will-power, she told me to choose my own date. I chose October 7, because October is when everyone has *kosa* [a ritual for home and family fortune].

Three *mansin* came over to do the *taegam kut* for me, but I was already possessed by my mother-in-law and by T'ŏju Taegam (the supernatural House Site Official). Through my lips, these spirits spoke to the three *mansin*: "Why are you *mansin* here? You came over to worship the T'ŏju Taegam of *this* house, but instead you are worshiping your own *taegam* spirits. What the hell are you doing here?" I grabbed them all by the collar and said, "Go away, I don't need you, I am T'ŏju and I am the ancestor. We don't need you!"

The *mansin* thought I was possessed by *hŏju* (false spirits), or some kind of evil spirit (*subi, magwi*). They wanted to drive the *hŏju* out of me, so they grabbed me by the hair and pushed my head down and said, "You get away from this lady. You are this or that evil spirit." They put the Spirit General's sword to my throat and said, "Go away, otherwise we will do something with this sword."

They covered me with a paper net. They wanted to drive out the *hŏju*. But my mother-in-law possessed me, and I said, "I am the ancestor. I am T'ŏju, not *hŏju*, and if you are not doing what you are supposed to, get away!" I was crying. I was really possessed by my mother-in-law. Mother-in-law said, "I came to help you and bring you good luck. You stop this *kut*. I will take care of my children; I will bring good luck to this household."

So the *mansin* who were supposed to continue the *kut* for three days stopped on the second day and fled, because I was possessed by my mother-in-law. Speaking *kongsu* [when a spirit speaks directly through a *mudang*], mother-in-law told them, "You are not here to do *taegam kut* but just to get money, so go away."

After they fled, I took out some rice and made some rice cakes, and offered the rice-cake steamer to T'ŏju and the ancestor. I worshiped these two spirits.

After a while, I was possessed by mother-in-law and spoke *kongsu*. I grabbed my husband by the collar, saying, "I am your mother. You are my son. I feel pity for you, both of you, my son and my daughter-in-law. I will take care of you and bring luck to you because you are my son and you are my daughter-in-law."

After this *kut*, I became possessed. I didn't do anything, didn't prepare breakfast, any meals, didn't wash, nothing. When peddlers came to our shop for supplies I would say, "Your family has such and such a problem," and they were surprised.

They asked my husband, "What happened to her?" and he said, "Oh, she had a *taegam kut*."

I said, "Oh you shut up. Don't say anything to these people." But the peddlers realized that what I was saying was correct, so they came to believe me.

Whenever the peddlers came in I told them what was going to happen. I did this as a precaution, to prevent evil spirits from coming into their houses. This went on for a year. The peddlers took my advice and were surprised that my predictions came true. To show their appreciation for my advice, they brought something to pay for it. They brought me money, rice, and candles. Those whose neighbors were ill would take me to see the sick.

For one year after the *taegam kut* I didn't do *kut*. I told peddlers' fortunes to protect them from evil spirits, and they showed their appreciation. One day Kaju Bosal came along and said, "You have been fortune-telling for a year and getting nothing, so why not start doing *kut* yourself? I will help you."

I came across a client who had *mubyŏng* [the sickness which signifies a "call" to become a *mudang*]. To recover the client must have a *naerim kut*,[6] so for the first time, I chose a date to do a *kut* for someone else. With Kaju Bosal and another woman, I conducted a *naerim kut*.

So after conducting that first *naerim kut* for my client, every October 7 I always hold a two-day *kut* to commemorate the day when I became possessed by the *taegam* and became a *mansin*. First I go to the mountain, to worship the Mountain Spirit (Sansin) and then I have *ant'aek kosa*, a ritual to bring good fortune to my house and family and to pray for prosperous business for the shop. On the second day I have a *kut* to please mother-in-law's spirit.

At this point in the interview, we were interrupted by the arrival of a client who had come for fortune-telling. She wanted a suitable date for her daughter's forthcoming marriage. When Mrs. Cho returned, we talked about other things, and I asked if she could tell me what kind of child she was.

I was the youngest. I was never beaten by my older sisters. I always won fights with my sisters and brother. I was a troublemaker, beating up boys in the village. I was a tomboy, my mother used to call me *sŏn mosum* [naughty boy]. I used to gather wood for the fire like a boy.

I have always wanted to be a man. Of course it is impossible now, but when I die, I want to be a male spirit. I want to be a great general like the Spirit General so I can lead hundreds of thousands of people.

My husband is a womanlike man. He's quiet and mild and never behaves like a man, but I act like a man, so I would like to be like a great general. I want to lead and tell people what to do. I hate my own status. I'm not educated, not physically strong, and on top of that, I'm a woman.

This segment of the interview ended here, but I have presented enough material, I think, to provide a basis for a brief discussion of the life of a Korean *mudang*, or at least of *this* particular *mudang*. I cannot pretend that Mrs. Cho is representative of *all* Korean shamans, but in meeting and working with *mudang* and reading about others, I find certain features recurring often enough to permit certain broad generalizations. I do not offer these generalizations as empirically-tested facts, but as impressions based on experience.

First, one is struck by the fact that Mrs. Cho's life has been one of almost unremitting hardship and deprivation. Born into a poor family, losing her father at the age of three, watching her mother eke out a bare existence working for wealthier people, seeing her sister given away out of economic necessity, Mrs. Cho must have very early formed the notion that life is a series of adverse events or obstacles to be overcome.

If psychiatry has taught us anything at all, it is that early experiences make lasting impressions and help shape adult personality and character. Mrs. Cho's life of poverty, loss, and deprivation enables her to identify with the clients who seek her aid. Most of them have backgrounds similar to hers. She is able to help her clients because she is one of them. The problems they bring her are, for the most part, similar to problems she has already faced and worked through herself. She has experienced the loss of father and child, physical illness, marital infidelity, mental and emotional stress. This last, the emotional strain of an increasingly bitter marriage, precipitated her initial attack of spirit sickness (*sinbyŏng*)[7] and her decision to become a -*mansin*. That decision, even if unconscious, was to radically alter her life.

Now, as *mansin*, she must take aggressive command of her own life, tapping her intuitive powers[8] to battle demons and control them. She must demand and receive the powerful assistance of the Spirit General (Changgun) and his Spirit Arrester (Sinjang); of the Mountain God (Sansin) and the Seven-star God (Ch'ilsŏng); the spirit officials (*taegam*), who like to be feted; the ancestors; and all the spirits of the house. It means, to use Mrs.

Cho's own phrase, "becoming a leader of hundreds of thousands." Now, for the first time in her life, she experiences freedom and power—freedom and power normally found in the male domain.

Mrs. Cho most passionately wished that she could have been born a man. Not penis envy, she wanted power and has acquired it now as a healer.

The power of the *mudang*, the "shaman-sorceress," is scorned by men but understood and utilized by women. One sees women at the rituals but not men. The women at *kut* dance, laugh, cry, and experience great outpourings of emotion, while the men stolidly gather in other rooms to drink and make derisive jokes about "those superstitious women."

The negative image of the *mudang* was formed generations ago, when men perceived shamanistic beliefs and practices as threats to the all-encompassing supremacy of Confucian ideology. The educated Confucian male was literate and "rational;" his social and spiritual universe was orderly and harmonious. In this system, the female was considered irrational and emotional; women's intuitive and potentially dangerous powers must be confined, controlled, dominated. In the legal codes of the last dynasty, shamans were designated "outcastes" and banned from the capital. Even so, shamans retained their popular appeal.[9]

The lives of Korean women have been, for centuries, carefully circumscribed with taboos, rules, and sanctions governing every aspect of their behavior, from cradle to grave. A woman's proper place was at home having babies—male babies, who would inherit their father's name and ancestry. There was very little outside the home for a woman to do in traditional Korea. A woman alone might become a man's concubine (*chagŭn manŭra*). She might become a *kisaeng*, a skilled entertainer, or she might become a less-accomplished prostitute. But these roles are still subordinate and demeaning; these women are playthings for men's amusement. But becoming a *mudang* is something else altogether. Rather than being subdued, it is she who subdues the evil demons—the *kwisin*, *magwi*, *subi*, and *chapgwi*.

Mrs. Cho took for her tutelary spirit her own mother-in-law. Now, when the spirit of her mother-in-law possesses her, Mrs. Cho speaks to her husband as a mother speaks to her child, using grammatical forms of address that a wife would never use in speaking to her husband.

Mrs. Cho told me that when her mother-in-law first possessed her, she started ordering her husband around, using the mother-child form of address. Her husband thought she had gone crazy, and beat her soundly. But she persisted. When she refused to have sexual intercourse with her husband, he beat her again. This unhappy state of affairs continued for about a year, until finally the husband accepted the authenticity of his wife's experience.

As Youngsook Kim Harvey has pointed out: "That these possessing spirits are often the ancestral ghosts of the victim's husband's lineage makes the coalition between the shaman-recruit and her possessing spirits a powerful one against which the other family members are quite helpless."[10] She describes a "gradual reversal" in "the hierarchy of power positions" within the family, with the *mudang* becoming the de facto household head.

I have seen Mrs. Cho's husband kneeling before her on the mountainside while she, speaking as her mother-in-law, invokes the protection and blessings of the mountain spirit on him and his family. It is a very rare thing in Confucianist Korea to see a husband kneeling before his wife in full view of the world. Such a radical role reversal is possible only where players temporarily suspend the conventional order of things in favor of a new order of reality imposed by a power transcending the man-made social order. The agent of this transcendental power is the *mudang*.

I began by talking about the negative fictional and popular images of Korean *mudang*. The life, character, and work of my informant, Mrs. Cho, do not sustain these negative images. She is neither insane nor psychotic. She does, by her own testimony, experience auditory and visual "hallucinations," but these "hallucinations," like the trance-state in which they usually occur, are culturally learned and standardized. To hear the voices of deceased ancestors is no more psychotic in an ancestor-worshiping culture than for saints and mystics to converse with God in a Christian culture.

Another of the negative stereotypes of *mudang* is that they are ignorant, illiterate women. Many are indeed illiterate or semiliterate, and many more have only the rudiments of an education, thanks to a sexist philosophy, which, for a thousand years, taught that women are inferior beings incapable of learning. With Mrs. Cho and a number of other *mudang* I have known, I am struck not by ignorance but by intelligence and very often by keen insight into the intricate workings of the human heart and mind.

Two Korean psychiatrists claim that one of the deficiencies of shamanism is that it does not encourage self-understanding in the resolution of intrapsychic conflict.[11] Physicians overlook the strength of shamanistic ritual where pain, sickness, alienation, loss, and a host of other problems that afflict human beings are actualized in the course of the ritual in the form of demons, ancestors, spirit entities, gods, and goddesses. One actually sees these carriers of disease, death, and misfortune made real in the "folk theater" of ritual. Here the confrontation between the forces of light and the forces of darkness always results in the defeat of the forces of darkness. Colorful costumes, swords and tridents, and drums and gongs help to create the illusion of a real battle.

In "Chom-Nye," the *mudang* is portrayed as a greedy, selfish, insensitive charlatan. Unquestionably, there are such *mudang*, perhaps a multitude of them. But again, my field experience suggests that there are also *mudang* who possess an almost missionary zeal toward their "healing ministry," heeding any call to serve the sick and needy. Such *mudang* claim that they are not really "paid" for their work; rather, they receive a gift-offering tendered in gratitude. Mrs. Cho, for example, did not like to discuss money; she did not consider the services she performed for clients a business transaction. She told me that she was called to this work and was therefore compelled to do it.[12] Whatever success she might have had was the work of the gods, not the fruit of her own effort.

The negative stereotypes of *mudang* are the combined product of centuries of systematic oppression of *mudang* and of women's powerlessness in traditional Korean society. Women are necessary for the continuation of the male line; they provide sons. And, although it may not be admitted among men, *mudang* are necessary; they minister to the afflictions of women crippled by the limitations placed upon their lives simply because they are women. The stereotype of *mudang* as ignorant, irrational, perverse creatures is but an extension of the Confucian stereotype for *all* Korean women. The *mudang* dares put her "ignorance" and "irrationality" on display, in dramatic form, for all to see and hear.

Notes

[1] See Choe 1961.

[2] See Kim Tong-ni 1972.

[3] Choe 1961: 27.

[4] Kim Tong-ni 1972: 32.

[5] Ibid.: 43.

[6] *Naerim kut* is the initiatory ritual performed by experienced *mansin* for a novice who has been diagnosed as having *sinbyŏng* (*mubyŏng*).

[7] For an analysis of *sinbyŏng*, see Harvey 1979: 235-40.

[8] Yoon Soon Young also comments on the intuitive skills of *mudang* in her "Magic, Science and Religion on Cheju Island." (Yoon 1976; see also Harvey 1979: 235-36).

[9] According to Chang, Confucianist opposition to shamanism had already appeared during the Koryŏ dynasty (918-1392), and "some *mudang* outside the court were banished for having deceived the people" (Chang 1974: 66). In the *Kyŏngguk taejŏn* (Great Code of Administration), *mudang* are designated among the "Eight Outcaste Professions," along with Buddhist monks, *kisaeng*, butchers, and slaves. The unrestrained emotional outpourings of shaman-led *kut* were banned, and, "because women were disregarded in this strongly patrilineally-oriented religion, natural religious feeling was suppressed" (Chang 1974: 66). The oppression of *mudang* continued under the Yi kings, and, for a time, "shamans were driven out of the city and formed a separate community outside the city walls" (Kim 1977: 129).

These attempts to eradicate shamanism failed. Every major town had its "chief female shaman," some of whom had access to the royal court. The need for their services was so great that kings T'aejong, Sejong, and Sŏngjong called on government shamans to pray for rain during dry weather (ibid.: 130, 133).

[10] See Harvey 1979: 238-39.

[11] Assessments of the therapeutic value of shamanistic ritual have been made by Rhi Bou-yong (1970) and Kim Kwang-iel (1972). Kim finds that Korean shamanism has "negative aspects;" it promotes "paranoid tendencies." Its "positive functions" include a projective system that "relieves anxieties."

[12] *Mudang* believe that if they are "called" to the *mudang* vocation and reject the "call," then others among their family or friends will suffer or perhaps even die. (cf. Harvey 1979).

Bibliography

Chang Chu-gŭn
    1974 "Mu-Sok—The shaman culture of Korea," in Chun Shin-yong, ed., *Folk Culture in Korea* (Seoul: International Cultural Foundation).

Choe Chong-hi
    1961 "Chom-Nye," in *Collected Short Stories from Korea*, vol. 1 (Seoul: Eomun-Gag Publishing Company).

Harvey, Youngsook Kim
   1979   *Six Korean Women: The Socialization of Shamans* (St. Paul: West Publishing Co.)

Kendall, Laurel
   1977   "Caught between ancestors and spirits: Field report of a Korean *mansin*'s healing *kut*," *Korea Journal*, 17(8): 8-23.

Kim Kwang-iel
   1972   "Shamanism and personality in Korea," in *The Modern Meaning of Shamanism* (Iri City: Won Kwang University).

Kim Tong-ni
   1972   "The tableau of a shaman sorceress" (trans. by Kim Yong-chol), *Korea Journal*, 12(10): 31-45.

Kim Yung-chung, ed. and trans.
   1977   *Women of Korea: A History from Ancient Times to 1945*, Committee for the Compilation of the History of Korean Women (Seoul: Ewha Woman's University Press).

Rhi Bou-yong
   1970   "Psychological aspects of Korean shamanism," *Korea Journal*, 10(9): 15-21.

Yoon, Soon Young S.
   1976   "Magic, science and religion on Cheju Island," *Korea Journal*, 16(3): 4-11.

Formal and Informal Korean Society: A Reading of *Kisaeng* Songs

David R. McCann

Two recent studies of contemporary Korean society have described its structure as dualistic, characterized on the one hand by a formal, "Confucian" mode of hierarchical interaction, and on the other by an informal, egalitarian mode.[1] This characterization is of considerable interest for the student of Korean literature, who must deal with the simultaneous and yet distinct traditions of Korean vernacular and *hanmun* (Chinese) literature. *Hanmun* literature was read and written primarily by men of the elite class. Women and nonelite men infrequently learned the classics and, if literate at all, tended to use only the simpler Korean alphabet, *han'gŭl*.

Even within the field of Korean vernacular literature, the dualistic structure appears as a significant motivating factor in the plots of such well-known stories as *The Tale of Ch'unhyang*,[2] or the *Tale of Hong Kiltong*. In this paper, the idea will be used to examine a group of song-poems, called *sijo*, that were written by—or at least ascribed to—Korean *kisaeng*, professional women entertainers, similar to the Japanese geisha. As we shall see, these *sijo* reveal something of both sides of Korean society and serve as a reminder of the extent to which all persons in the hierarchical world of Yi dynasty Korea, from the king on down, ultimately depended for their positions in life upon someone else's favor.

The *sijo* is a brief, three-line vernacular lyric form,[3] some thirty of which are ascribed in various collections to named, as opposed to anonymous, *kisaeng*. Fourteen of these *sijo*, which treat the subject of loneliness, or of longing for a lover, reflect the *kisaeng*'s peripheral status in the formal Confucian social order. A second group of *sijo*, disparate in accomplishment as in subject matter, reflect, in contrast, the informal, ground-level arena of social interaction which Brandt has termed the "egalitarian, community ethic."[4]

In reading the *sijo* in the first group, one encounters a persistent sense of vast distance between the speaker/singer and the person being addressed. A *sijo* by Kyerang contains a rich mixture of temporal and spatial images, into the midst of which the singer propels her lonely dreams—the song itself:[5]

> As pear blossom rains fell and scattered
> I wept and held the love now gone.
> In autumn winds and falling leaves
> I too might dream of flight,
> though over the countless miles
> only these lonely dreams pass to and fro.

Representative of the less artistically accomplished songs of longing is a *sijo* by Hongnang, a *kisaeng* who is said to have become involved with a Ch'oe Kyŏng-ch'ang, an official who had been posted far from the capital. Upon his recall, she composed the following:

> I will take one branch of the willow
> and send it to you, my love.
> Plant it beneath your window,
> and imagine when new leaves come
> in the night rain
> it is I.

The story associated with this *sijo* is an example of a common type in which a virtuous *kisaeng* becomes involved with a member of the scholar/official class.[6] In such stories as *The Tale of Ch'unhyang*, the male lead is a young man, not quite old enough to have taken the *kwagŏ* examinations and established thereby a position in the bureaucracy, yet just the age to be tired of studying, out wandering in spring—the model adolescent. The man and the woman in these stories occupy mutually contrasting situations with regard to the capital, the center of the Confucian world. In a relationship with an official sent away from the capital, or with a student not yet summoned to it, a *kisaeng* would come to participate in the official, court-centered life, though only at a literal and figurative distance. When the man is summoned to the capital upon successful completion of the examinations, or when he is recalled, in the case of the banished official being forgiven, the woman is left behind to lament the end of a relationship that was conditional upon the man's being away—from the capital.

Numerous *sijo* by exiled officials sound a similar lament, longing for the ruler's good graces as the *kisaeng* longs for a vanished lover. A song by Chŏng Ch'ŏl, whose career in and out of office was a model of uncertainty and change, seems cut from the same bolt of cloth as Hongnang's:[7]

> Snow has fallen in the pine woods;
>   every branch has blossomed.
> I would break off one branch
>   and send it to my lord.
> If he should only see them,
>   what does it matter if the flowers melt away?

At any point in the cycle from favor to dismissal, either a man or a woman—an official or a *kisaeng*—could stop and compose a song of parting or loss. In this highly stylized process, furthermore, both the official and the *kisaeng* would use the same term—*im*—to refer to ruler or lover, according to the circumstances. Not surprisingly, many of the *sijo* written in such circumstances are passive, conventionalized, and dull. One needs to travel away from the capital, and turn away from thoughts of returning to it, to discover the songs that express the well-known vivacity and wit of colloquial Korean culture.

A song by a *kisaeng* known as "Pine Tower Spring," Song Taech'un, makes just such a journey.

> Butterfly from Seoul
>   sampled Myriad Flowers,
> stopped with Milky Way Moon,
>   now rests on top of Pine Tower
> and bit by bit forgets
>   his Plum Blossom's lure.

In this *sijo*, thoughts of Seoul are quite literally hidden away behind a catalogue of *kisaeng* names. What butterfly would care to remember the capital, after all, if to get back he first had to pass again Plum Blossom, Pine Tower, and the others? One lingers, too, over the pun in the last line, so thoroughly prepared in the preceding lines: *saeke*, which I have translated as "lure," means, variously, color, appearance, sexual attraction, or passion.

The "outgoing, often unrestrained"[8] expressiveness of this song and of much of Korean vernacular, oral literature affirms a sense of commonality, rather than hierarchical separation. The following *sijo* by a *kisaeng* named Munhyang, for example, explicitly locates both the speaker and her (soon-to-be) former lover on the same ground, under the same skies, and surrounded by equal numbers of persons of the opposite sex:

> I hate it when you answer me
> as you would a child. Can't you change?
> Were you alone beneath the skies
> well might you boast "I am all!"
> But in all that the heavens provide,
> can there fail to be another love for me?

A decidedly "unrestrained" example of earthy humor is to be found in a *sijo* by a *kisaeng* known as Kuji. The Chinese characters for her name could be translated as something akin to "Seeks It"; the Korean word *kuji*, without the characters, is an adverb meaning "firmly." Kuji is said to have had a lover named Willow Limb, Yu Ilji, a tree whose droopy, threadlike branches suggest a double reading for the verb *maeda* in the original, which can mean to tie, as well as to stiffen a thread with wax or paste for sewing.

> From a long pine you built your boat
> and launched it on the Taedong.
> Where Willow Limb hung down limp,
> tight and firm I fixed it.
> But now you act like a fool!
> To say you prefer that Pond!

This song provokes the suspicion in one reader, at least, that some male musician made it up, along with the *kisaeng* named Kuji and the lover named Willow Limb. Who performed this *sijo*, after all, under what circumstances, and for what kind of audience? Not Kuji, I would venture. Indeed, we must recall that the stories about liaisons with *kisaeng*, whether bawdy or refined, are just as much elements of the oral tradition as the songs themselves. The significance of any given story, therefore, lies not in its historicity, but in its function as a setting for a song. Songs of melancholy longing are to be found in settings that allude to the formal, hierarchical axis of the social order, which made everyone an exile; songs having a humorous effect, or at least a light-hearted intent, are situated locally, among the members of a group or community.

A similar biaxial division is apparent in Chinese oral verse as well. In fact, such bawdy puns as were found in Kuji's song are especially suited to the Chinese language, with its vast number of homophones. One example from a Ming dynasty collection of "Mountain Songs" (*shan ko*) turns for its effect upon the meaning of "fur" or "body hair" for the word *mao*, the common surname:[9]

> The groom was named Mao, the bride was named Mao.
> With the dowry was a serving girl, also named Mao.
> Mao family girls came in marriage into a Mao family.
> Through the middle of the night it was bodies turning,
>   Mao against Mao.

An example from a Ch'ing dynasty collection, *Shi Xing Ya Ya You*, sounds, in contrast, like any number of heartsick *kisaeng sijo*:[10]

> Since we parted I am always lonely.
> My spirit wanders after you.
> In daylight I can bear to think of you.
> But I am afraid of the midnight hours
>   with those thoughts of painful love.
> How bitter. Tears
> have soaked through my half of the pillow.

In the case of the two Chinese songs, the different flavors of the pieces reflect different historical attitudes toward life: the risque Ming song about *mao* resembles other examples from that more free-spirited period, while the Ch'ing collections, reflecting the dynastic return to more formal, restrained amusements,[11] contain songs like Kyerang's or Hongnang's. One can find historical shifts in Korea which resemble those between Ming and Ch'ing, as for example between Koryŏ and Yi.[12] The *kisaeng sijo* have come down to us, however, in relatively late collections, the *Ch'ŏng'gu yŏngŏn* (1728),

Haedong kayo (1763), and *Kagok wŏllyu* (1876), all of which antedate the *kisaeng* to whom the songs are ascribed by two centuries or more. The *sijo* cannot, therefore, serve as evidence of historical attitudes.

Although they cannot be used to demonstrate historical change, the *kisaeng sijo* do reflect the social structure; they are useful in synchronic, if not diachronic, terms. The biaxial structure they reflect has a special resonance in Korean society because of the high degree of formality represented by the Confucian strand, but at the same time this structure corresponds to a general contrast found in any culture:[13]

> Formality and revelry are perceived as being counterparts of the same occasion, "contrasted opposites." Both involve the assumption of roles and masks, but in the case of formality, these epitomize the usual social role and order, while in masquerade they comment on it ironically at the same time they provide a release from everyday social restrictions.

In the Korean case, it happens that the formal, epitomizing function is associated with Chinese models of government, social order, and individual responsibility; by default, therefore, the numerous ways in which individuals have sought "release" have been labeled "native Korean." Historically, the native traditions have been denigrated precisely because they seemed to run counter to the officially accepted standards of the Confucian social order. No doubt they did. Dante's troubled efforts to find a place in the hierarchical structure of *The Divine Comedy* for the "pagan" poets show, however, that the problems in accommodating native traditions to a new normative system are universal.

The problematic nature of the relationship between epitomization and ironic comment is well represented by the status of the *kisaeng* themselves. Although the *kisaeng*'s formal training in etiquette, painting, singing, verse-writing, and other arts was an imitation of the training through which a male in Yi Korea became an official, repeated attempts to cleanse official society of these women indicate that the *kisaeng* were viewed as being subversive of proper decorum.[14] Both of these contrasted, conflicting opposites are revealed in a *sijo* by the *kisaeng* Hwang Chini, which epitomizes both the Chinese and the native vernacular aspects of Korean culture in a most intriguing fashion. A reading of this *sijo* will provide the conclusion of this paper.

The first feature to be noted in Hwang Chini's song, which is perhaps the best known of all *sijo*, is that the first half of each line is in Chinese, while the second half is in Korean. The *sijo* looks as follows:[15]

青山裏碧溪水야　수이감을 쟈랑마라
一到滄海하면　　도라오기 어려오니
明月이滿空山하니　수여 간들 엇더리

Translated parallel to the Chinese/Korean structure of each line, the song reads:

>Jade Green Stream among the blue hills
>　Don't be so proud of your easy going.
>Once you reach the vast seas
>　to come back again will be difficult.
>Since the bright moon fills the empty hills
>　why not pause, and then go on?

The story associated with this *sijo* relates how a respected Confucian scholar-official, whose title happened to be Pyŏkkye, a homophone for *jade green*, had boasted that he was immune to the charms of the famous *kisaeng* Hwang Chini, whose pen name, in turn, was "Bright Moon." When she heard that he was passing through the area where she lived, she sent him this song, which is said to have knocked him off his mule in the middle of a stream.

The story fits the sterotype, certainly; upright Confucian scholar beguiled by witty *kisaeng*. The contrast between the Chinese and the Korean halves in each line reinforces this theme, with the rhetorical point of the "other," Korean, half actively countering or challenging the assumption of the Chinese half. We may note that the first half of each line speaks of a static limit of some kind—the hills, the sea, and then again the hills—which the second half breaks through. If we read only the first half-lines, we must make our way through a disjointed sequence of associated images; the argument carried by the three Korean half-lines, in contrast, could not be more plain, and might occur, in fact, in the normal speech of anyone trying to persuade another not to leave. Not just anyone, however, could manage it with so elegantly simple a trick as the grammatical transformation of a phrase of parting—*sui kamŭl* ("easy going")—to one of staying—*suyŏ kandŭl* ("taking your ease and then going").

The remarkable appeal of this *sijo* is due in part to the story, no doubt, but the *sijo* itself is an extraordinary tour de force. No other *sijo* better exemplifies the magical qualities of song—its *charm*, in the figurative as well as the literal senses of that term. The majority of *kisaeng sijo* express either the psychic ennui of peripheral life or the limerick-like phrases of the wine house. Yet in giving us both—and through the songs of Hwang Chini in giving us far more, a distinctive poetic voice—the *kisaeng sijo* provide a poignant glimpse of Yi dynasty society from inside, and inside-out.

Notes

[1] See Vincent S. R. Brandt, *A Korean Village: Between Farm and Sea* (Cambridge, Harvard University Press, 1971); Charles D. McBrian, "Two Models of Social Structure and Manifest Personality in Korean Society," *Occasional Papers on Korea Number Five* (Seattle, University of Washington, 1977).

[2] Jae-on Kim, "The idea of chastity in Korean folk tales: A study of a popular ideal and its social implication," *Occasional Papers on Korea Number Five*, 1977.

[3] For further discussion of the structure of the *sijo*, see David R. McCann, "The structure of the Korean *sijo*," *Harvard Journal of Asiatic Studies*, 36 (1976).

[4] Brandt 1971: 230.

[5] Translation by the author. Except where noted, the translations of *kisaeng sijo* are reprinted from David R. McCann, ed., *Black Crane: An Anthology of Korean Literature*, Cornell University East Asia Papers 14 (Ithaca, N.Y.: 1978).

[6] See Kim 1977, passim.

[7] Original text in *Song'gang kasa* ("The Poems of Song'gang"), included in *Han'guk kujŏn ch'ongsŏ II siga ryu* (Seoul: 1973): 81.

[8] McBrian 1977: 1.

[9] John McCoy, "The linguistic and literary value of the Ming dynasty 'Mountain Songs'," *Journal of the Hong Kong Branch of the Royal Asiatic Society*, 9 (1969): 112.

[10] Translation by John McCoy, to be published in the folksong section of an anthology of Ch'ing-dynasty poetry, by Indiana University Press.

[11] See McCoy, "The linguistic and literary value," passim.

[12] For a discussion of the changes in the status of women between Koryŏ and Yi Korea, see Martina Deuchler, "The tradition: Women during the Yi dynasty," in Sandra Mattielli, ed., *Virtues in Conflict: Tradition and the Korean Woman Today* (Seoul, Royal Asiatic Society, Korea Branch, 1977): 1-47.

[13] Roger D. Abrahams, "Folk dance," in Richard M. Dorson, ed., *Folklore and Folklife: An Introduction* (Chicago, 1972): 399.

[14] For a succinct description of the *kisaeng*, see Byong Won Lee, "Evolution of the role and status of professional female entertainers (*kisaeng*)," *The World of Music*, 2, 1979 (International Institute for Comparative Music Studies, Berlin).

[15] Original text in the Encyclopedia of Korean Literature, *Han'guk munhak tae sajŏn* (Seoul, 1973): 950.

City Women and Divination: Signs in Seoul

Barbara E. Young

Miss Im, an unmarried graduate student, hopes that her parents will successfully arrange a marriage for her this year and though she looks forward to it, she adds, "I am prepared to accept my blows from my husband." Mrs. Lee, a forty-five-year-old mother of four and a woman with no formal education, wonders whether or not this is a good time to sell an apartment building she owns. Mrs. Han, a full-time secretary and mother of two toddlers, is the only person to see in the office of a small company, because only she among four men and two other women has a grasp of all aspects of the business; if you want something done, you go to Mrs. Han. Miss Moon, an abstract expressionist painter who lives alone in a downtown apartment and supports herself doing office work, intends never to marry. Mrs. Kwak, wife of a bus driver, has just delivered her fourth daughter and already is hoping for a son next time, for her mother-in-law is disappointed. What do all these women have in common? Among other things, they are Korean, they live in Seoul, they are all strangers to each other, and they were found chatting among themselves one Saturday morning. Where? In the tiny waiting room of a fortuneteller, just off a thoroughfare of fish vendors, executives, schoolchildren, and women shoppers—some tattered and some elegant. The changes, paradoxes, traditional and modern values and expectations, strengths and weaknesses, adaptability and intransigence of women in a rapidly modernizing economy can be *surmised* with a glance at the sidewalk traffic, but it can be *chronicled* with a few visits to a diviner's establishment. Men, too, grapple with new and old, west and east, south and north—they also are capable of creative solutions, dogged inflexibilities, and wondrous contradictions—but it seems to be Seoul's women who make franker and more extensive use of divination as they cope with Seoul's transformation from a farmland crossroads into an industrial and commercial metropolis of seven and a half million people.[1]

Diviners—Male and Female

Koreans traditionally acknowledge two main categories of significant influences affecting human fortune; first, temporal and spatial location; and second, the actions and will of gods, lesser spirits, ghosts, and ancestors (see Appendix I). The first category is primarily the province of horoscope readers. Horoscope readers rely on esoteric divination manuals to plumb the relationship between individual fortune and the properties of a given hour, day, month, year, and direction. Since this is a literary and systematic technique, horoscope diviners must have an extensive reading knowledge of Chinese characters. In Seoul, most horoscope diviners are men, a situation compatible with traditional Korean sex roles. Men traditionally and in the present attain higher formal education than women, and knowledge of Chinese texts has long been a prestigious activity for men, not women.

Women, more often than men, become inspirational diviners, contacting the supernatural on behalf of their clients.[2] Most women diviners report that they would rather not pursue this occupation, but that ever since a "spirit came down" they have felt compelled to divine. Many suffered repeated illnesses, dreams, and visions with recurrent ferocity until a shaman or diviner diagnosed the descent of a spirit and suggested a supernatural occupation. The women often claim, "I don't want to be a diviner but if I didn't do this, I would die;" their spirits would harass them to death.

Inspirational divination is one of the few ways in which an uneducated woman or poorly educated woman without capital or a married woman with children can earn a living. Tied to the home by child-rearing responsibilities and household duties, a woman who must also support her family cannot enter the work force as an office or factory worker. Rather, she must produce goods or services in or very close to home. Telling fortunes is a skill admirably suited to such circumstances.[3] There are problems, however. A woman diviner reported, "It is difficult to get customers without advertising, but my children don't want me to advertise, and they beg me to return to taking in sewing because this occupation is an embarrassment to them."

Ironically, while divination provides income to women in financial difficulties—those whose husbands are ill, unemployed, or dead, or who have abandoned the family—the "shameful" nature of the occupation disrupts family relationships. In fact, few of the women diviners I met in Seoul lived with their husbands. It was often unclear whether an individual diviner took up the occupation after her husband left her or whether her becoming a diviner precipitated their separation.[4]

While the tendency for men to become horoscope readers and for women to become inspirational diviners approaches a sexual division of labor, the two systems of causation are not mutually exclusive (see Appendix II). Since harmony in daily life depends upon both supernatural and temporal/spatial influences, most diviners take both influences into account. A horoscope reader examines a birthdate, which reveals a dearth of parental support caused by unfeasted ancestors. An inspirational diviner petitioning the spirits receives a vision cautioning the client to avoid the southeast.

To predict and advise with accuracy, reliability, and sensitivity requires that both intellectual and intuitive skills be demonstrated by male and by female diviners, regardless of their specialties. Let us consider how a variety of Seoul women—the women from the crowded waiting room and others like them—perceive and utilize diviners.

Women Clients

Mrs. Pak, a thirty-two-year-old Christian, is married to a businessman and has two young children. She does not herself consult diviners. When her parents and parents-in-law arranged her marriage with the help of a matchmaker, her mother consulted a horoscope reader about *kunghap*, the potential compatability of spouses. A university graduate, Mrs. Pak has gone to a diviner only once, with her mother, just before she married. Just for fun, she and her husband read the *T'ojŏngbigyŏl* (*Secrets of To'jŏng*) divination manual predictions for the new year printed in the January issues of popular magazines. Her mother goes often to a *paksu* (male shaman). Mrs. Pak reports, "I don't go to diviners, but whenever we have some family problem, my mother goes. Now, when my mother goes to ask about her own family's fortune, she asks about my family when the diviner finishes with hers. I don't take it seriously, but I listen for fun."

Mrs. Kim, a thirty-six-year-old farm wife, lives on the outskirts of Seoul with her husband, their four children, and her husband's parents. Her husband objected to her discussing divination. Mrs. Kim said that she herself does not consult diviners but that her mother-in-law visits a *mansin* (shaman) three or four times a year. "If we have problems which require visits to diviners," she explained, "my mother-in-law goes. When our children are sick or we have other problems, she consults a *mansin*. She discusses the *mansin*'s advice and predictions with her husband and then tells my husband and me. My mother-in-law makes the final decisions in our household."

Mrs. Lee, a forty-three-year-old widow, supports her two sons and her mother by selling household articles in a small shop near a city market. She visits various kinds of diviners, both shamans and horoscope readers. Her relatives recommend good diviners to her. She goes, she says, "because I've nobody to discuss things with." She also visits a Buddhist temple twice a month and goes there for ancestor rites (*chesa*) on the death anniversaries of her husband, father, and two brothers.

Mrs. Lee has consulted diviners about illness in the family, about her son's schooling, about business problems, and whenever she is having difficulties or feels distressed. "I can trust diviners somewhat. It's worth paying for," she said, and then explained:

> My father and my two brothers died in accidents. Of my parents' children, only my sister and I were left, and I am the eldest. . . [Since there is no living male descendant] no one holds ancestor rites for my father and brothers. I visited a diviner who threw rice, and the grains stood up on the table. The diviner said the grains stood up because ghosts in my natal family were unhappy, not properly feasted. I visited another diviner and he said the same thing. I went to the temple and asked a monk to do ancestor rites. Afterward, I visited a shaman and asked about my fortune. She didn't say anything about my natal family's ghosts, so now I feel comforted.

Most of Mrs. Lee's female relatives visit diviners—her mother only occasionally, her sister-in-law twice a year, and the others at intervals unknown to her. She claims that she, herself, does not take horoscope projections from the *T'ojŏngbigyŏl* seriously, but she does try to follow the suggestions and remedies that diviners give her. As she says, "I want to do everything I can."

CITY WOMEN AND DIVINATION

Mrs. Hong, now seventy-two years old, resides in Seoul with her "salary man" son and his wife. Born in a village on the East Coast, she and her family moved to increasingly larger towns, then to the outskirts of Seoul, and two years ago, when her son found employment, into Seoul itself. Mrs. Hong never went to school or learned to read. Her husband died when she was forty-three. She has given birth to nine children, but five children died of childhood diseases.

Although Mrs. Hong converted to Catholicism when she was fifty-six, she retains her belief in the power of ancestral spirits, her individual horoscope, and the predictive value of divination manuals, "because it comes from books." Whenever she feels worried (*taptaphada*), she goes to a cathedral and prays. Though she no longer consults horoscope readers or inspirational diviners as she once did, she still refers to the shaman who lives near her house as her "regular shaman" (*tan'gol*). She still holds ancestor rites because, "even Catholics have ancestors." As one might expect, since the church disapproves of divination, Mrs. Hong prefaced her remarks about diviners with skepticism:

> A diviner is a bad man. When I was young, I knew nothing so I visited diviners. Shamans are bad too. They have evil spirits. Shamans said that if I held *kut* [a ceremony to placate and feast various spirits] my children would live. I held *kut*. But my children died.

When she became a Catholic, she had visited diviners more than thirty times:

> When I was thirty-five years old, a diviner told me my fate was to be childless, but if I had a child after age forty, he would be male and would live. Two years later, I was pregnant. I thought, "I'm near forty so the baby could live." It was a boy.
>
> I visited diviners and prayed. Now he is my only surviving son. Most of the diviners I visited said my dead children had early-death fates.

Mrs. Hong attributes her difficulties to *sajup'alcha*, a personal horoscope based on temporal/spatial analysis of birthdate. Her horoscope is "the worst—White Horse," a particularly inauspicious birth year for women, recurring only once every sixty years.

Mrs. Chang, a thirty-five-year-old housewife married to a businessman, has two children. Her family resides in a comfortable, relatively large, modern house in midtown. Mrs. Chang is a high school graduate, proud of her own education and her husband's university degree. She was quick to say, "I never visit diviners." She continued, however, with the following account:

> I never visit diviners, but in the spring of last year, I visited many shamans and diviners. After my father-in-law's funeral, my husband fell ill. We went to four or five hospitals, but he didn't recover. My neighbors and relatives recommended shamans. So all day long I visited diviners and shamans. When I walked along the street and saw a diviner's sign, I entered. Every shaman and diviner said the same thing. In the third lunar month, my husband's fortune was awful, so every bad spirit would visit him. That is why he was sick. The shamans proposed remedies—I held an exorcism (*p'udak-kŏri*), and for three days, I prayed in my husband's room. After that, he recovered.

Mrs. Chang consulted more than twenty diviners that spring. Her husband's sister and her husband's brother's wife both consult diviners two or three times a year, but now Mrs. Chang no longer does. She explained that after her husband recovered from his illness, she trusted shamans and wanted to visit the shaman's house on Buddha's birthday. Her husband objected. "Even if you treat the spirits well," he told her, "they will bother me again. The spirits always want another exorcism and they want *kut* again and again." So Mrs. Chang never goes to diviners.

These descriptions of women in five different families illustrate the wide variation in use and frequency of consultation: one woman has never consulted a diviner; one "never does," but did visit twenty this year; one has gone twice; one goes very often; and one consulted diviners when she was middle-aged but has given it up. Furthermore, all of these women reported other female relatives who consult diviners with varying degrees of regularity, sometimes on behalf of the respondent herself. None of the women reported that men in their families consult diviners, either on their own or on behalf of their families. This greater use of divination among women than among men is typical. Fewer men than women (22 out of 41 men; 85 out of 106 women interviewed) admitted experience with diviners, and forty-two diviners (27 horoscope diviners; 15 spirit diviners) reported an average ratio of women to men clients of two to one.[5] Traditional Korean sex roles partially account for this difference. Women are responsible for household matters and men for affairs outside the home. Divination discerns the presence or correctable absence of harmony in household and family. Responsible for family harmony, women feel it their duty and desire to keep tabs on family fortunes and to take appropriate measures if something goes askew.

Women discuss all aspects of family life with diviners. In addition to such nonspecific problems as feeling worried and depressed or seeking a sounding board, women also ask about their own or their husbands' jobs, their children's education and marriages, physical illness of family members, moving their residences, money, the future, and problems in family relationships. Much more frequently than men, women consult with diviners about family members other than themselves (see Appendix III). When a problem concerns a child, an unmarried adult man or woman, a married man, a grandmother, a grandfather, or the household in general, the senior woman, not the senior man, consults a diviner. Women are responsible for matters within the household compound. Going to a diviner is a logical extension of a woman's role in the family.

Women seem to have greater familiarity than men with divination procedures. When a woman looks for a diviner, she has probably already heard about, if not witnessed, one or several divinations. Most women thus have a more sophisticated view of what constitutes a good divination, and they tend to use personal recommendations and referrals more often than men when choosing diviners. Men make selections based on advertisements, or by entering an office upon seeing a signboard. Both men and women are often drawn by a diviner's fame, information which is common knowledge. Women also drop in on neighborhood diviners, are more often at home when itinerant diviners knock, and frequently have flexible work schedules which can better accommodate daytime consultations. More city women than men seem to have divination information and to have had divination experiences.

Women have a wide range of divination experience. Some women try out all kinds of diviners, both spiritual and horoscopic, sometimes over a period of years, sometimes over a period of days. Sometimes they shop around, for some women believe only what two out of three diviners tell them. Some go for entertainment or diversion, and some are regular and faithful patrons of one diviner. Some women go to horoscope readers for their yearly fortunes and to spirit diviners when they face a crisis. Other women have a preference for one kind or the other. There seems to be much more variation—the variation that results from greater overall exposure—in women's behavior as clients than in men's.

These patterns suggest a pragmatic and efficient use of divination and of the social networks for finding diviners, but the social aspects of divination also have some appeal in and of themselves. This is not to suggest a lack of seriousness of purpose, but only that the social interaction that takes place in diviners' waiting rooms adds an important dimension to the custom.

Visits to diviners' offices or homes are often social occasions. A popular diviner, or nearly any diviner during peak seasons like the Lunar New Year, will have a bustling waiting room. The anticipated wait prompts many women to bring along friends and sometimes also snacks, so that the occasion may take on the air of a picnic, what with chatting and sharing food with friends and strangers. Old women pinch the cheeks of babies and offer advice on assorted topics; middle-aged women—some in furs, some in sweaters—discuss their children; and giggling school girls—usually in flocks, not merely in pairs—gaily speculate about their matrimonial futures. In the waiting room, a woman may discuss her situation, her children, or her husband. She may glean such "unrelated" information as how the newest downtown department store compares with other stores or which medical clinic charges the most reasonable fees. It would be difficult not to consider waiting-room encounters a resource in themselves.

Divination and Hardship

There are, of course, differences in women's use of divination. Age, educational level, financial situation, and religious affiliation affect divination practices. Not all city women use divination to the same extent, nor is consulting diviners necessarily a consistent practice throughout a woman's life. The following observations, based on information obtained from middle-class women living in Seoul in 1976 and 1977, should suggest possible patterns as well as areas for further research.

Financial circumstances affect the use of divination in several ways: a financial crisis might propel a client to a diviner to find out why or what to do, but slim finances might also curtail visits. In Seoul, people say that the most frequent patrons of diviners are middle- or upper-class women who have money and time to spare. This generalization, however, is somewhat hard to document or to disprove, because of the disproportionately more difficult access to very wealthy and very poor individuals. Extreme poverty does seem to reduce use of divination or to limit inquiry to the least expensive diviners, street vendors who peddle preprinted divinations for as little as twenty *won*, or neighborhood shamans.[6] Very wealthy individuals may never appear at diviners' homes or offices. Instead, they call diviners in for "home consultations" or consult them by telephone. The very rich may thus use divination, although one would never find them in diviners' offices downtown.

Age, since it is related to life crisis events, seems to affect use of divination. Graduation from school, first job, marriage, birth of children, children's school entrance, graduation, and death of family members are among the events that send a woman to consult a diviner (see Appendix III, Parts B and C).

Attitudes toward divination change with age, or, at least, different purposes for visiting diviners are expressed by young and old. Young women, particularly unmarried women, find social or entertainment value in divination, visiting diviners in groups, and cheerfully teasing each other about their futures. Women in their middle thirties to early forties take consultations more seriously, with the weight of the whole household's problems on their shoulders. In old age, divination again has a social attraction—a nonrestrictive atmosphere in which to gather for bawdy jokes and cigarettes—as well as a kind of philosophical appeal. Often the pragmatic, problem-solving motivations of the middle years have been supplanted by a more relaxed attitude. The age variable is, however, crosscut by differences in educational background, religious affiliation, and economic circumstance, all of which require further consideration.

Education and religion, from what I could observe and from interviews, seem less influential than one might expect. Women with college degrees, for instance, appear in diviners' offices, as do women with little or no formal education. There is some slight indication that educated individuals prefer horoscope diviners, but many educated women—high school graduates or above—use both kinds of diviners. Women with few educational or economic resources are more often restricted to lower-cost neighborhood shamans. Education thus may not curtail a woman's inclination to use divination as much as limited financial resources may limit a woman's capacity to do so.

Citing proscriptions against "other gods," ministers forbid women to consult diviners. A few Christian women visit diviners anyway or gain information about their situation from relatives who ask on their behalf. Some dutifully avoid spirit diviners but feel free to consult horoscope diviners, because the presence of "other gods" is not as obvious. Many Christian women, however, reported that they avoid divination because of their religion.

Though many scorn its usage or its validity, divination remains a viable traditional Korean institution serving individuals and families. Clients use divination when a crisis occurs or after a long series of difficulties. Individuals use divination when they feel distressed, stifled, anxious, or bored—these are the reasons most frequently mentioned by urban clients (see Appendix III, Part A). Finally, by incorporating philosophical and religious beliefs about the nature of the universe and about individuals, divination provides an ethical support system to help individuals cope with illness, death, and physical, economic, and social inequities. In sum, for a few women, divination provides a real economic base; for a fairly large number it provides a social network, with its own sources of information and support; and for an even greater number it serves as a counseling service and family support system.

Appendix I. Characteristics of the Two Main Divination Specialties in Seoul

	"Spiritual" Divination	"Horoscopic" Divination
Place of Divination:	Diviner's Home	Diviner's Office
Location:	Residential Neighborhoods, Outskirts of Seoul	Along Arterials, Downtown
Method of Attracting Clients:	Word of Mouth	Advertisements, Signs
Divination Technique:	Primarily Inspiration, Secondarily Analysis	Primarily Analysis, Secondarily Inspiration
Sex of Diviner:	Majority Are Female	Majority Are Male
Subject of Divination:	Frequently Whole Family	Usually Individual, Occasionally Family
Services Offered:	Advisory and Curative, i.e. Divination and Other Rituals	Primarily Advisory, i.e. Divination Only
How Skills Acquired:	Spirit Descends, Apprenticeship to Shaman	Self-taught, through Reading Books; Instruction by Diviner or Institute

Appendix II. An Outline of Korean Divination

There are many forms of divination practiced in Seoul, the most popular of which are (1) horoscopic divination (2) divination through spirits (3) physiognomy (4) divination by lots, and (5) numerology. The following is a brief catalog of the most widely practiced of these five types:

(1) *Horoscopic divination*

Horoscopic divination is based on the premise that the moment of birth carries implications for an individual's whole life: his personality, temperament, character, and general destiny. Interpretations of the meanings associated with particular times of birth most commonly follow principles originally established in China but adapted by Koreans—the system of *sajup'alcha* (the four pillars and the eight characters) or *saju* (the four pillars) for short. The term *saju* refers to the year, month, day, and hour of birth, which are each assigned one character out of ten and one character out of twelve (creating a cycle of sixty possible combinations), depending upon where they fall in established cycles. An almanac is needed to determine the eight characters of any individual birthdate. Meanings consist of multiple and overlaid sets of associations (i.e. elements, directions, colors, body parts, temperaments, feelings, and so on). A second branch of horoscopic divination consists of using the birthdate (again as expressed in four pillars and eight characters) as a key to particular passages of the *Chuyŏk (Book of Changes)*, which the diviner then interprets. (For another means of access to this divination text, see *Divination by lots*.)

(2) *Divination through spirits*

Various techniques are used in Seoul to call down spirits and to interpret their messages, the main source of information in these divinations. Chanting, instrumental music, and dancing are among the most common methods of calling spirits (especially in the course of a large ceremony), but burning incense, lighting candles, fasting, imbibing rice wine, offering food, and making certain kinds of noises should also be listed as frequently-used techniques, particularly in Seoul, where clamorous, large-scale ceremonies often incur objections from neighbors or police. Once the presence of the summoned spirit or spirits is recognized, the diviner describes the client and the client's situation, often including the birthdate as part of the description. Often the descriptive information is chanted, thus serving both to get the spirits' attention and to acquaint the spirits with the issues in question. Interpreting the responses of spirits to various queries put to the diviner by the client is done in many ways—in fact there are so many ways that it would be impossible to catalog them all. Within the course of one large ceremony, for instance, shamans learn the comments and intentions of particular spirits through voices, through the shaman's own bodily reactions and behavior changes, in grains of rice, in five colored flags, or in the balancing of a knife, scimitar, cup, or other implement on a blade, a pig's snout, a kimchee jar, or some other precarious place. Outside of religious ceremonies, diviners most frequently interpret the opinions of spirits from grains of rice tossed on a small table, from coins rhythmically shaken and thrown to the table, or occasionally from the quality of movement in a bowl full of water. No matter which of these interpretive techniques is used, divination through spirits is heavily dependent not only upon the diviner's special knowledge, but also upon the diviner's special relationship with one or more spirits. This latter aspect of spirit divination results in substantial variations in the exact manner in which the spirit's messages are read in coins or rice. Some diviners, for instance, report that visual images appear before their eyes; some see patterns in the grains of rice—a pair, a path, a circle, a scattering—which suggest things to them; some get insights or ideas in their minds as they turn the coins over, one by one; and still others interpret the odd and even numbers of objects that fall together on the table. The diviner as an intermediary between clients and spirits is the common element in all of these techniques.

(3) *Physiognomy*

Such physical characteristics as conformation, color, proportion, texture, and markings are considered significant and interpretable indicators of personality, character, and temperament, and of past, present, and future events. Several portions of the anatomy—in Seoul most often the face and hands—are examined by diviners for such signs, though there is also a tradition in Korea of bone reading, feet reading, and fingertip reading. In Seoul, diviners who are specialists in face reading can be found, but more frequently interpretation of the hands and face is used in conjunction with horoscopic divination.

(4) *Divination by lots*

The interpretation of chance events within some well-defined context (often believed to be the workings of fate, spirits, "synchronicity," or the natural interactions of the cosmos masquerading as chance) is not unknown in Seoul. Though this may be seen to overlap with divination through spirits, various kinds of lot drawing are also used by nonshaman diviners. Shamans themselves most often use such techniques in the course of ceremonies (see Lee 1976 for a description of such techniques). Several randomizing devices are used by "analytical" diviners to gain access to the appropriate passages of divination texts, especially the *Book of Changes*. The most popular of these randomizing devices seem to be: three coins thrown from a "turtle box," patterned count of forty-nine (fifty with one first removed) bamboo sticks, and six throws of eight tiny metal rods. Most of these techniques yield a hexagram, which is then used as an index to 384 passages of a version of the *Book of Changes* or some other standardized set of fortunes, such as those in the *Taehanminyŏk* (a yearly almanac). Drawing lots is also the basic principle behind "*saechŏm*" (bird divination); a coin dropped into a cage prompts a diviner to release a small bird, which chooses one of many small pieces of paper printed with fortunes.

(5) *Numerology*

Numerology, whereby the occurrence or recurrence of particular numbers is interpreted by a diviner, does not seem to be practiced in Seoul as a separate divination specialty, but it is used as an interpretive tool in horoscopic divination, in divination through spirits, in divination by lots, and even, though to a lesser extent, in physiognomy. It figures significantly in name divination wherein the three Chinese characters of a person's name are interpreted according to sound harmony, stroke number, and aspects of horoscopic divination.

In actual practice, of course, these five kinds of divination are difficult to disentangle. A *saju* reader, for instance, may work within the framework of horoscopic divination, but he or she is free to use spiritual inspirations, a little numerology, and assessments consciously or unconsciously derived from physiognomy to round out a particular client's fortune; likewise, a shaman probably uses spirit-inspired insights as the main ingredient in her divinations, but when it seems appropriate, she may very well add a pinch of *saju* analysis, a dash of numerology, a little physiognomy, and a liberal sprinkling of interpreting "random" events. However, most diviners have a specialization, and in Seoul, the first two methods described (horoscopic divination and spirit divination) seem to be the most popular and the most widely practiced. The latter three methods—physiognomy, divination by lots, and numerology—are slightly less popular and are more often used in conjunction with one of the other two methods than they are used separately. Physiognomy and numerology, for instance, are most frequently combined with horoscopic divination, while divination by lots, with *Book of Changes* divination as a major exception, is usually encompassed by spirit divination.

Appendix III. Occasions for Divinations

A. Reported Reasons for Seeking Divinations by Sex of Client (Reasons in Rank Order)

Urban Men	Urban Women
1. *Taptaphada*: State of being (anxious, stifled)	1. *Taptaphada*
2. Need for someone to listen to problems	2. Need for someone to listen to problems
3. Job, business matters	3. Job, business matters
4. Desire to know the future	4. Physical illness
5. Marriage (own)	5. Marriage (children's or own)
6. Entrance examination (own)	6. Family problems, household matters
7. Physical illness	7. Desire to know the future
8. Moving residence	8. Moving residence
9. Curiosity	9. Entrance examinations (children's)
10. Family problems	10. Curiosity
11. Name interpretation	11. Loneliness
12. Loneliness	12. A wish for good luck*
	13. Name interpretation
	14. Determination of baby's sex*

*Not mentioned by any men interviewed.

Appendix III. Occasions for Divination (cont.)

B. Diviner Observations of Reasons for Divinations by Age and Sex of Clients

Age	Male	Female
Under 18	Whether to go to college, college entrance examinations, aptitude for academics	Boyfriends, college entrance examinations
19-24	Making friends with girls, college major, choosing a wife, jobs after college	Choosing a spouse, college major
25-35	Business affairs (especially promotions, salary increases, changing jobs)	Love affairs, choosing a husband, husband's love affairs, naming children
36-55	Business affairs (especially business failures, whom to hire, commercial contracts)	Husband's business, husband's love affairs, children's health and future, illness, luck in general, family problems, life expectancy
56 and over	Life expectancy, illness, Marriage of grandchildren	Life expectancy, illness, marriage of grandchildren

Appendix III. Occasions for Divination (cont.)

C. Divinations by Kin Relationships

For a Problem Concerning:	Person Who Consults Diviner:
A child	The mother, the paternal grandmother, or (occasionally) the father
An unmarried adult man or woman	The person himself (herself), or her mother
A married man	Himself, his wife, his mother
A married woman	Herself, her mother-in-law, her mother
A grandmother	Herself, her daughter
A grandfather	Himself, his son, his daughter-in-law, his daughter, his wife
The household	The eldest resident female, the mother of the male head of household (even if not in residence), sometimes the male head of household (though rare)
Events outside the household	The person involved (usually male), the wife of the man involved, the mother of the man involved

Notes

[1] The material presented in this paper is based on fieldwork done in Seoul during the summer of 1975 and from June 1976 to September 1977 and on library research through January 1978. These efforts were funded, respectively, by a travel grant from the Department of Anthropology, University of Washington; a Fulbright-Hays Dissertation Grant; and a grant (PHS-NIH-MH-05896-01) from the National Institute of Mental Health. I am very grateful for this assistance, as well as for the cooperation and contributions of numerous individuals in Korea and in the United States. All errors are of course my own.

[2] These two kinds of diviners have also been characterized as "learned" and "possessed" fortunetellers. See, for instance, Janelli (1977).

[3] The *Seoul Statistical Yearbook* (Seoul Metropolitan Government 1977: 180) reported a total of 2,623 diviners in 1976, of which 1,099 were men and 1,524 were women.

[4] Research on how women in Korea become shamans, including case histories, is reported in Harvey (1976).

[5] Interviews were conducted in Seoul during the fieldwork periods noted in n. 1, above. Diviners were located through advertisements, signs, and word of mouth; about 50 clients were interviewed in diviners' establishments; and 155 urban residents, primarily in three Seoul neighborhoods (one central, two peripheral), were questioned about their use of divination.

[6] At many large ceremonies by shamans, there are points in the ritual when divinations for spectators are performed.

Bibliography

Chang Chu-gŭn and Ch'oe Kil-song
    1967 *Kyonggido chiyŏk Musok* [Shaman Practices of Kyŏnggi Province] (Seoul: Ministry of Culture).

Chang Chu-gŭn
    1974 "Min'gan sin'ang" [Popular beliefs] in D. H. Lee, C. G. Chang, and K. K. Lee, eds., *Hanguk Minsokhak Kaesol* [Introduction to Korean Folklore] (Seoul: Minjung Sŏgwan): 128-96 (in Korean).

Chung Cha-whan
    1977 *Change and Continuity in an Urbanizing Society: Family and Kinship in Urban Korea* (Ph.D. dissertation, University of Hawaii).

Harvey, Young-sook Kim
    1976 *Korean Mudang: Socialization Experiences of Six Female Shamans* (Ph.D. dissertation, University of Hawaii).

Im Sŏk-jae
    1971 "Han'guk Musok Yon'gu Sosol" [Introduction to the Study of Korean Shamanism], *Journal of Asian Women*, 10: 161-217.

Janelli, Dawnhee Yim
   1977 *Logical Contradictions in Korean Learned Fortunetelling: A Dissertation in Folklore and Folklife* (Ph.D. dissertation, University of Pennsylvania).

Kendall, Laurel
   1977a "Caught between ancestors and spirits: Field report of a Korean *mansin*'s healing *kut*," *Korean Journal* 17(8): 8-23.
   1977b "*Mugam*: The dance in shaman's clothing," *Korea Journal* 17(12): 38-44.

Kim Tae-gon
   1978 "Shamanism in the Seoul area," *Korea Journal* 18(6): 39-51.

Kim Yung-chung, ed. and trans.
   1976 *Women of Korea: A History from Ancient Times to 1945* (abridged and translated version of *Hanguk Yŏsŏng-sa*) (Seoul: Ewha Woman's University Press).

Kinsler, Arthur
   1976 *A Study in Fertility Cult for Children in Korean Shamanism* (Ph.D. dissertation, Seoul, Yonsei University).

Lee Hyo-chae and Cho Hyoung
   1977 "Fertility and women's labor force participation in Korea," *Korea Journal* 17(7): 12-34.

Lee Jung-young
   1976 "Divination in Korean shamanistic thought," *Korea Journal* 16(11): 5-11.

Lewis, I. M.
   1971 *Ecstatic Religion: An Anthropological Study of Spirit Possession and Shamanism* (Middlesex, England: Pelican Books).

Seoul Metropolitan Government
   1977 *Seoul Statistical Yearbook* (Seoul: Seoul Metropolitan Government).

Yi Nung-hwa
   1927 "*Chosŏn musok-ko*," *Kaemyong*, 19: 1-85.

Yoon Soon Young Song
   1977 "The emergence of the Fourth World: Korean women in development," *Korea Journal* 17(2): 35-47.

Korean Women, Conflict, and Change: An Approach to Development Planning

Hesung Chun Koh

"Male dominance and female subordination" has been the recurring theme in studies on Korean women by both Korean and Western writers. Similarly, the problems of Korean women have too often been characterized as a lack of equality with men. Thus, recommendations for social change have usually been aimed at the elimination of the barriers that prevent equality.

Many Koreans, however, still acknowledge considerable ambivalence about the desirability of the social changes suggested by these studies, which are aimed directly at the elimination of some of the barriers to equality. Many Koreans, both men and women, still feel that the goal of equality is a Western ideal, imposed from without, rather than one required by Koreans' own social needs. For example, Koh Yong-bok, in his article on "Traditionalism and De-Traditionalism," expresses this ambivalence by observing that "in Korea the compromising attitude that Western culture is too idealistic and the traditional culture more realistic openly dominates the intellectual world" (Koh 1976: 132).

As a result, neither the intellectuals nor the general public see social equality as a desirable or necessary goal, because they see no harmful effects from the present inequality. Many legislators, political leaders, and scholars, for example, do not sense any urgency to change social institutions, on the assumption that sustained economic development will inevitably lead to the improvement of the well-being of *all* individuals, including women. This assumption mistakes mere economic development for development in the true sense.

Boserup (1970), Tinker (1976), and several others have pointed out that women have often been adversely rather than positively affected by so-called economic development in developing countries. Yoon Soon-Young, in two articles (1977a and 1977b), has demonstrated that improved social, political, or legal well-being for Korean women has *not* necessarily accompanied rapid economic development in South Korea. Lee Hyo-chae and Cho Hyoung, in their study of fertility and women's labor force participation in Korea (1977), found that the more children a woman had, the more she participated in the work force, countering prior assumptions that the fewer children a woman had, the more likely she was to seek outside employment.

The aims of this paper are to present a method of delineating the area most in need of change from the Korean perspective and to suggest a means to achieve this change. The area most in need of social change is that of the practices in the family and the household. Change can be effected through reform in legislation, communication through mass media, and active public education, once the appropriate areas of conflict are determined.

Hanna Papanek and others have stressed the need for a new approach to the study of women, new systems of analysis, and new methods of data collection and classification (Papanek 1977: 18). This paper simply demonstrates one new approach through an analysis of a psychological case and a legal case. These cases will be analyzed as illustrations of the internal conflicts experienced by women in Korea. Special attention will be paid both to the nature of the conflicts manifested in these cases and to an analysis of the social institutions, cultural assumptions, and values that have generated these conflicts.

According to the late Dr. D. S. Hahn, a Korean psychiatrist, the manifestations of Korean women's emotional conflicts can best be seen in cases of hysterical neurosis (Hahn 1964). According to a series of clinical studies on Korean psychiatric patients discharged from Seoul National University Hospital between 1958 and 1973, 75.6 percent of the hysterical neurosis cases were female. During this fifteen-year period, the number of cases almost tripled, and they are still rapidly increasing (Rhi 1977: 129-30). Dr. Rhi Bou-yong, Professor of Psychiatry at Seoul National University Medical College, has analyzed some of the cases from the perspective of how to cure the patient rather than what caused the illness. He and other psychiatrists viewed the sociocultural factors that contributed to the emotional disorders in the women as a single collective consciousness, representing one aspect of the patients' psyches.

Whether or not we accept the diagnosis category, "hysterical neurosis," the women who appear in these case records were clearly experiencing emotional conflict. In this study, in contrast to Dr. Rhi's approach, I seek to analyze this "collective consciousness" that has affected Korean women by asking: What specific attitudes, beliefs, social practices, and social institutions affect Korean women adversely, and under what conditions? How, and in what direction, can these values and institutions be changed to improve the condition of women? These are my primary concerns in this paper.

I will present and analyze two actual cases, one psychiatric and the other legal. The two cases are representative of the conflicts that many Korean women face, but my aim in presenting them is not simply one of illustration. I will also use these cases to present a methodological approach that will tease out the conflicts and contradictions inherent in Korean women's social and legal status. The methodology permits non-culture-bound suggestions for reform.

Summary of a Psychiatric Case[1]

Diagnosis: Hysteria

History of disturbances and symptoms
The patient, a fifty-two-year-old woman, had suffered from various physical disorders for about ten years. The symptoms first occurred five months after the birth of her last child, but a medical doctor found no physical disorder. Her symptoms fluctuated and seemed to occur in relation to emotional conflicts. She was referred for psychiatric treatment by her doctor, although her husband, who was a doctor himself, did not think it was necessary.

The patient's personal and family background
The patient was the youngest child and only daughter among four children of a landowner in a village in South Korea. Her father was a member of the county council under the Japanese colonial regime. Her marriage was arranged by her family, and she married four years after her high school graduation. Her husband was a medical student and the son of a landed aristocratic family that had had no other sons for the last three generations.

The patient's married life

For the first five years of the marriage there were no children. The patient's parents-in-law were extraordinarily anxious and suggested that their son consider having another woman bear a son, although the wife's relationship with them was good. Her husband was against this idea and asked his family to wait until his wife reached thirty-nine years of age. She became very depressed and cried secretly.

Her first pregnancy ended in a miscarriage. The second child, a daughter, died soon after delivery. The patient was severely ill during both pregnancies and the delivery. The third child was another daughter, who was delivered safely. The husband's parents claimed that by that time they did not care about the sex of the child. Another daughter was born and then a son. The last child was delivered when the patient was forty-three years old. Because of the age difference between herself and this last child, she felt particularly sorry for him.

The patient claimed to feel no frustration regarding her husband. He was described as taciturn and sincere, a little careless about household matters, and usually indifferent to the family's economic state. He had grown up in a wealthy family and had never experienced financial hardship. However, she had suffered from poverty, due to her husband's unsuccessful political activities (in which he was more interested than in his medicine). His social standing was good, however, and they were economically stable at the moment. She described her sexual relations with her husband as satisfactory. However, she asked in a later session whether it was harmful to her health to have sexual intercourse only rarely. Her husband felt that sexual contact disturbed the health, an idea he had gotten partly from an herb medicine practitioner.

The patient's psychological state

The patient described herself as a rather introverted, unyielding person. She was intellectually ambitious and became very jealous if she was "defeated" by someone else. In her dreams, she was reproached by middle-aged women, her mother and a school teacher. She could not express her frustration easily and attributed it to having to keep up appearances. She considered this to be due to her conservative education.

Summary of a Legal Case[2]

Child Custody and Divorce
Facts

In the summer of 1972, Mr. Kim M.D. (hereinafter Mr. Kim A), his wife, and their two daughters (ages three and one year and nine months), visited Korea on what seemed to be a summer vacation. (The Kim A family had lived in New York for seven years.)

Some days after they arrived in Korea, Mr. Kim A, together with his sister, her husband (Mr. Moon), his parents, and his brother (hereinafter Mr. Kim B), told Mrs. Kim A that she was being divorced through annulment procedures. To Mrs. Kim A it was a bolt from the blue. They expelled Mrs. Kim A from the house; they hid one daughter, so that Mrs. Kim A could not take her; and they took the other daughter away from Mrs. Kim A against her will. Mrs. Kim A was alone, and had no alternative but to go to her parents' house. Mr. Kim A entrusted an attorney with his marriage annulment case, which immediately was brought into the Seoul Family Court, and then left Korea for New York, leaving his two daughters in the care of his eldest brother Mr. Kim B, and his brother-in-law, Mr. Moon.

The alleged grounds for seeking an annulment was Mrs. Kim A's insanity. Though ordinarily Mrs. Kim A could have asked an attorney to represent her in the annulment proceedings and could have then returned to the United States, she had to stay in Korea to prove she was not insane. She was put through two mental examinations, each of which required two weeks of hospitalization. Both examinations showed that Mrs. Kim A was not insane.

While the marriage annulment case was pending in Family Court, Mrs. Kim A was very much concerned about her daughters. She visited Mr. Moon's residence many times, asking to see her daughters. But Mr. Moon and his wife did not allow it. Since Mrs. Kim A could not predict when the legal action against her would end, she tried to see her daughters at any cost. At last she decided to bring legal action herself. Finding that there were difficulties in contending a parental right of recovering her children and keeping them as a mother, Mrs. Kim A brought a suit of kidnapping against Mr. Kim B and Mr. Moon, arguing that they had seized her daughters by violence and had prohibited her from seeing her own natural children.

Arguments for both sides

Mrs. Kim A argued that when Mr. Kim A expelled her to her natal home, his sister and brother-in-law took the children away from her by violence. Mrs. Kim A also argued that when she visited Mr. and Mrs. Moon's house to see her own children, they would not let her into the house. Mrs. Kim A argued that those acts constituted kidnapping.

The defendants argued—with the testimony of Mr. Kim A, who flew back to Korea to appear for the defendants—that they had been legally entrusted by Mr. Kim A with the care of the children and they were following the instructions of Mr. Kim A, the children's father.

Judgment

The decision reads partly as follows: "the defendants are not guilty. . . . Mr. Kim A, the person who possesses and is entitled to exercise parental authority, committed to these two defendants the responsibility of caring for the children. . . . Defendants kept the children in their custody, and, even though they had resorted to violence to take and retain the children from the mother, rejecting the mother's demand to surrender the children to her, it cannot be considered kidnapping as provided in the . . . Criminal Code."

Even though Mr. Kim A had stayed abroad so long that he was not able to exercise, personally, his parental rights and duties toward his children, the request of the defendant's brother to retain custody of the children was legally sufficient to award custody even over the claim of the children's mother. Therefore, the charge of kidnapping was not applicable in this case.

Analysis of the Psychological and Legal Cases and Their Implication for Social Policy

What is the nature of the conflicts faced by Korean women as reflected in these cases?

I. *Imbalance of Goals and Means*

One of the characteristics of the psychological case seems to be the imbalance between the role that is expected of the patient and the lack of sociocultural means available to her to achieve that expected role. What are some of the social beliefs and attitudes that shape this woman's expected role in society? One that is most noticeable is the Korean value of male child preference. Much of the literature on population and family planning has identified male child preference as the major deterrent to family planning in Korea (Kwon and Lee 1975). Classical teaching, folklore, and historical documents also amply disclose the social norm of strong preference for sons. (Lee Kyu Tae 1973). Being sonless was also pointed out as a source of severe emotional strain for Korean women by Cha, Chung, and Lee (1977: 113). Korea is one of the few countries in the world, besides India, the People's Republic of China, and Taiwan, where the preference for male children is still great (Lee Kyu Tae 1973; Kwon and Lee 1975; Cha, Chung, and Lee 1977; Parish and Whyte 1978).

To understand this phenomenon, we must first examine a number of Korean values and related social institutions. Koreans share three basic assumptions with people of other East Asian countries (namely, China and Japan): (1) an individual is a critical link between the past and the future; (2) the family is a basic social institution, through which this linkage is maintained; and (3) the family can only be continued through the male line. These assumptions are institutionalized both in Korean customs and in the laws of succession, inheritance, and adoption. Despite the common acceptance of these assumptions in all three countries, the situation in Korea can be differentiated from those in Japan and China.

Korea, compared to Japan and China, has had more structured and less flexible rules of descent. The rules of descent are currently part of the inheritance and succession laws of the Civil Code. In traditional Korea, the family headship was succeeded to only by lineal male descendants. Rank of succession was determined by age and sibling order. In Korea, unlike China, it was very important to be the first son. Although a female can now become family head under the Civil Code, a female successor loses the headship as soon as she marries. Thus, female succession is only provisional in nature and not a common or permanent practice. In traditional Japan, it was usually the eldest son who succeeded to the family headship, but when the eldest son was not suitable, one of the younger sons was chosen to become the heir. Also, when there was no son, a son-in-law could be adopted into the family at the time of his marriage. Thus, non-kinsmen could succeed to the family head position. This Japanese practice would be rare in Korea. It was not practiced before the Japanese period, and it has been practiced only rarely since; those who have practiced it in recent years seem to be ashamed of it. Under Korean adoption laws, only a single male bearing the same surname and clan seat could be adopted to succeed to the family headship. The Civil Code of 1958 does provide for the adoption of a son-in-law (Article 876), but there have been only a few cases where this was actually practiced. More recently, the Civil Code as revised in 1977 permits both the adoption of someone with a different surname and the entry of the husband's name into his wife's family register. However, several hundred years of practice and beliefs regarding adoption in Korea, based on neo-Confucianism, make change rather slow.

In short, the position of family head, assumed only by the eldest son, has in the last three centuries been more powerful in Korea than in Japan or China. In Korea, sons are essential. With respect to the option of adoption, Koreans have been far less flexible than Japanese, perhaps even less flexible than the similarly descent-preoccupied Chinese. There is an extreme imbalance between the needs of a Korean family and the availability of means to meet them when no male child exists. Under the circumstances, it is hardly surprising that the conclusion is often reached that Koreans have the strongest male child-preference values among East Asian societies. Korean families or couples without male children traditionally seem to suffer more than those of Japan and China.

II. *Responsibility Assigned for Conception vs. Inability to Control It*

A Korean assumption, which causes undue emotional burdens for women in relation to childbirth, is the unscientific notion about the determination of a child's sex. Koreans of *both* sexes often attribute failure to bear a son primarily to the wife. Furthermore, the Korean wife is almost always held primarily responsible for the childlessness of a couple. Biological facts concerning reproduction and conception carry little weight in a society where there are deeply entrenched beliefs that the women are to blame for any reproductive "failures." When reminded that men, not women, provide the "Y" chromosomes, a young Korean husband responded, "Yes, but it is the woman's job to catch the right one" (Cha, Chung, and Lee 1977: 113).

Such an interpretation regarding conception has provided a legitimate excuse for men to seek concubines, extramarital relationships, and even divorce, often with the encouragement and support of kinfolk, neighbors, and peers. The amount of emotional insecurity and pressure generated for a sonless woman by this notion and the fear of the possible loss of her husband is too extensive to elaborate on here.

Nevertheless, from the psychiatric case at hand, we can see that the patient internalized this cultural attitude to the detriment of her emotional tranquility. Considering the fact that the patient's husband was the only son in his family for three generations, the couple had a heavier than normal responsibility to continue the family line, and the wife in particular experienced an unusual degree of social and psychological pressure due to their prolonged sonlessness.

The tragedy of this situation is compounded when we appreciate the fact that exclusive succession through the male line was, in Korea, a fairly recent phenomenon (cf. Peterson, in this volume). Social historian Martina Deuchler has described how during the Koryŏ and early Yi periods a married woman often not only remained in her natal home but also inherited and managed wealth from her natal family:

> She received the same share of inheritance in the form of slaves and land as her brothers. Thus she was economically independent from her husband and had absolute control over the raising and the education of her children. This system placed heavy emphasis on the wife's family and accorded the woman an important social and economic role [Deuchler 1977: 8].

Ch'oe Chae-sok (1972), in his analysis of seventeenth- and eighteenth-century land records (*punchaegi*) in southern Korea, finds that the system of equal succession to property by all legitimate sons and daughters continued until the middle of the eighteenth century. Mark Peterson, in his analysis of genealogies (in this volume), finds a similarly significant mid-Yi shift in inheritance practices, with increasing discrimination against women and the sons of secondary wives. This increasing rigidity in Korean inheritance practices over the last several centuries has had an increasingly adverse effect on Korean women.

III. *Wider Range of Options vs. Scarcity of Resources to Achieve Them*

According to Confucian values, the dominant ideology of the traditional Korean ruling class and a normative model for most present-day Koreans, a woman should be a "wise mother and good wife." The patient, too, acquiesced as to the importance of this value and its accompanying role requirements when her parents arranged her marriage during her teens. In recent years, however, values have changed, and there are more women in Korea who are successfully assuming both mother/wife *and* professional roles.

The patient seemed to be preoccupied with a reassessment of her situation; she could see that her own role choice had been dictated to her, and she recognized that there are new options today. But despite changing career options for women, it remains extremely difficult for a middle-aged Korean woman to prepare herself for a new lifestyle. Her conflict, then, may be characterized as a growing multiplicity of possible goals, due to changes in society's expectations of women, accompanied by a slower development of the social institutions through which women can achieve such new goals (i.e. a scarcity of resources available to women who desire to achieve these new options).

Still other factors apart from the cultural values may be related to the patient's midlife transition. Rhi (1977) noted that many midlife Korean women experience a haunting sense of regret or of unfulfilled wishes, a condition Koreans call *"han."* The patient in the case study, being middle-aged, has already met to some degree the traditional Korean cultural expectations of a woman by bearing a son. Yet even though she has this longed-for son, she may now fear making some mistake in rearing him or discovering a lack of adequate psychological reward for her effort.

In the U.S., studies on adult developmental stages, conducted by Levinson and others (1977) at Yale, also indicate that men and women seek new and different life course directions when they reach their middle years. (Hennig and Jardin [1976], Pincus [1980], and Hall [n.d.] have conducted other studies, leading to similar conclusions.) In light of these and other studies, it is not presumptuous to suppose that one of the difficulties this patient is facing is the lack of means to achieve these new options.

IV. *Imbalance of Responsibilities and Rights*

The divorce case above applies Part I of Article 909 on Parental Authority (Civil Code, p. 260), which states:[3] "A child, who is a minor, shall be subject to the parental power of his or her *father* with whom the child is residing" (emphasis mine). Even though the child is not residing with the father, it may be interpreted that as long as the father is living, *even when he is not in a position to care for the child himself*, the mother cannot exercise any right over her own child, even when she is ready, willing, and able to do so.

Unlike the situation in the United States, where custody of the children would be awarded to the mother at the time of divorce, in Korea, the practice is reversed, to accord with patriarchal and patrilineal principles. Who would take better care of the children or how the children might be affected by such a decision are considerations secondary to the father's legally-enforced parental authority.

If this decision exemplifies child custody practices in Korea, it is also a classic case of the imbalance between the responsibilities and the rewards that are given to a mother. According to Korean custom, there is no question that the mother is expected to nurture, educate, and give affection to her children. The strong emotional attachment in the Korean mother-child relationship is well documented by Takahashi Toru. This renowned Japanese scholar concluded from a comprehensive survey of Korean folklore from all regions that the most intense and frequent theme of Korean folklore is the love and intimate attachment between mother and child. He concluded that the essence of Korean folk songs was the expression of mother and child love, rather than the love between friends, father and child, or even man and woman (Takahashi 1936).

Furthermore, according to Lee Hyo-chae's 1970 survey of urban Korean women, mothers regard their primary purpose in life as ensuring the success of their children. When asked: "What kind of woman is most blessed?" the highest percentage of middle-class respondents from Seoul answered that it was the "woman whose children are grown up and successful." By comparison, having an "amicable relationship with one's husband" was considered to be of only secondary importance.

In short, by Korean cultural expectations, a woman is responsible not only for the bearing of children (and male children, at that) but also for rearing them, nurturing them, and, as far as possible, ensuring their ultimate success in life. If a couple has no children or no male heirs, or if none of their children survives to maturity, or if they have successful children, the blame is placed largely, if not totally, on the mother. Even though a Korean mother is burdened with virtually *all* of the responsibility for bearing and rearing her children, she has no corresponding legal right to their custody. The system deprives a separated or divorced mother of the legal right to rear her own children, even when she desires to and is clearly able to do so.

Clearly, the Civil Code's provision regarding parental rights serves the well-being of neither women nor their children; rather it serves only to strengthen the patriarchal system at their expense.

Summary and Conclusion

The above analysis suggests four broad types of related conflicts experienced by Korean women. (1) *Imbalance of goals and means*: The paramount goal of continuity of the family is achievable only by limited means. The family headship carries considerable authority, and the laws of descent are relatively inflexible, even when compared to the organizational principles of Chinese and Japanese families or to an older Korean system. Most families can attain continuity only if women give birth to sons.

(2) *Responsibility assigned for conception vs. inability to control it*: Korean women are held responsible for *sonlessness* or *childlessness* (and hence for any failure in family continuity), even though they have no real control over conception or the sex of the child. (3) *Wider range of options vs. scarcity of resources to achieve them*: Due to the changes in society and the wider range of role options now available to women, Korean women who previously dedicated themselves solely to the mother/wife role are longing for self-fulfillment in their post-child-rearing years. But without adequate educational and job-training programs, through which midlife women can pursue these new options, they end up with a haunting sense of regret (*han*). (4) *Imbalance of responsibilities and rights*: Korean women are expected not only to bear children but also to rear them and take responsibility for their future success. However, they have no legal right to custody in the event of separation or divorce. The effect of this child-custody practice is inhumane, both from the mother's and from the child's point of view.

These conflicts are generated by the following six institutions, which are embodied both in law and in custom: (1) family headship (2) parental authority (3) inheritance (4) household and family succession (5) constraints on adoption, and (6) the educational system. To alleviate the types of conflicts portrayed above, each of these institutions should be a major target of social change. The goal of changing each of these six institutions should be part of any coherent development plan that purports "to bring about sustained improvement in the well-being of the individual and of society and to bestow benefits on all" (United Nations 1975: 4-5).

1. The institution of the *family head* in Korea needs to be carefully examined. The power and responsibility of the family head ought to be limited to serve only essential functions, as in Japan, while the responsibility of other family members should be enhanced. This can be done by revision of the civil code, especially where it is related to succession, inheritance, and adoption.

2. *Parental authority* laws ought to be amended to take children into account and to bring the mother's legal rights into balance with her responsibilities for child-rearing.

3. *Inheritance rights to the family property* should be distributed equally among all offspring, as in China.

4. Laws governing *succession to the family head* should be revised so as to provide the opportunity for either a man or a woman to be the family head on a more permanent basis, even after marriage, as long as the individual is capable of assuming the responsibilities assigned to the position, regardless of sex or sibling order.

5. *Adoption practice* should be liberalized to allow families to go outside blood relatives when necessary to adopt successors, since the current adoption law does allow adoption of sons-in-law (*teril-sawi*). The real need here is to lessen the gap between the legal provision and the actual practice of adoption.

6. *The educational system* should be developed in two areas: (a) Active public education and public information programs should present scientific facts on reproduction and conception (including sex-determination). They should also illuminate the inflexibility, age bias, and sex bias of the present system of succession, inheritance, adoption, and parental authority by presenting the legal developments and social practices not only in other East Asian societies but also in pre-Confucian Korea. (b) Career counseling and job training for women in midlife should be provided to offer more flexible and continuing educational opportunities for mature women.

Clearly the cases presented here must be taken only as illustrations of the problems that are presented by the laws, social institutions, and cultural values that define a woman's role and limit her options in the Korean family. Further examination should be made of a wide range of cases in both the psychiatric and the legal fields, to see where the detrimental effects of Korean civil codes and social practices are most clearly manifested. If the objective of the development process is to improve "the well-being of the individual and of society," it must first target those areas in which individuals are suffering under the present system, and focus on reform of the social institutions and values that are causing this suffering.

When these conflicts are examined in terms of the forces promoting and resisting social change, we may be able to pinpoint the areas requiring change without importing policy goals that have been established outside the society. This would allow us to formulate systematically a strategy for integrating women into a development goal that is more acceptable to the people of the society being changed.

Notes

[1] Summary of a psychological case in Rhi Bou-yong, 1977.

[2] Seoul Criminal District Court, 72 Kodan 18142 (July 7, 1972); Seoul Family Court, 77 De 326 (October 20, 1977). For Korean Civil Code, see Korean Legal Center 1975.

[3] Korean Legal Center 1975.

[4] I wish to acknowledge the kindness of Professor Rhi Bou-yong, for reading the earlier version of this paper and providing valuable comments, as well as giving me permission to summarize and use one of his psychological cases. I am also indebted to Judge Gui Won Kang, who provided the legal case used in this paper, and who also provided legal source materials.

References

Boserup, Ester. *Women's Role in Economic Development* (New York: St. Martin's Press, 1970).

Cha Jae-ho, Chung Bom-mo, and Lee Sung-jin. "Boy preference reflected in Korean folklore," in Sandra Mattielli, ed., *Virtues in Conflict: Tradition and the Korean Woman Today* (Seoul: Royal Asiatic Society, Korea Branch, 1977): 113-46.

Ch'oe Chae-sŏk. "Chosŏn sidae ŭi sangsokche e kwanhan yŏn'gu — punjaegi ŭi punsŏk e ŭihan chŏpkŭn [The institution of inheritance during the Yi dynasty: an analysis of inheritance records]," *Yŏksa Hakpo*, 53/54 (1972): 99-150.

Chŏng Chu'ung-nyang. "Tosi chubu saenghwal e kwanhan silt'ae chosa [A study of the life of housewives of urban middle class families]," *Ihwa Yŏja Taehakkyo, Han'guk munhwa Yŏn'guwŏn Nonch'ong* (Seoul), 16 (1970).

Deuchler, Martina. "The tradition: Women during the Yi dynasty," in Sandra Mattielli, ed. *Virtues in Conflict: Tradition and the Korean Woman Today* (Seoul: Royal Asiatic Society, Korea Branch), 1977: 1-47.

Fukutake Tadashi. *Nihon no noson no shakaiteki Seikaku* (Tokyo: Tokyo Daigaku Shuppansha, 1967).

Hahn Dongse. "Hanguk toshi sahoe e issŏsŏ ŭi hysteria imsangjŏk kŭp illyuhakchŏk yŏngu [A clinical and anthropological study of hysteria in Korean urban society]" - *Neuropsychiatry* (in Korean), 3, 1 (1964): 327-39.

Hall, Douglas T. *A model of coping with role conflict: the role behavior of college-educated women*, Report No. 35, Ford Foundation funded research at the Yale University Department of Administrative Science (mimeographed) n.d.

Han'guk Yŏsŏng Tanch'e Hyŏpŭi Hoe, Yŏsŏng Chiwi Hyangsang Uiwŏnhoe [Korean National Council of Women, the Committee for the Promotion of Women's Status]. Segye Yŏsŏng ŭi Hae Kinyŏm Charyojip [Observance of the International Women's Year, Resource Material Collection] (Seoul, 1975).

Hennig, Margot, and Anne Jardin. *Women Executives, Pioneers in Management* (New York: Anchor Press, 1976).

Kim Haing-ja. "Role analysis of female politicians in Korea: A comparison with U.S. Congresswomen," *Korea Journal*, 17, 7 (1977): 35-43.

Kim Yong-han. "The succession system of Korea," in Chun Shin-yong, ed., *Legal System of Korea*, Korean Culture Series 5 (Seoul: International Cultural Foundation, 1975): 37-57.

Koh Yong-bok. "Traditionalism and de-traditionalism," in Chun Shin-yong, ed., *Korean Society*, Korean Culture Series 6 (Seoul: International Cultural Foundation, 1976): 129-46.

Korean Legal Center. *Laws of the Republic of Korea* (Seoul: Korean National Council on Women [Hanguk Yŏsŏng Tanch'e Hyŏpŭi Hoe], 1975).

Kwon Tai Kwan and Lee Hae Young. "Preference for number and sex of children in a Korean town," *Bulletin of the Population and Development Studies Center*, 5 (1975): 1-12.

Lee Hyo-chae and Cho Hyoung. "Fertility and women's labor force participation in Korea," *Korea Journal*, 17, 7 (1977): 12-34.

Lee Hyo-chae and Kim Chu-suk. "The status of Korean women today," in Sandra Mattielli, ed., *Virtues in Conflict: Tradition and the Korean Woman Today*, (Seoul: Royal Asiatic Society, Korea Branch, 1977): 147-55.

Lee In-ho. "Women's liberation in Korea," *Korea Journal*, 17, 7 (1977): 4-11.

Lee Kwang-gyu. "Comparative study of rule of descent in East Asia: China, Korea, and Japan," in *Hanguk kajok ŭi kujo punsŏk* (Seoul: Iljisa, 1975): 382-400.

Lee Kyu-tae. "Minsok'e nat'anan nama non sasang [Boy preference in Korean folkways]," *Korean Institute for Research in the Behavioral Sciences, Research Bulletin* (Seoul, 1973).

Lee Tai-young. "The legal status of Korean women," in Chun Shin-yong, ed., *Legal System of Korea*, Korean Culture Series 5 (Seoul: International Cultural Foundation, 1975): 83-114.

Levinson, Daniel, C. N. Darrow, E. B. Klein, and M. H. Levinson. *Seasons of a Man's Life* (New York: Knopf, 1977).

Pak Pyŏng-ho. "Nama chonjung sa sang kwa kajok kyehyoek silch'ŏn [Boy preference and its relations to family planning]," *Korean Institute for Research in the Behavioral Sciences, Research Bulletin* (Seoul, 1973).

Papanek, Hanna. "Development planning for women," *Signs: Journal of Women in Culture and Society*, 3, 1 (1977): 14-21.

Parish, William L., and Martin King Whyte. *Village and Family in Contemporary China* (Chicago: University of Chicago Press, 1978).

Pincus, Cynthia. *Some Factors Affecting Mid-Life Change among a Population of Adult Women*, Ph.D. dissertation, Goodwin Watson Institute (typewritten), 1980.

Rhi Bou-yong. "Psychological problems among Korean Women," in Sandra Mattielli, ed., *Virtues in Conflict: Tradition and the Korean Woman Today* (Seoul: Royal Asiatic Society, Korea Branch, 1977): 129-46.

Takahashi Toru. "Chosen min'yo no utaeru boshi no aijo [Mother-child love in Korean folk songs]," *Chosen*, 255 (1936): 14-36.

Tinker, Irene. "The adverse impact of development on women," in Michele Bo Bramsen and Irene Tinker, eds., *Women and World Development* (Washington, D.C.: Overseas Development Council, 1976): 22-34.

United Nations, World Conference of the International Women's Year, Mexico City, June 19-July 2, 1975. E/CONF. 65/5 Provisional agenda, item II, paragraph 13.

Yoon Soon Young S. "The role of Korean women in national development," in Sandra Mattielli, ed., *Virtues in Conflict: Tradition and the Korean Woman Today*, (Seoul: Royal Asiatic Society, Korea Branch, 1977a): 157-67.

Yoon Soon Young S. "Study of the role of young women in the development process, especially in industries (Republic of Korea)," Report Submitted to ESCAP/Division of Population and Social Affairs, 1977b (unpublished typescript).

Glossary

We have provided Chinese character glosses for Sino-Korean and mixed words, expressions, and phrases found in the text. Respecting our authors' stylistic choices, alternative romanizations are provided where appropriate. Since pure Korean expressions, rendered in *han'gul*, can be retrieved from the romanized terms used in the text, they have not been included in the glossary. A few Chinese terms are so indicated. The Korean style of alphabetization for ch/ch', k/k', p/p', and t/t' has been used for this glossary, but not for the index, in which English-language terms predominate.

We gratefully acknowledge the expert help of Eugene H. Chai in preparing the final version of this glossary.

The Editors

GLOSSARY

anbang, anpang 안房, 안방
an chuin, anjuin 안主人
Andong Kwŏn 安東權
Andong Kwŏn-ssi sebo 安東權氏世譜
ant'aek kosa 安宅告祀
bosal, posal 菩薩
changnye, changrye 葬禮
chapkwi, chapgwi 雜鬼
chesa 祭祀
Chin (surname) 陳
chokpo, chokbo 族譜
chŏm 占
chŏmsulga 占術家
Chŏng Ch'ŏl 鄭澈
Chŏng In-ji 鄭麟趾
chung pulsa, chung-bulsa 중佛師
chosang 祖上
chosang malmyŏng / chosang manmyŏng 祖上말명, 祖上萬明
Chosŏn 朝鮮
chubu 主婦
Chuyŏk 周易
ch'arye 茶禮
ch'ilgŏ chi ak, ch'ilgŏ-chiak 七去之惡

ch'ilsŏng 七星
Ch'ing (Chinese) 清
Ch'oe Kyŏng-ch'ang 崔慶昌
ch'on 寸
<u>Ch'ŏnggu yŏngŏn</u> 青丘永言
ch'ŏnmin 賤民
ch'ulga oein 出家外人
ch'ung 忠
<u>Haedong Kayo</u> 海東歌謠
haenyŏ, henyŏ 海女
haesan'gwi, haesan'gi 解産鬼
han 恨
hanmun 漢文
hoju 戶主
Hong Cham 洪暹
Hongnang 洪娘
hoengsumegi, hoengsumagi 橫數메기, 橫數막이
Hsü Ching (Chinese) 徐兢
hubu 後夫
Hwang Chini 黃眞伊
hyo 孝
ijang 里長
ippuhon 入夫婚
<u>Kagok wŏllyu</u> 歌曲源流
Kangwŏn (province) 江原

katsangja	나箱子
kisaeng	妓生
Koryŏ	高麗
Koryŏ togyŏng	高麗圖經
kosa	告祀
Kuji	求之
kunghap	宮合
kŭngnak	極樂
kwagŏ	科擧
kwisin	鬼神
Kwŏn Chŏl	權節
kye	契
Kyehu tŭngnok	繼後謄錄
Kyerang	桂娘
Kyŏnggi (province)	京畿
Kyŏngguk taejŏn	經國大典
Kyujanggak	奎章閣
Ma (surname)	馬
magwi	魔鬼
malmyŏng, manmyŏng	말명, 萬明
mansin	萬神
Mao (Chinese)	毛
Ming (Chinese)	明
mubyŏng	巫病
mudang	巫堂

muhu	無後
Munhwa Yu-ssi Chongch'in Hoe	文化柳氏宗親會
<u>Munhwa Yu-ssi sebo (Kajŏng p'an)</u>	文化柳氏世譜 (嘉靖版)
Munhyang	文香
munjung	門中
myŏnjang	面長
namjon, yŏbi	男尊女卑
namnyŏ ch'ilse pudongsŏk	男女七歲 不同席
oeson	外孫
oeson pongsa	外孫奉祀
pakkat chuin	박갓主人
paltong hada	發動하다
Pannam Pak	潘南 朴
pŏmnye	凡例
pon	本
posal	菩薩
Puan Kim-ssi	扶安金氏
pujo	扶助
pujŏng	不淨
punjaegi, punchaegi	分財記
pun'ga	分家
Pyŏkkye	碧溪
Pyŏn Nam-nyong	卞南龍
sadae pongsa	四代奉仕
saejŏm, saechŏm	새占

GLOSSARY

Saengnyuksin, Saengryuksin 生六臣
saju 四柱
sajup'alcha 四柱八字
sanggun, sang'gun 上君
Sansin 山神
sarangbang, sarang-bang 舍廊房
Sejo 世祖
shan ko (Chinese) 山歌
Shi Xing Ya You (Chinese, pin-yin rm.) 時興呀哟
sihyangje 時享祭
sije 時祭
sijip 媤집, 시집
sijo 時調
sillyŏng 神靈
sim-pua (Chinese, Hokkien) 媳婦仔
Sin Suk-chu 申叔舟
sinbyŏng 身病
Sinjang 神將
sŏng 姓
Song Taech'un 松臺春
taegam 大監
Taehan millyŏk, Taehanminyŏk 大韓民曆
taesin 大神
taesin malmyŏng 大神말명
tan'gol 丹骨

GLOSSARY

taptap hada, taptaphada 沓沓하다
todŭngnyŏ 도둥女
tongja 童子
tonggun, tong'gun 舌居
tubu 豆腐
T'ŏju 터主
T'oegye Yi Hwang 退溪 李滉
T'ojŏng pigyŏl, T'ojŏngbigyŏl 土亭秘訣
wit'o 位土
yakchu, yakju 藥酒
yangban 兩班
Yejo 禮曹
Yi (surname) 李
yin (Chinese) 陰
yŏbu 女夫
yŏl 烈
Yŏm Che-sin 廉悌臣
yŏngsan 靈山
yŏt'am 豫探
Yu Hŭi-jam 柳希潛
Yu Ilchi, Yu Ilji 柳一枝
Yun Kyŏng-yŏn 尹景淵

Index

abuse, of *minmyŏnuri*, 48-52, 57-59
adolescents, 130
adoption, 33-34, 40-43, 43 n.4; documents, 38-39; in genealogies, 26-27, 31, 38-39; intralineage, 35-36; and *minmyŏnuri*, 47, 49, 58; of nephews, 38; retroactive, 27; rules and laws of, 67-68, 165-72; of sons, 26, 37; of sons-in-law, 171
affinal household, 9, 12, 50, 98; ties to the, 42, 107-08
agnatic kin, 1, 9, 65-66
agriculture, 68-70; wet-rice, 68
almanacs, 150-52
alphabet, Korean (*han'gŭl*), 129
anbang (inner room), 5, 8, 69-70
ancestors, 12-13, 64, 66, 102, 104-05, 120-21, 123, 125-26, 140-41; bilateral, 104; ghosts or spirits of the, 125, 143; in *kut*, 97, 102-15; restless, 97, 99-101; tablets to the, 11; on the woman's side, 97-111
ancestor worship, 8-9, 11-12, 15, 66, 72-73, 97-111; ceremonies for (*chesa, sihyangje, sije*), 9, 35-37, 39-42, 44 n.10, 44 n. 11, 72-74, 81, 85-86, 142-43; by an "outside grandson" (*oeson pongsa*). 37. 40; sacrifices for, 66; women's role in, 39-42
anch'ae (inner quarters or inner wing), 51, 70
an chuin ("inside master"), 70, 77
Andong Kwŏn, 23-32, 38; genealogy of the (*Andong Kwŏn-ssi sebo*), 23-32
annulments, of marriages, 163
ant'aek kosa (ritual), 122
anthropologists, 9, 14, 89
aunts, 41, 54-55
authority, 64-65; of the house head, 74-75; paternal, 91
autonomy, female, 81-94
avoidance relationships, 49

babies, 118-19; care of, 86, 89-90; and divination, 153-54; male, 124
bachelors, 100, 102
Bae Kyung Sook, 17 n.1
beliefs, social, 36, 161, 164-66
Biernatzki, William E., 8
"big house" (*k'ŭnjip*), 9
birth, 25, 36-37, 147, 153; age at, 59 n.1; dates, 143-44, 150; and divination, 147, 153; order of, 25, 36-37. See also childbirth
birthdays, 102, 103; Buddha's, 144; sixty-first, 111 n.8
Board of Rites (Yejo), 38, 47
Book of Changes (Chuyŏk), 150-53
boys, 8-9, See also sons, males
Brandt, Vincent S.R., 8, 129, 136 n.1
bridegrooms, 10, 111 n.8, 117; of *minmyŏnuri*, 45-61
brides, 9-13, 64, 104, 111 n.8; *minmyŏnuri* as, 45-61; "tomorrow's," 17
brothers, 77 n.4, 87; and *kut*, 102; legal rights of, 163-64, 167; relationships among, 73-74
brothers-in-law, legal rights of, 163-64
Buddhist temples, 88, 100, 114, 142
capital, the, 130-31. See also Seoul
capital investment, 74
career, 93-94; concept of, 93, 94 n.8; counseling, 148, 171; diving as a, 93
Catholicism, 143
cattle-tending, 86, 90
Central Korea, 63-77
ceremonies, religious, 150-51. See also ancestor worship
chagŭnjip, (branch house or collateral descent line, literally "little house"), 9, 36, 72, 97, 109
chagŭn manŭra (concubine), 88-89, 124
Chang Chu-gŭn, 127 n.9
"Chang, Deaconess," biography of, 7
change, and Korean women, 159-72

182

changnye (funerals), 85-86
chants (shamans'), 97, 101, 150
charlatans, shamans as, 113, 115, 126
Cheju Island, 10, 15, 81-94
Cheng brothers, 43 n.2
chesa (ancestor ceremonies), 9, 81, 85-89, 92, 93 n.3, 97-98, 101-02, 111 n.1, 142
childbirth 82, 104, 161, 166-67, 170-72
childlessness, 34, 36, 143, 166, 169-70
children, 70, 77, 88, 92-93, 108-09, 116, 140-41, 160-62; and ancestor worship, 37; care of, 63-66, 68, 86, 171; custody of, 163-64, 168-72; dead (*tongja*), 104, 111 n.8; and divination, 143, 145, 153-54; in genealogies, 25-26, 28, 31; illegitimate, 28, 31, 114; and marriage, 46-48; of *minmyŏnuri*, 53-56; of widows, 35
ch'ilgŏ chi ak ("seven offenses"), 34
Ch'ilsŏng (Seven-star God), 123; ritual for, 99
China, 150, 165-66, 170-71
Chinese, the, 8-10, 134; influence of, 8-10, 75, 134; and marriage, 46, 48-49, 52, 58
Chinese, classical (language), 77 n.5, 86, 133, 140, 152
Ch'ing dynasty, 133-37
chip (family or household), 66, 97-102, 106, 108, 111 n.1, n.8
Ch'oe Chae-sŏk, Professor, 27, 30-31, 167
Choe Chong-hi, 113, 115
Ch'oe Kyŏng-ch'ang, 130
Cho Haejoang, 10, 13, 15
Cho Hyoung, 160
Cho, Mrs., the story of, 15-16, 116-26
chokpo (lineage genealogies), 23-32, 37-38, 44 n.11
"Chom-Nye," the story of, 113-14, 126
ch'on, 87, 93 n.4
Chŏng Ch'ŏl, song by, 131
Ch'ŏng'gu yŏngŏn (*sijo* collection), 133-34
ch'ŏnmin (outcaste), 16
chosang (ancestors), 100-03

chosang-gŏri (ancestors' sequence), 97, 105
chosang malmyŏng, 100-01, 111 n.7
Chosŏn. *See* Yi dynasty
Christianity, 114-15, 125, 141, 148
Chu Hsi, 43 n.2
"*ch'ulga oein*" (once married, an outsider), 64, 98
ch'ung (loyal subjects), 35
Chungju, 119
Ch'unhyang, The Tale of, 129, 130
Chuyŏk (Book of Changes), 150-53
Civil Code, 165-66, 170, 172 n.2
civil service examinations (*kwagŏ*), 29, 34, 43 n.5, 130
clans, 23-32, 166
clients, of diviners or shamans, 97, 113, 115, 122-23, 141-48, 150-55
codes, 37-38. *See also* Civil Code, Criminal Code
collective consciousness, 160-61
commercialization, of the rural economy, 71
commoners, 5-6, 48
Communists, 117-18
comradeship, in diving, 82-84
conception, responsibility for, 166-67, 170-72
concubines (*chagŭn manŭra*), 6, 11, 28, 50, 88-89, 119, 124, 166
conflicts, emotional, 87, 101, 123, 159-72
Confucianism, 1-3, 8, 10-11, 15, 33-35, 38, 42-43, 60 n.5, 63-66, 125-26, 127 n.9; ideology of, 2, 8, 86, 90-93, 124, 167-68; rituals of, 34, 85-86, 92; and social structure, 63-66, 129-30, 134-35; and women, 16
Confucianization, 1-3, 25, 33-39, 42, 43 n.2
cooperation, 67, 90, 92
cottage industry, 14-15
court cases, 16-17, 163-72
cousins, 102; and adoption, 39
co-wives, 89. *See also* concubines, "little wives," wives

INDEX

Criminal Code, 164
cruelty, 113. *See also* abuse
cultural assumptions, and conflict, 160
custody, child, 163-64, 168-72
customs, 17; and conflict, 170-72

dancing, 150; of shamans, 115, 124
Dante, *The Divine Comedy*, 134
daughters, 9-11, 33-36, 98, 113; and ancestor ceremonies, 39-42, 101-03; and divination, 139, 155; in genealogies, 24-31, 35-38; and inheritance, 37, 39-42, 43 n.1, 167-71; lineages of, 25-26; married, 103-05; and mothers, 82, 87-88
daughters-in-law, 45-60; and divination, 155; and *kut*, 106
dead, the, 97, 99, 101-05, 107-08, 111 n.5, n.7, n.8; land of, 113
death, 97-101, 103, 126; anniversaries, 103, 142; and divination, 148; early, 143; and *kut*, 99-101
demographic factors, in social change, 33
demons, 115, 123-24, 126; evil (*kwisin*), 124
dependence, psychological, 90-91, 93
descendants, in genealogies, 30-31; lack of (*muhu*), 26-28, 31
descent, lines of, 25-28, 36, 40-43, 165-72; collateral, or secondary (*k'ŭnjip*), 36, 40-42; direct, or primary (*chagŭnjip*), 36, 40-42; rules concerning, 165-72. *See also* lineage

Deuchler, Martina, 10, 11, 16, 167
development planning, economic, 159-72
discrimination, 167
diseases, 126; childhood, 118, 143. *See also* illness
dividing the household (*pun'ga*), 68, 77 n.4
divers, women, 10-11, 15, 81-94; songs of the, 89, 93 n.5
divination, 139-57; and city women, 139-57; and hardship, 146-48; by hexagram, 152; "horoscopic," 140-41, 143, 145-46, 148-53; inspirational, or "spiritual," 140-41, 143, 145-46, 148-53; *mansin*'s 103-05; manuals, 140-41, 143; occasions for, 153-54
diviners, 16, 120-22, 139-57; Buddhist-style, 120-22; female, 140-41; male, 140-41; *mansin* as, 103-05
division of labor, 13; sexual, 81-86, 141
divorce, 30, 33-34, 38, 43 n.3, 88-90; and children, 163-64, 166, 169-70
Dix, Griffin, 8, 10
domain, domestic and public, 63-66, 124
domestic sphere, the, 16, 66, 74-77, 104
dominance, 90-93, 159; male, 90, 93, 159; of wives, 89-90
dowries, 35, 133
dreams, 140, 162
drinking, 86, 90-91, 114-15; ritual, 85-86

East Asia, 165, 171
economic life, 8, 75-76, 81-85, 87; agricultural, 66; on Cheju Island, 81-85, 87, 91-92; development and, 159-60; and divination, 147-48, 153-54; modernization of, 139; problems in, 148; and social change, 33; surplus and, 13, 75-76; of villages, 92
education, 15, 75-76, 88, 125, 147-48; and change, 160, 170-72; of women, 15, 140
egalitarianism, 129
Eight Peaks Village, 66-77; description of, 66; a farmhouse in, 69-70, 79
elders, 65, 67; lineage, 34; village, 81, 86
elite classes, 2, 23, 64, 129
employment, of women, 2, 15-16, 160
endogamy, village, 87-89
entertainers, professional. *See kisaeng*
Ewha Women's University, 17 n.1
ethnographers, 8. *See also* anthropologists
examinations, 130; entrance, 153-54. *See also* civil service examinations
exogamy, 87

184

INDEX

exorcism, 2, 99, 115, 144; minor (*p'udak-kŏri*), 99
extramarital relationships, 166

families, 87-89, 116-17, 140-41, 148-49; on Cheju Island, 87-89; and divination, 140-41, 148-49; matrifocal, 87-89; of *minmyŏnuri*, 48-53, 57-58
family, the, 23-32, 67-70, 97-98; and adoption, 39; and ancestors, 101; and change, 43, 160; Christian, 6; Confucian, 3, 6; and divination, 145, 153-54; headship of, 165-72; and kinship, 17, 43; and law, 88; and *minmyŏnuri*, 48-53; nuclear, 72, 92; problems of, 83, 88; planning, 165; and shamans, 113-15; as social institution, 107, 165-72; stem, 72; uterine, 57, 60 n.7; woman's role in, 10, 33-34, 171
Family Court, Seoul, 163-64, 172 n.2
farmhouse, arrangement of the, 69-70; diagram of, 79
farming, 72, 81-85, 113; tenant, 72, 113
fate, 151-52. *See also* fortune
fathers, 54-56, 97, 109, 116-17, 123, 155, 163-64, 168-72; as ancestors, 97, 109; and divination, 155; legal rights of, 163-64, 168-72; of *minmyŏnuri*, 54-56
fathers-in-law, 55-56, 144
females, 1-3, 81-94, 165-72; autonomy of, 81-94; as diviners, 140-41; as "inferior," 33, 36, 42; as shamans, 98-99; subordination of, 159; and succession, 165-72. *See also* girls, wives, women
feminism, 81
fertility, 160
fiction, 113-15
filial piety (*hyo*), 92-93; of sons, 35
food, 65-70; and *chesa*, 85, 101
fortune (*chŏm*), 120, 140-41; family, 141, 144-45; -telling, 120, 122, 139, 141, 152, 156 n.2
friendships, 82-85, 90
funerals (*changnye*), 85-88, 102, 116

Gale, James S., 7, 13
Gamble, Sidney D., 8
gambling, 85, 91
gender personality, 89-91
genealogies (*chokpo*), 10-13, 23-32, 34-38, 64, 66-67, 167; compilers of, 23-24, 29-30, 37; in the Yi dynasty, 23-32
generations, 27, 39-41, 102, 109; and *kut*, 109
geomancy, 81, 120
ghosts (*yŏngsan*), 12-13, 101-03, 140, 142; and *kut*, 102-05; restless, 97-101. *See also* spirits
Gifford, the Reverend Daniel, 6
girls, 45-61, 82-84; as divers, 82-84; as *minmyŏnuri*, 45-61
goals, and means (imbalance of), 164-66, 170-72
gods, the, 99, 101, 126, 140, 148; and goddesses, 126
government, 63, 74, 86, 130, 134
grandchildren, 17, 25, 37, 101; and divination, 154-55; in genealogies, 25; -great-, 55-56; of *minmyŏnuri*, 55-56
grandfathers, 74, 97, 102, 109; as ancestors, 97, 109
grandparents, 74, 97, 101, 103-05, 108-09, 145, 154-55; as ancestors, 103-05; and divination, 145, 154-55; and *kut*, 108-09
grandsons, 17, 25, 37; in genealogies, 25; "outside" and patrilineal, 37

Haedong Kayo (*sijo* collection), 134
haenyŏ/henyŏ ("women of the sea"), 82, 84, 90. *See also* divers, women
haesan'gi (childbirth), 104
Hahn, Dr. D. S., 160
han (sense of regret), 101, 168, 170
Han Sang-bok, 8
han'gŭl (Korean alphabet), 129
hanmun (classical Chinese), 75, 77 n.5; literature, 129

INDEX

Harvey, Youngsook Kim, 7, 10, 12, 14, 16, 17 n.1, 125
headship, 67; house, 63, 67, 155; town, 67; village, 67. *See also* house head.
healing, by shamans, 2-3, 124, 126
heirs, 39-42. *See also* inheritance
henyŏ. See haenyŏ
hierarchal interaction, 129, 133
history, women in, 9
hoju (house head), 67, 70
hŏju (false spirits), 120-21
home, 13; natal, 48, 64, 98, 100, 103-05, 164, 167
Hong Kiltong, Tale of, 129
Hongnang (a *kisaeng*), 130-31, 133
house, arrangement of the, 70. *See also* farmhouse
house head (*hoju*), 63, 67, 77 n.1, n.4, 155; authority of the, 70-71, 77; room of the (*sarangbang*), 70
households, 9, 29, 63, 65-68, 77 n.4; aristocratic, 2; and change, 160; and divination, 145, 153; functions of, 63, 67-68, 76-77; gods of, 99, 107, 111 n.4; headship of, 9, 63, 67, 155; of *minmyŏnuri*, 45-60; pantheons of, 100, 107, 111 n.4; problems, 147; and shamans, 98-99, 121; and women, 17, 46-48. *See also* affinal household
housekeeping, 86, 90
housemaids, 15, 117
house mistress, 70, 76-77
House Site Official (T'ŏju Taegam), 120, 121
"*hubu*" ("later husband"), 28
humor, in *sijo*, 132-33
husbands, 7-8, 72-76, 87, 105, 116-24, 167-71; and adoption, 38; on Cheju Island, 88-94; and conflict, 161-62, 167-71; and divination, 139-46, 154; natal homes of (*sijip*), 64; in genealogies, 24-25, 35-36; in *kut*, 108-09; "later" (*hubu*), 28, of *minmyŏnuri*, 45-60; second, 28-30

Hwang Chini (or "Bright Moon," a *kisaeng*), 134-36; *sijo* by, 134-36
hysterical neurosis, 160-62

ideology, Confucian, 2, 8, 90-91, 93, 124, 167-68
ijang (village head), 67
illiteracy, in women, 125
illness, 2, 88, 92, 99, 106, 116, 122-23, 140, 142, 144-45; and divination, 148, 153-54; and *kut*, 99-101, 103; mental and emotional, 160-62
immigrant women, 17 n.1
incest, 52
income, 68; cash, 82, 84-85, 89; from divination, 140; from farming, 72; household, 68, 72-75
Independence Movement, 48
India, 165
industrial development, 63-66
inequality, of the sexes, 148, 159
infancy, marriages in, 46, 48
inferiority, of females, 33, 36, 42
inheritance, 9, 11, 35-37, 68, 74, 87; by daughters, 35, 43 n.1; documents, 37, 39-40; laws, 77 n.4, 165-72; rules, 1-2; by women, 33
intiation (or spirit) sickness (*sinbyŏng*), 10
inner quarters, or wing (*anch'ae*), 1-3, 51, 69-70, 73
inner room (*anbang*), 1-3, 5, 64, 69-70
insanity (*mich'ida*), 115, 163

Janelli, Roger L. and Dawnhee Yim, 8
Japan, 165-66, 170-71
Japanese, the, 116-17; regime of, 48, 161, 165; women, bibliography of, 17 n.1
job training, need for, 171
Jones, George Heber, 6-7, 14

Kagok wŏllyu (*sijo* collection), 134
Kangwŏn (province), 66
Kendall, Laurel, 10, 12, 16
kidnapping, 163-64

INDEX

Kim Kong Soo, 17 n.1
Kim Ku, 48
Kim Taek-kyu, 8
Kim Tong-ni, 113
kin, 12-13, 15, 87, 103-05, 107-08, 155; and ancestors, 97-98, 103-05, 107-08; bilateral, 107; and divination, 155; fictive, 15, 87; male-linked, 105; natal, 12-13
kings, 15, 129, 131
kinship, 9, 11-12, 64-65; bilateral, 11-12, 107; categories of, 105, 108-09; on Cheju Island, 87; diagrams, 9; patrilineal, 11, 64; terms, 58
kisaeng (professional women entertainers), 2, 15-16, 124, 127 n.9, 129-37; descriptions of, 137 n.14; songs by (*sijo*), 129-37
Knez, Eugene, 8
Kofyar, 92
Koh Hesung Chun, 10, 16-17, 17 n.1
Koh Yong-bok, 159
Korean War, 56, 117
Koreans, and *minmyŏnuri* marriage, 46-49, 52, 58-59
Koryŏ dynasty (917-1392), 1-2, 43 n.2, 47, 127 n.9, 133, 137 n.12, 167; late, 26, 28, 29
kosa (ritual, offerings), 99, 120
Kuji (a *kisaeng*), 132; *sijo* by, 132-33
k'ŭnjip (direct descent line, literally "big house"), 9, 36, 72, 73, 97, 109
kunghap (compatibility of spouses), 141
k'ŭn mudang (great shaman), 99
kut (shaman ritual), 12, 97-111, 120-24, 127 n.9, 143-44; ancestors and ghosts in, 102-05; examples of, 99-101; and the living, 101, 106
kwagŏ (examinations), 130. See also civil service examinations
kwisin (spirits, ghosts, demons), 124. See also *magwi*
kye (loan associations), 14
Kyerang (a *kisaeng*), 130, 133; songs by, 130, 133

Kyŏnggi (province), 66, 97, 98, 111 n.3
Kyŏngguk Taejŏn (Great Code of Administration), 28-29, 127 n.9
Kyujanggak, 23-24, 44 n.7, n.12, n.18

labor, 32, 68-70, 72, 160; agricultural, 68-70; division of, 63-77, 81-86; skilled, 82, 84; surplus of, 65; teams (*su-notta*), 85; wage (*p'ump'ari*), 32, 72; and women, 160
land, 11, 65-68, 72, 75, 167; -lords, 119; ownership, 66-67, 113; records (*punchaegi*), 37, 39, 167
law, 9, 17, 39-42, 160-61, 165-72; and conflict, 165-72; suits, 39-42; women and the, 6-7, 9, 17 n.1, 161. See also legal case, legal status
Lee Hyo-chae, 160, 169
Lee Man Gap, 8
legal case, analysis of a, 39-42, 163-72
legal status, of women, 6-7, 9, 17 n.1, 40, 161
legislation, for change, 160
liberation, 93, 116; Korean, 116
life crises, and divination, 147, 153-54
lifestyle, 2; for midlife women, 168-71
lineage (*munjung*), 8-9, 23-32, 41, 43, 63-64, 66; and adoption, 38-39; elders, 34, 67; exogamy, 67; functions of the, 67, 76-77; genealogies, 10-11, 31, 37-38; local, 72; female, 31; male, 27, 30-31, 39, 42, 124-26, 165-72; and marriage, 34-36; origins (*pon'gwan*), 44 n.9; position, 13, 72-75; rites, 9, 67; structure, 8, 23-32, 65; woman's natal, 35-36, 39, 42. See also patrilineage
literature, 3, 129-37; Chinese (*hanmun*), 129, 133; oral, 129-37; vernacular, 129-34
"little houses" (*chagŭnjip*), 9
"little wives," 88-89, 124. See also concubines
loan associations (*kye*), 14
lots, divination by, 150-53

187

INDEX

Lotus Paradise (*kŭngnak*), 99-103, 106, 111 n.5, n.9
love, 169; affairs, 119, 154
lovers, 15, 114-15; in *sijo*, 129, 131
lower classes, 2, 5-6
loyal subjects, 35
luck, 120-22; and divination, 153
Lunar New Year, 146

madness, 114-15. See also insanity (*mich'ida*)
magwi (evil spirits), 120, 124. See also *kwisin*
males, 1, 124, 159; associations of, 8, 92-93; as diviners, 140-41; dominance of, 90-93, 159; and lineage, 27, 30-31, 39, 42, 124-26, 165-72; preference for, 164-66; secret societies of, 92-93; as shamans (*paksu*), 98; superiority of, 33, 36, 42. See also husbands, men, sons
malmyŏng (restless ancestor), 101, 103, 111 n.7
mansin (professional shaman), 2, 15, 98-107, 111 n.5, n.7, n.8, 127 n.1, 141-42; as an informant, 115-16. See also *mudang*, shaman
marketing, 14, 71
marriage, 11-12, 34-36, 64-65, 68, 101, 108, 117-18, 122-23, 171; arranged, 7, 161, 167-68; ceremonies, 10, 50-59; on Cheju Island, 15, 87-90; child, 12, 45-60; consummation of, 50; difficulties, 52, 58-59, 89; and divination, 139-41, 145-47, 153; dominant form of, 45, 47, 49-50, 58; *minmyŏnuri*, 12, 45-60; patrilocal, 8-9; rules of, 68, 87-89; second, 28-30; in *sijo*, 133; *sim-pua*, 48-59; uxorilocal, 58, 77 n.1, 87, 89, 107. See also remarriage, weddings
mass media, the, and change, 160
match-makers, 15, 117, 141
matriarchal society, 107
matrifocal families, 15, 87-89
matrilateral concepts, 105

matrilocal society, 107
Mattielli, Sandra, 11, 17 n.1
McCann, David, 15-16
McCoy, John, 137 n.10
means, and goals, imbalance of, 164-66, 170-72
medical treatment, 2, 88, 106
memorial tablets, 35
men: adopted, 34; and *chesa*, 85-86, 97, 102; childless, 34; in genealogies, 26-27; in the lineage, 36, 42; liberation of, 93; and property, 44 n.10; superiority of, 33, 36, 42; urban, 145, 153. See also husbands, lineage, males
menarche, 50
menstruation, 82
methodological approach, 161
middle class, 169
midlife transition, 168-71
Ming dynasty, songs of the, 133, 137 n.9
minmyŏnuri, 12, 45-60, 116; marriage, 12, 45-60; novel about, 46, 48
miscarriages, 106, 162
misfortune, 99, 126
missionaries, 6-9, 14, 48
modernization, of the economy, 139
modesty, 6, 14
Mohwa, the sorceress (the story of), 114-15
money, 82, 116, 118-19, 121, 126; borrowing, 82, 85; control of, 71-72; problems concerning, 145, 148; saving, 88, 92; and shamans, 126
monks, 142; Buddhist, 127 n.9
mothers, 2, 7, 116-17, 123; and children, 87-89, 169; and daughters, 82, 87-88; deaths of, 105; and divination, 139, 141, 155; and *kut*, 103-05; legal rights of, 163-64, 168-72; and *minmyŏnuri*, 45-50; and shamans, 114-15
mothers-in-law, 7-9, 12, 120-22, 124; and divination, 139, 142, 155; of *minmyŏnuri*, 45-60

INDEX

"Mountain Songs" (*Shan ko*), 133, 137 n.9
mubyŏng, or *sinbyŏng* (initiation or spirit sickness), 127 n.6
mudang (professional shaman), 2, 15, 98-99, 113-27
"*muhu*" ("no descendants"), 26-28, 31
Mundurucu, 92-93
Munhwa Yu, genealogy of the, 24-32
Munhwa Yu-ssi Chongch'in Hoe, 24
Munhwa Yu-ssi sebo (Kajŏng p'an), 24-32
Munhyang (a *kisaeng*), 132
music, 150
mutual aid, 85-87; allowance (*pujo*), 85

naerim kut, (initiary ceremony), 122, 127 n.6
namjon, yŏbi, 33, 36, 42
natal home, 48, 64, 98, 100, 103-05, 164, 167; husband's (*sijip*), 64; wife's, 33-34, 98, 111 n.9
natal kin, 33-34, 97-98, 142
neighbors, 67, 150
neo-Confucianism, 10, 43 n.2, n.6, 166
nephews, 38; and *kut*, 102
New Guineans, 92
new year, 59 n.1, 141, 146; Lunar, 146; predictions, 141, 146
nieces, and *kut*, 102
nobility, 48
"no descendants" ("*muhu*"), 26-28
non-kinsmen, 165
North Korea, a village in, 8
North Koreans, 117
numerology, 150-53

oeson (an "outside grandson," the child of a daughter), 40-42
oeson pongsa (ancestor ceremony via an "outside grandson"), 37, 40
offerings, 64, 99
officials, 2-3, 5, 134; in *sijo*, 130-31, 134; wives of, 5. *See also* scholar-officials
options, role, 167-68, 170-72
organization, social, 87-89

orphans, 54-55
Osgood, Cornelius, 8
outcastes (*ch'ŏnmin*), 5-6, 16, 127 n.9; shamans as, 124
Outer (or Outside) Wing (*pakkatch'ae*), 70

Pae Kyŏng-suk. *See* Bae Kyung Sook
Pak Ku-hyuk, 8
pakkat chuin ("outside master"), 70
paksu (male shaman), 98, 141
palace women, 9
Pannam Pak clan, 25
Papanek, Hanna, 160
parent household (*pun'ga*), 77 n.4
parents, 103-05, 163-72; and ancestors, 103-05; authority of, 163-64, 168-72; rights of, 163-64, 168-72
parents-in-law, 162
patriarchy, 6, 30, 63-66, 70, 81, 107, 169-70
patrikin, 72, 74, 77
patrilateral bias, 105, 107
patrilineage, 1, 30, 34-36, 42, 87, 103, 169; and adoption, 39; and the ancestors, 97-98, 102; and childlessness, 34; and descent, 36, 76, 87; and the family, 8-9, 26, 68, 76; and marriage, 34-36; and society, 39, 63-66
peasants, 14; and social structure, 63-66. *See also* rural life
peddlers, 16, 117-21, 147
People's Republic of China, 165
personality, 7-8, 151; gender, 89-91
Peterson, Mark, 11-12, 167
physical disorders, 161-62
physicians, 15, 125-26
physiognomy, 150-53
planning, 159-72; for development, 159-72; family, 165
politics, 63-64, 67, 75-76; local, 6, 13, 86; women in, 17
pollution (*pujŏng*), 99
polygyny, 88-89
pon (clan seat), 64

INDEX

pon'gwan (lineage origin), 44 n.9
possession, of shamans, or *mansin*, 97-98, 105, 107, 113, 120-25
poverty, 57, 113, 147, 162
power, 7, 13, 50, 65-66, 70-72; in the household, 70-74; private, 13; public, 13; of the sexes, 7, 50, 65-66, 70-74; of shamans, 124-26; of women, 7, 50, 65-66, 126
pre-Confucian society, 25-26, 42-43, 171
pregnancy, 82, 104, 143, 162
principles of compilation (*pŏmnye*), 29
privacy, 6
promiscuity, 114-15
property, 35-37, 42; ceremonial, 39-42; inheritance of, 35-37, 40, 87; ownership of, by women, 37, 42; rights to, 44 n.10
prostitutes, 16, 124
proverbs, women in, 9
psychiatry, 16-17, 123, 125, 160-62, 164-72; analysis of a case in, 161-62, 164-72
Puan Kim-ssi lineage, 39
public domain, 6, 10, 74, 76-77; power in the, 13; women in the, 16
p'udak-kŏri (exorcism), 97, 99, 104
pujŏng (pollution), 99
punchaegi (land records), 37, 39, 167
p'ump'ari (day labor for wages), 68, 72
pun'ga. See dividing the household
Pyŏkkye, 135
Pyŏn Nam-nyong, 29, 44 n.14

quarrels, 120
quarters: inner (*anch'ae*), 51; male (*sarang-bang*), 51
queens, 38

reform, suggestions for, 161
Register of Adoptions, 38-39, 44 n.15
relatives, 116-19; and *chesa*, 86; and diviners, 142, 144, 155; and farming, 85
religion: and divination, 147-48; traditional, 3

remarriage, 28-30, 35-38; and children, 28-29; of widows, 35-36, 38; of women, 28-30, 38, 42, 43 n.1. See also marriage
residence patterns, 1-2; rules of 87
resources, 71-72; allocation of, 71-72; household, 77; scarcity of, 167-72
responsibilities and rights, imbalance of, 168-72
restlessness, in ancestors and ghosts, 97, 99-101
Rhi Bou-yong, Dr., 160-62, 172 n.1
rights, and responsibilities, imbalance of, 168-72
rituals, 1, 9, 24, 92-93, 98-99, 111 n.5, 114-15, 120; Confucian, 85-86, 92; curative, 149; and land, 35; manuals of, 75-76, 98; roles in (male and female), 10, 16, 98; shamanistic, 98, 125-26, 127 n.11. See also ancestor worship; *chesa*; *siyang*
"robber woman" (*todŭngnyŏ*), 9
roles, of women, 24, 27, 164-72. See also sex roles; work roles
ruling class, 167; members of the, in *sijo*, 129, 131. See also *yangban*
rural life, 8; economy of the, 71; and women, 16. See also peasants
sacrifices. See ancestor worship
saju (four pillars), 150-52; -*p'alcha* (personal horoscope), 143-44, 150-52
sarangbang/sarang-bang (house head's room, or male quarters), 13, 51, 56, 67-74
scholar-officials, 2-3, 15, 38, 130, 135-36
secret societies, male, 92-93
sedan chairs, 2, 5-6
segregation, by sex, 60 n.5
seniority, in the family, 64
Seoul, 53, 98, 117, 130-31; signs and divination in, 139-57
separations, marital, 140-41, 170
servants, 2, 5-6, 94 n.6, 133
"seven offenses" (*ch'ilgŏ chi ak*), as cause for divorce, 34

190

INDEX

sex: of a child, 166-67, 170-72; of clients, in divination, 153-54
sex roles, 24, 27, 164-72; on Cheju Island, 81-94, 140-41; dichotomy of, 14; and divination, 145; and division of labor, 13-14, 81-86, 141
sexual intercourse, 55-56, 125, 162; aversion to, 52, 58-59
shamans and shamanism, 2-3, 6, 10-11, 15-16, 56, 113-27, 140-44, 147-49, 151-53, 156 n.4; and ancestors, 97-111; ceremonies (*kut*) and rituals, 10-12, 97-99; great (*k'ŭn mudang*), 99; hereditary families of, 98; lives of, 17 n.1; male (*paksu*), 98, 141; "regular," 143. See also *mansin, mudang*
shan ko ("Mountain Songs"), 133
Shi Xing Ya Ya You (Chinese song collection), 133
siblings, 103-05, 171; dead, 104-05, 111 n.8; order of, 171; relationships among, 49, 54, 60 n.5
sickness, initiation or spirit (*sinbyŏng*), 10, 123, 127 n.6, n.7. See also illness
signs, diviners' (in Seoul), 139-57
sihyangje, sije (graveside rites), 9, 66, 72-73
sijip (husband's natal home), 64
sijo (*kisaeng* songs or song-poems), 129-37; structure of, 136 n.3, n.10
Silla dynasty, 43 n.2
sillyŏng (spirits, gods), 99
sim-pua marriage (Chinese), 48-49, 52-53, 57-59, 59 n.4
sin. See *sillyŏng*
sinbyŏng, or *mubyŏng* (initiation or spirit sickness), 10, 123, 127 n.6, n.7
Sinjang (Spirit Arrester), 123
sisters and sisters-in-law, 87, 103, 116-18, 122; of *minmyŏnuri*, 45-58
siyang (ritual for the dead), 111 n.5
socialization, 66, 81; and divination, 146, 148; female and male, 64; of *minmyŏnuri*, 58-59

society, 1-3, 5-10, 17, 98, 129-37; and change, 1, 5, 33-44, 159-61, 165-72; and order, 2, 10, 133-34, 148; peasant, 63-66; shamans' place in, 113-27; structure of, 63-67, 76-77, 87-89, 91, 165-72; traditional, 33, 42-43, 126; village, 67, 76-77; and women, 1-3, 6-7, 10, 64-65, 75-76, 101, 161
Song June-ho, 10
Song Taech'un (a *kisaeng*), 131
song: of divers, 89, 93 n.5; "Mountain," 133, 137 n.9; or song-poems, of *kisaeng* (*sijo*), 129-37
sonlessness, 33-36, 124, 126, 162, 165-70
sŏn mosum (naughty boy), 122
sons, 9, 114-15, 124-26, 164-70; adoption of, 26, 37; and ancestors, 97, 102; and conflict, 33-36, 162, 164-67, 169-70; and divination, 139, 155; eldest, 9, 36, 41, 72, 77 n.2, 88-89, 97, 165-72; filial (*hyo*), 35; in genealogies, 25-27, 30-31, 38; importance of, 33-44, 124, 126; and inheritance, 37-42, 167-71; and shamans, 114-15, 121; women without, 33-44
sons-in-law, 24-25, 28, 30, 165, 171; adopted (*teril-sawi*), 50, 58, 171; and descent, 165; in genealogies, 24-25, 28, 30
sorceress, the story of a, 113-15. See also Mohwa
Sorensen, Clark, 13
souls, 100, 107, 113
Spirit Arrester (Sinjang), 123
Spirit General (Changgun), 120, 122, 123
spirit official (*taegam*), 99-100, 120-24
spirits, 99, 111 n.4, n.7, 113-15, 120-26, 148-53; divination through, 140-53; evil (*subi, magwi*), 2, 6, 120, 143-44; false (*hŏju*), 120-21; kindred, 102; tutelary, 124
status: groups, 2; of men, 15, 64, 93-94; of women, 1-3, 5-17, 23-32, 37-38, 89, 123, 137 n.12
stepdaughters, 56-57
stereotypes: Confucian, 1-3; of scholars,

136-37; of shamans, 15, 115, 125-26; of women, 1-3, 12
Strathern, Marilyn, 81
subi (evil demons, or spirits), 120, 124
subjects, loyal, 35
subordination, female, 159
subsistence needs, 77
succession, 33; laws of, 165-72
suicide, 115
Sung dynasty, 43 n.2
Sunoo, Harold Hakwon, 17 n.1
su-notta (labor team), 85
superiority, of males, 33, 36, 42
supernatural, influence of the, 16, 104, 114, 140-41
superstition, 3, 6, 98, 113, 124
surnames, 165-66; in genealogies, 30-31

T'aebaek Range, 66
taegam (spirit officials), 120-24; and *kut*, 120-22
Taehanminyŏk (a yearly almanac), 152
taesin (deities), 111 n.7
Taiwan, 12, 52-53, 58-59, 59 n.4, 165
Takahashi Toru, 169
taxes, 14, 63
tchok (hairdo), 45-46, 48, 50, 53, 55-56, 59
teril-sawi (adopted son-in-law), 50, 58, 171
Thematic Apperception Test (T.A.T.), 90, 94 n.7
Three Kingdoms period (37 B.C.—677 A.D.), 47
todŭngnyŏ ("robber woman"), 9
T'ojŏngbigyŏl (Secrets of T'ojŏng), 141, 142
T'ŏju Taegam (House Site Official), 120, 121
tongja (dead children), 104
topknots, 7
township head (*myŏnjang*), 67
traditionalism, 33, 42-43, 126, 159
translations, of *kisaeng*'s *sijo*, 136 n.5
travelers, accounts by, 6-9, 14

Udo Island, 81
uncles, and adoption, 38
Underwood, Lillias Horton, 7, 13
unions, 82, 85, 86
upper class. See *yangban*
usury, 14
uxorilocal marriage, 50, 58, 77 n.1, 87, 89, 107

values: and conflict, 160-62; male-centered, 104-05; of women, 25, 139, 160-62, 165-72
vernacular literature, 129, 132, 134
Village Association, 86
villages, 8, 13, 87-91; agricultural, 63-66; endogamy and exogamy in, 87-89; heads of (*ijang*), 67; leaders and elders in, 67, 81, 86; life in, 52, 54, 86, 89-91; *min-myŏnuri* in, 50-52; rural, 16; social structure of, 13, 67-77
virilocality, 87

Wagner, Edward W., 11-13
weddings, 50, 86-87, 102-04, 113. See also marriage, ceremonies
Werbner, Richard P., 107
Westerners, 1, 6-9; culture of, 159; as "devils," 114
widowers, 56-57, 88
widows, 14, 35-39, 86-88; and adoption, 38-39; chaste (*yŏl*), 35; and diviners, 142; and farming, 85; and remarriage, 35-36
wills. See inheritance documents
Wilson, Brian, 14-16
witches, shamans as, 113
wives, 2, 6-8, 13, 72-76, 111 n.10; and adoption, 38-39; and ancestors, 104-05; and divination, 139-40, 155; natal families of, 33-34, 87; in genealogies, 28, 35-36; in *kut*, 106-07; legal rights of, 163-64, 167-72; "little," 88-89; responsibilities of, 88-94, 166-72; secondary, 28, 88-91, 124

Wolf, Arthur P., 59, 59 n.4
Wolf, Margery, 49, 59-60 n.4, n.7
women, 2, 5, 42, 124; and ancestor rites, 85-86, 97-111; autonomous, 81-94; bibliography of, 17 n.1; childless, 33-34; and divination, 16, 139-57, 145, 147; and diving, 81-94; as inferior, 33, 36, 42; liberation of, 93; lineages of, 42-43; and inheritance, 37, 42, 44 n.10; and marriage, 45-46, 106-08; older, 83; quarters of, 5, 8, 69-70; and remarriage, 35-38, 42-43; sonless, 33-44; status of, 33, 44 n.17, 126, 137 n.12; studies on, 9; urban, 16, 139-57, 169; and work, 84-92. *See also* females, wives
Women's Association, 82
work roles, 10, 68-71, 84-92; of diving, 84; of farming, 84-86; inside (*annil*), 69-71; outside (*pakkanil*), 68-70; and women, 84-92
yangban (upper class), 14, 23, 25, 26; women, 5, 28-31
Yejo (Board of Rites), 38
Yi (Chosŏn) dynasty (1392-1910), 1-3, 10-11, 47-48, 129-37, 137 n.12, 167; codes of the, 37-38; early, 23-33, 36-43; late, 33-36, 38-43; middle, 33; society of the, 2, 23-44, 63; women of the, 10-11, 42
yŏl (chaste widows), 35
yŏngsan (ghosts), 101-03
Yŏngsŏ (region), 66
Yoon Soon-young S., 10, 127 n.8, 159-60
yŏt'am (offerings), 104, 111 n.8
Young, Barbara, 16
Yu Island, 15